Knotted

Knotted

MICHELLE
HOLMAN

Copyright © Michelle Holman 2009

Michelle Holman asserts the moral right to be identified
as the author of this work.

All rights reserved. No part of this publication may be reproduced,
stored in a retrieval system or transmitted in any form or by any means,
electronic, mechanical, photocopying, recording or otherwise, without
the prior written permission of the author.

Published by: Michelle Holman
ISBN: 978-1-0670071-1-9
First published 2009
Second edition published 2024

Produced by: Indie Experts Publishing
www.indieexpertspublishing.com

Cover design by Ammie Christiansen
Cover artwork by Katie Fisher
Typesetting by Fast Forward Design
Typeset in 10pt Minion Pro

National Library of New Zealand Cataloguing-in-Publication Data
Holman, Michelle. Knotted / Michelle Holman

*This one is for my dad, Arthur (1924–2009),
and my mother-in-law, Ethel (1926–2009).*

Chapter 1

When Daneka Lawton was awakened at 6 a.m. by her radio alarm clock and Lily Allen singing 'Smile', she was unaware that her personal nemesis had just stepped off a 747 at Auckland airport.

As she unglued her eyes and swore at the clock, smiling wasn't high on her personal agenda. Her twin sister, Daniella, had died six months earlier, at the age of thirty-two, leaving Danny responsible for her eleven-year-old nephew, Matt, and his eight-year-old sister, Mia, a pile of debt and a house crumbling around her ears like a mouldy cake. Danny was still reeling from her sister's death, unable to even begin to come to terms with it. Like Einstein's Theory of Relativity, it was just too much for her brain to process.

Nella's death had been avoidable. Their mother, Rose, had died from breast cancer when they were nineteen, and so the girls knew they were at risk. Danny kept her breast-screening appointments and had thought her sister did, too. But Nella threw away the letters and ignored the lump she found in her breast. By the time Danny realized her sister was sick, it was already too late. Like their mother, Nella had spent her entire life avoiding anything unpleasant, leaving Danny to run the reality checks and fight any family battles.

But this time it was a battle Danny couldn't win.

When Danny took extended leave from her job as a nurse at the local Emergency Department to care for her sister, Nella refused to let her contact Patrick Fabello, her American partner, to tell him about the cancer.

'I don't want him to see me like this,' she'd said. 'He'll hate it.'

In Danny's opinion, Nella's relationship with her irresponsible, wastrel lover was one-sided. Patrick's visits to New Zealand were infrequent and brief, and Nella could go for months without hearing from him. Danny suspected Patrick only turned up when he had nothing better to do and had worn out his welcome elsewhere.

'Does he ever work?' she'd asked.

'I think his family has money,' Nella answered vaguely. 'You worry too much about material things.'

'And you don't worry enough.'

Like a hothouse flower that needs careful nurturing and fertilizer to keep it blooming, Patrick needed somebody to feed him constant bullshit, and confirm his place at the centre of the universe. He also needed a supersized plasma television, home gym and hot tub.

'Why?' Danny asked him, when Nella handed over her precious savings to buy the tub. 'You're never here to use it.'

'It's not just for me; it's for the whole family,' Patrick said.

Nella hovered nervously, trying to decide whether to defend him or hide in her garden. Nobody with any sense took on her younger-by-eight-minutes-sister. Danny's brain sprinted where other people's jogged, her tongue honed to a scalpel-like sharpness that usually left her opponents red-faced and stuttering.

Danny's brows rose and her lip curled. Patrick began to sweat. He hated Nella's sister. She reminded him of his brother. 'I take personal fitness very seriously.'

One brow rose still higher, hanging like a mocking question mark. Patrick took everything about his personal appearance very seriously — Danny suspected he'd been a supermodel in a previous life. 'The only body parts I see getting a work-out are your thumb on the remote control and your hair-dryer arm — *that* gets plenty of exercise.'

Long black ringlets hung about Patrick's shoulders — at Nella's insistence, Danny had only just stopped referring to him as D'Artagnan.

Patrick threw a tantrum and threatened to leave.

Nella burst into tears. 'Stop it! Why do you have to be so difficult?'

As Danny was forced to back down, Patrick slid her a look of triumph. He might not be the sharpest tool in the shed, but he knew the power he held over Nella, and that Danny was jealous of him. Patrick treated Matt and Mia much the same way as he treated their mother: he was all over them for the first day or two until the novelty wore off. Patrick didn't like having to compete for Nella's attention, but Danny had realized it was a waste of time trying to get Nella to make sure the children weren't pushed out — she was like a giddy, besotted teenager where Patrick was concerned. Danny's comments only caused more arguments and widened the rift between the sisters. Nella might have been at the back of the queue when they were handing out the grey matter (Danny wondered if that was where her sister first met Patrick), but she'd been first in line for stubbornness.

'You don't understand,' Nella said. 'I don't want a boring, predictable relationship with a stay-at-home man. I want what Mum and Dad had. I want fun and spontaneity. I want passion!'

'I'll remind you about that the next time you're crying because Patrick hasn't sent his half of the mortgage payment,' Danny replied angrily. 'And exactly which part of Mum's relationship with Dad was fun? All I remember is a lot of fighting and crying before he abandoned us.'

'You always twist what I say! Why can't you be happy for me?'

Because I don't like him and I don't trust him, Danny thought.

'What about his family? He never mentions them.'

Nella hesitated. 'They're estranged.'

Danny's brow rose. 'Really?'

Estranged was just the kind of crap Patrick would come out with. Danny substituted pissed off for estranged. If she had to live with the knowledge that she shared genetic material with Patrick Fabello, she'd be estranged too.

'You're impossible!' Nella accused. 'You make Patrick feel as if he isn't welcome in his own home.'

It seemed to have slipped her mind that the only reason she and the children had a roof over their heads was because Danny had insisted on Patrick coughing up half the money for the deposit.

'I'll find the other half and contribute to the repayments provided my name is alongside yours and Nella's on the deeds,' she told Patrick. It was the only way to make sure he didn't sell the house out from under them if he was short of cash.

Patrick sulked and threw more tantrums, but Danny wouldn't give in. Nella did what she did best — sat on the fence, climbing off at regular intervals to soothe Patrick's hurt feelings. Danny watched as Nella manoeuvred Patrick right where she wanted him, still maintaining her role as good cop. Once Danny had sown the seed, Nella was determined to have a house and Danny was going to get it for her. Patrick might be the sun in Nella's personal solar system, but Danny was the gravity keeping everything in its rightful place. Patrick eventually came up with the cash, but only after he'd made it clear it was money he'd put aside to finance climbing Mount Everest.

Danny just about wet her pants laughing. 'Even you can't seriously believe Patrick wants to climb Mount Everest! There wouldn't be a pub on the way to the summit and there'd be nowhere to plug in his hair-dryer.'

Good-cop Nella took offence. 'Just because you don't have any dreams, it doesn't mean you can make fun of Patrick's.'

Danny was tempted to say that watching out for her and the children didn't leave much time for daydreaming, and it would be nice if Nella stepped up to the mark for once. But out of respect for the mystical link that pulsed between Danny and her twin, she kept silent. And besides, Danny didn't trust her sister to make good decisions for Matt and Mia.

In the weeks following Daniella's death, Danny spent hours on the telephone and internet trying to find Patrick. She eventually discovered he'd taken a drunken tumble off a yacht in the Solomon Islands and drowned.

Matt and Mia had never received so much as a birthday card from the States, so Danny was unnerved when letters began arriving from lawyers representing a Ross Fabello, requesting information about and access to the children. Danny ignored the letters. A family that produced Patrick had nothing to offer Matt and Mia. If Ross Fabello was anything like his brother he was a moron with an encyclopaedic knowledge of hair products.

That was a serious miscalculation on Danny's part. The letters became more frequent, and right now, sitting on her bedside table, was another one. Only this time, it was from a law firm based in downtown Auckland.

'Get out of there! What are you doing?'

Danny looked through the side window of the truck at the yellow-hatted workman and mouthed a classic New Zealand salutation. *Bite your bum.*

If she wasn't wearing her nursing uniform and the truck wasn't outside the Emergency Department, Danny might have given him the finger for good measure. She was past being polite, past waiting for the site supervisor to move the Criterion Construction truck straddling the kerb leading to the Emergency Department. Inside, the ED was wheelchair-to-walking-stick with patients. As the nurse in charge of the morning shift, Danny was responsible for keeping the flow of patients moving and ensuring that the ambulances could unload and get back out on the road again. She'd spent the past twenty minutes dealing with irate paramedics, ambulance control staff, and disgruntled relatives and patients, because the truck was blocking the main access road to and from the ED. The hospital manager wasn't having any luck contacting the management at Criterion Construction, the site supervisor had disappeared with the keys, and the truck was an automatic, so pushing it wasn't an option.

In the ambulance bays outside the ED, hospital orderlies, paramedics and workmen milled around trying to come up with a solution. What had started as a Cold War was about to erupt into hand-to-hand combat.

When the cellphone she carried as nurse in charge rang, Danny thumbed a button and lifted it to her ear.

Vanessa Cooper, her best friend and fellow ED nurse, said, 'We've just had a Blue Call. A forty-seven-year-old cardiac arrest is on the way. Be here in five.'

Danny pocketed the phone and marched towards the nearest workman. She pointed at a yellow digger tearing up chunks of earth at the bottom of the slope beside the road where the foundations were being laid for the new Emergency Department. 'Get that thing up here and haul this truck out of the ambulance bay. *Now!*'

He looked shocked. 'We can't do that! The boss'll go apeshit!'

A second workman jogged up the slope. He held up a set of keys. 'Found a spare set.'

Danny wanted to kiss him. '*Brilliant!*' She yanked open the truck door and looked at him expectantly.

The workmen hesitated.

'What are you waiting for?' She gestured impatiently at the truck.

'The boss'll have our guts for garters,' one of them said.

Danny took a step closer and said menacingly, 'Not if I pull them through your nostrils first.'

He reddened and backed away. 'Now listen here lady—'

His colleague cleared his throat nervously. 'The supervisor's real touchy about anybody driving his truck. It's brand-new; he only got it last week.'

In the distance the wail of an ambulance siren was coming closer. Danny snatched the keys, jumped into the cab of the truck, slammed the door and snapped the locks.

And mouthed her suggestion about his bum.

She started the engine and headed onto the grass and down the slope towards the building site. The vehicle felt heavy compared with her Nissan, but Danny figured she'd be OK, she'd done a defensive driving course a couple of years ago and she only needed to move the truck to the bottom of the hill. Unfortunately, days of heavy Spring rain and a steady traffic of tractors, diggers, trucks and steel-capped work boots had turned the earth into a brown, gluey mess.

The truck picked up speed. Danny gripped the steering wheel and tried to remember if the instructor on her defensive driving course had offered any advice on piloting a speeding truck down a muddy slope. She heard his disembodied voice say inside her head: *In a skid situation, it is important that the driver remains calm and under no circumstances slams on the brakes. Gently depress the brake pedal . . .*

Danny gently depressed the brakes. Nothing happened.

She pressed harder.

The truck slewed sideways, slamming the concrete blocks stacked in the back into the side of the flatbed like cannonballs. The wheels on the driver's side lifted as gracefully as a ballerina's arm during a performance of *Swan Lake*.

'*Oh!*' she gasped. '*Ohhh sheeyitt!*'

Too late she realized that driving the truck was a completely different proposition to driving her car, and that the defensive driving course hadn't covered slaloming down a muddy slope in a truck packing a shitload of concrete blocks. Dying was not an option. If something happened to her, there would be nobody to look after Matt and Mia.

Danny wrenched the steering wheel to the right and the wheels of the truck thudded back to earth. It shot forwards across the face of the slope, sending workmen diving for cover. She spied a pile of earth and a stack of concrete blocks like the ones in the back of the truck at the bottom of the slope. A big Monty Pythonish finger seemed to break through the heavens and point at the pile of dirt. Danny aimed the truck straight for it.

'I can do this,' she said grimly. 'I can do this!'

She gently depressed the brakes and the truck slowed. The ominous sound of the concrete blocks sliding forwards made her cringe. They slammed into the cab as the front wheels hit a particularly gluey patch of earth. The wheels spun and the truck aquaplaned down the slope and straight into the wall of concrete blocks.

Danny wasn't wearing a seat belt. The impact lifted her out of the driver's seat, her forehead collided with the windscreen and lights exploded in front of her eyes as she was catapulted back into the seat. The truck rocked violently, flinging her backwards and forwards like a glove puppet. Danny opened her mouth in a silent howl as her face banged once, then twice, into the steering wheel.

She grabbed hold and clung on to keep from being flung backwards again, her fingers curled in agony. Somewhere in the distance a car horn blared, but it wasn't nearly as loud as the buzzing in her ears, as if somebody had left a telephone off the hook in her head.

Danny moaned.

She wanted her money back from that driving instructor.

Somebody was trying to get in.

'Unlock the door!'

A man's rough, gravelly voice shouted.

'Unlock the door!'

Danny didn't move. She concentrated on distancing herself from the burning sensation in her forehead. It felt like a match had been lit there. Dimly, she heard the man shout, 'Cover your head! We're going to break the window!' She screamed as glass exploded around her.

The door was wrenched open and the rough voice demanded, 'Are you OK? Can you hear me?' He sounded American.

Danny slowly raised her head and the horn stopped blaring. She gazed at it in surprise before slowly looking up into the face of the man with his head thrust inside the cab. 'Somebody . . .' she quavered, 'left the phone . . . off the hook.'

He lifted his heavy black brows, purpose-built for scowling. 'Hell, you're a mess.'

His voice sounded a long way off. The inside of Danny's head felt like a piece of Swiss cheese — it was as if her brain had leaked through the holes. There wasn't enough left behind to make sense of what he was saying. The lucid part of her stood alongside, watching what was happening. Danny's ears still buzzed. Her heart thudded erratically against her breastbone, keeping time with the throb in her head.

The buzzing suddenly changed to a whine and then a twittering noise, as if birds were circling her head. Danny patted the air above her, still woozy. 'Are there birds in here?' she asked faintly.

Lucid Danny buried her face in her hands and shook her head. The man caught her hand and drew it gently downwards. Danny was surprised at how warm he felt and how cold she was. She studied the chunky black sweater covering his chest and felt like burrowing into it. From behind him came the sound of raised voices. He chafed her hand between both of his and shouted over his shoulder. 'We need a doctor!'

Lucid Danny took a closer look. With bloodshot black eyes in a swarthy face covered in five o'clock shadow, she decided he didn't do the designer-stubble look well — in fact he looked more like a serial killer. Something was definitely wrong with her if she thought it was OK to snuggle up to a serial killer. And would you look at that nose? It stood like a monument in the middle of his face. He looked vaguely familiar and Danny decided she'd probably seen his face on *Crime Watch*.

'You look like a serial killer.'

Danny didn't realize she'd spoken aloud until the Serial Killer stopped chafing her hands. 'I look a whole lot better than you do. What the hell were you thinking?' he demanded. 'You could have killed somebody.'

It was as if he'd slapped her. She pushed his hands away and licked her lips. 'I want to get out.'

'Wait until the paramedics get here: you're bleeding.'

Danny stared at him, surprised. 'I am?'

He looked at her forehead and nodded.

Right on cue, something trickled down her nose. Blood? Danny raised her hand and touched her face.

He caught her wrist and pulled it away. *'Careful.'*

She looked at the sticky, red smear on her fingers and squeezed her eyes shut. It felt as if blunt needles were being driven into her face. When she opened her eyes again, the Serial Killer had been replaced by another face topped by thinning brown hair and dominated by a pair of large brown cocker-spaniel eyes watching her anxiously through glasses.

The Cocker Spaniel pressed a handkerchief gently against her forehead and asked in an American accent, 'Are you OK?'

Danny took the handkerchief from him, wondering where the Serial Killer had gone and why there were so many Americans around. She swallowed a giggle.

Concussed, slightly hysterical, Lucid Danny decided.

The Cocker Spaniel held up his hand. 'How many fingers?'

Her teeth began to chatter. 'Why? H-have you lost s-some?'

The Serial Killer wedged himself in beside the Cocker Spaniel. 'The paramedics are on the way, let them do that.' He noticed Danny's shudders and disappeared again. Then CS disappeared and SK reappeared, minus his sweater.

Danny giggled. 'Do . . . do you rehearse your m-moves?'

'Stop it.' SK growled.

'I *can't!*' She laughed, then whimpered as the pain increased.

'All that wriggling around is only making things worse,' SK said.

Danny cracked open an eyelid. Worse for who? Him? Or her?

He leaned forward to cover her with his sweater and stopped when he saw the ID badge attached to her blue uniform tunic.

Danny noticed a spreading patch of scarlet soaking his shirt-sleeve at the wrist. 'Y-you're bleeding.'

SK didn't answer.

She gritted her teeth against the pain and touched the edge of his sleeve. '*You're bleeding.*'

He looked at her fiercely, 'Daneka Lawton? *You're* Daneka Lawton?'

Her hand dropped to her lap. 'Yes. W-what's it t-to you?'

The Cocker Spaniel popped up again behind SK to peer intently at Danny's ID. His eyes widened. He placed a restraining hand on SK's shoulder. 'Not now, Ross, she's hurt.'

His words seemed ominous, but Danny couldn't hold the thought. The Serial Killer's face swam in and out of focus as her stomach started doing a Mexican wave that slowly spread up her oesophagus. She took deep breaths and tried to concentrate. Ross? His name was Ross? That was significant, but she couldn't remember why. Her stomach cramped — she had to get out of the truck.

'Sit still!' Ross the Serial Killer snapped. 'The paramedics are here.'

Suddenly the name in the letter Danny had received that morning popped into her mind. Ross Fabello. She stared at Ross, her stomach churning.

He gazed back stonily.

She had to ask. 'Who *are* you?'

His black eyes bored into hers. 'I'm Ross Fabello,' he said. 'I'm Patrick's brother.'

Danny grabbed her mouth.

Ross Fabello leapt backwards a moment too late.

She leaned out the door.

And threw up on his shoes.

Chapter 2

'Four hours,' Vanessa Cooper told Ross. 'Charge Nurse Lawton will have four hours of neurological observations before the doctors will even consider letting you see her.' Her nostrils quivered as if she'd smelt something nasty. 'It's up to you if you want to wait or not. You're in the queue to get your arm checked, but it'd be quicker to go to the private Accident and Medical Centre across the road.'

It would also get rid of him. 'I'll wait.'

Vanessa didn't look happy. 'If I get a moment, I'll dress it myself.' It sounded like a threat.

Obviously, Ms Cooper was a friend of Daneka Lawton's. She'd come barrelling down the hill after the crash and stayed while the paramedics transferred their patient to the ED. There were several more staff members waiting when they got there, including the hospital manager. Now that he'd finally tracked her down, Ross wasn't going to let four little hours stop him from speaking to Daneka Lawton.

Vanessa looked down at his battered trainers and said, 'Oh dear, did the vomit ruin your shoes?'

Ross gave her a filthy look and went to find a seat amongst the walking wounded in the waiting room. Jeff had loaned him an old pair of running shoes he'd found in the trunk of his car, but they were too small and pinched his toes. He sank onto an orange plastic chair and thought irritably that blisters were all he needed right now to add to the smell of puke clinging to the bottom of his pants.

He knew Daneka Lawton hadn't planned to throw up on him, he'd just had the bad luck to be in the wrong place at the wrong time, but he'd seen the ghost of a smile on her small, battered face as he helped the paramedics transfer her from the truck to the red plastic scoop. Before they'd moved her, they'd put her into a hard collar. Ross thought it should have been a straitjacket.

One of the paramedics called her Danny, and he thought it suited her far better than *Daneka* — *Danny* made him think of scrappy, troublesome boys.

He stared moodily at Jeff's shoes. If Breda, his mother, had been there she'd have seized the opportunity to pull her wise Irish mammy act and trot out some inexplicable proverb, along the lines of : *You must crack the nuts before you can eat the kernel.* Ross felt like his nuts had been in a vice ever since he'd been handed the job of coming to New Zealand to gain access to Patrick's two children. Hell, everybody knew that if aliens ever landed on Planet Earth Ross Fabello would not be the people's choice to make first contact. If he was in a good mood he'd watch from a distance and take notes, but if they arrived on a bad day he'd yell at them to get the hell off his front lawn. Deirdre, the youngest of his sisters, would've been a much better candidate, but she'd been a step ahead of him and ruled herself out by claiming her latest boyfriend might be the one. It was all that was needed to whip Breda into a marital frenzy and Ross onto a plane headed across the Pacific Ocean.

Nothing was going to get in the way of Ross seeing Ms Lawton now that he'd found her. He couldn't believe his luck, or decide if it was good luck or bad luck. He'd been trying to reach her ever since Patrick had died and the family had discovered he had two children in New Zealand, of all places. That Patrick had never thought to pass this little bit of information on to his parents wasn't surprising: Patrick enjoyed playing the black sheep. Whenever he came home he fell out with the rest of the family and left in a huff.

Nothing was ever his fault — he was misunderstood. He was also lazy, selfish and jealous of his older brother's success as a writer. Each time Ross looked at the devastation and bewilderment on his parents' faces he wanted to wring Patrick's neck. His brother had done some lousy things in his time, but keeping Breda and Vito ignorant about the existence of their two grandchildren was the worst. They were desperate to contact Patrick's children, their last link with their dead son.

It was pure chance that Ross was at the hospital construction site. Jeff Roseman was a long-time friend; they'd grown up on the same street and gone to school together. When Jeff married his New Zealand-born girlfriend, Christine, and moved to her home country, Ross kept in touch. Jeff, who co-owned Criterion Construction with his father-in-law, had met Ross at Auckland Airport when he'd arrived earlier that morning, and when Ross said he planned to stay awake until night rather than hit the sack Jeff suggested he might like to come with him to visit Criterion's hospital project.

They arrived in time to see the truck careering down the slope and were the first to reach it after it crashed. It was Ross who smashed the window to get to the nutcase who'd taken the vehicle on a sleigh ride down the hill, cutting his wrist in the process. He was relieved when the woman slumped over the steering wheel moved and was taken aback when he got a good look at her. She had blue hair — or at least, short, spiky fair hair tipped with blue — and wore silver safety-pin earrings. When they stopped rolling around in her head, her golden-brown eyes reminded Ross of the toffees his Granny O'Rourke sent from Ireland every Christmas. But the biggest surprise was the name on the ID tag clipped to the front of her uniform: *Daneka Lawton, Clinical Nurse Specialist,*

Emergency Department.

Ross was stunned. When he'd helped the paramedics lift Danny Lawton from the truck, she'd felt as light as a feather, fine-boned and with the graceful limbs of a ballerina. And the battered face of a prize-fighter.

He cradled a polystyrene cup of piss-poor coffee against his chest and tried to get comfortable on the plastic chair. The hospital manager had prevented him from following Danny into the examination cubicle. The truck had hit the concrete blocks like a freight train and she hadn't been wearing a seat belt, so it was a miracle she hadn't come flying through the windscreen, although she had a nasty cut and one hell of an egg on her forehead.

Ross studied the waiting room and reflected that, no matter where you were in the world, hospital waiting rooms looked the same: tired, badly decorated, and filled with a combination of frustrated desperation and plain old boredom. Despite the circumstances, the writer in him soaked it all up, tucking it away into his mental file to be pulled out the next time he was setting a scene in a hospital or needed to recall just how desperation or boredom looked, felt and — he grimaced at the coffee in the cup — tasted. Although God only knew when he'd write anything decent again — he wasn't so much suffering writer's block as writer's drought, it had been so long.

He watched a harassed young mother struggle to keep a fractious toddler occupied in the play area while pretending that if there hadn't been a room full of people watching she wouldn't have been yelling at Junior by now. Alongside Ross, a plump, matronly looking woman was knitting something purple on fat plastic needles. Her fingers flew and her elbow kept digging Ross in the arm, but she'd given up apologizing. Her eyes darted about the room as purple wool continued to unravel magically from a large tapestry bag at her feet, reminding him of Mary Poppins. He entertained fantasies of her delving inside the bag and pulling out a hat rack.

In the corner opposite the play area, a tall, cylindrical fish tank bubbled while fat, golden fish serenely ignored the children who pressed their faces against the glass or tapped to get their attention. A large television was chained to a shelf high on one wall, with the volume turned down low. Tired, dog-eared magazines and old newspapers littered several low tables and spilled onto the carpet beneath them. A long wire rack half-filled with information leaflets leaned at a drunken angle, the childish scribble on several of them testament to parents using them to distract bored children.

Vanessa Cooper watched Ross through the glass window surrounding the triage desk. He noticed she had a smile for everybody but him, but he was indifferent to her venomous looks, and continued to tally up his personal grievances. He was jet-lagged; his stomach soured by bad coffee; his feet hurt; he stank of puke and his ass was numb from sitting on the hard chair. What the hell had Danny Lawton been thinking? And why had the freakin' truck been parked by the ambulance bay in the first place? Ross heard the hospital manager explain to Jeff that the message Danny had received to say a critically ill patient was en route to the ED had prompted her to take matters into her own hands. In her place, Ross would have done the same thing, but it wasn't the kind of behaviour that inspired confidence in a person with sole responsibility for two young children. He shook his head, still struggling to believe that Pat had been a father. Responsibility and Patrick were two words that didn't sit happily together.

When the hospital manager mentioned that Daneka Lawton had suffered a recent bereavement and been under a lot of stress lately, Jeff sent Ross a meaningful look. Jeff always had been a soft touch, but Ross thought he might be less sympathetic if he'd seen what Pat's death had done to his parents. When the manager said that Danny was the nurse in charge, Ross thought he must be kidding. He wouldn't leave her in charge of a lemonade stand let alone a busy Emergency Room.

When the manager then proceeded to cover himself by hanging Danny out to dry, Ross thought he was a jerk.

Jeff suddenly appeared in the waiting room, looking grim. He snagged the empty chair beside Ross. 'I found the supervisor and fired him. The patient they were bringing in is in the heart unit and he's doing OK.' Jeff paused, looked over at Vanessa in her glass prison and smiled. She nodded back. 'Heard anything yet?' he asked.

'No.'

'How's the arm?'

'Thanks to the icy blasts coming from Ms Cooper's direction, I don't feel a thing. How's the truck?'

'Write-off,' Jeff grimaced. 'There was blood on the windshield. She took one helluva knock.'

Ross recalled the blood trickling down Danny Lawton's face and the cold, clammy feel of her skin. Vomiting wasn't a good sign following a head injury. 'What sane person pulls a stunt like that?' he demanded irritably.

'She didn't feel she had a choice,' Jeff said. 'You heard what the manager said — a seriously ill patient was arriving any minute by ambulance. If my foreman had been doing his job properly there would never have been a problem in the first place.'

Ross grunted. He was in a very bad mood and had been ever since the writer's block set in. 'She's got *blue* hair.'

'Yes, I noticed.'

'And safety pins in her ears.'

Jeff's brows rose. 'Real ones?'

'No,' Ross admitted, grudgingly. 'I bet she's got a bolt through her navel and tattoos on her ass, though.'

Jeff gazed at him in disbelief. 'When did you turn into such a judgemental pain in the butt? One of your old girlfriends had her nipples pierced and wasn't shy about showing them either.' He looked pointedly at Ross. 'If you ask me, Danny Lawton isn't the one who should be worrying about how she looks.'

Ross was unshaven, his eyes were bloodshot and his clothes rumpled. When Jeff had picked him up at the airport, Ross had refused the invitation to be dropped at the city apartment overlooking the harbour which he was renting. Jeff's wife Christine had wanted Ross to come and stay with them, but Jeff explained Ross liked his privacy.

'I thought I left my mother stateside,' Ross said.

Taking a leaf from Breda Fabello's book, Jeff replied bluntly, 'You look like hell. If you insist on talking to Danny Lawton now, she'll probably call security.' He sniffed. 'And you stink.'

'That's too bad. It's taken me months to find her, and I won't let a little thing like wrinkled clothes, five o'clock shadow and *her* puke put me off now.'

Jeff wondered what the hell was wrong with Ross. He could be moody, but he'd never been nasty, and he had the best sense of humour of anyone Jeff knew, but at the moment it seemed to have deserted him, right along with his manners. He seemed . . . *jaded*. Jeff reminded himself that Ross had just stepped off a long flight from the States at 5.30 that morning and that he'd been given a painful and difficult task by his family. Pat and Ross had never been close, largely due to Pat's refusal to grow up and his jealousy of his older brother's success. Jeff raised his hands in defeat. 'OK, but don't be surprised if the poor woman runs screaming from the room.'

Ross snorted. 'Give me a break! Do you really think a woman

who just ran a truck into a pile of concrete blocks is going to be frightened off by five o'clock shadow and rumpled clothes?'

Vanessa interrupted them to say that Danny was ready to see Ross.

Jeff beat him to it by asking, 'How is she?'

'She's got concussion, a head laceration and contusions all over, so she's going to be sore for the rest of the week.' Her cold green eyes speared Ross. 'She does not need any more stress. If it were up to me, you wouldn't get within six feet of her. Unfortunately, it isn't up to me.'

Ross smiled at her. 'Guess it must be my lucky day, then.'

Vanessa led him to a room with a sign on the door with *CLINICAL NURSE SPECIALISTS* written in capital letters. She made Ross wait while she went in and pushed the door to behind her. He heard her say flatly, 'He's here.'

Ross heard Danny Lawton ask, 'Which one? The one with the Cocker Spaniel eyes or the Serial Killer?'

He'd chalked up her earlier comment about his resemblance to a serial killer to the concussion, but now he wasn't so sure. Ross touched the stubble on his jaw self-consciously. He didn't look that bad. Did he?

'The Serial Killer. The Cocker Spaniel,' Vanessa's voice rose, *'the nice one*, seems to be his friend.'

'Just my luck,' Danny said.

'Shall I tell him to go away?' Vanessa asked hopefully.

You can try, Ross thought grimly.

'No.' Danny sounded weary. 'Best get on with it.'

Ross felt a treacherous stab of sympathy and told himself to toughen up. There was no way he would allow her to prolong this nightmare for his parents. He pushed the door open and stepped into the room. 'Sorry to break up the party, but we serial killers have busy schedules.'

Danny sat behind one of four desks ranged along the opposite wall. When she saw Ross, her upper lip curled. She tried to look down her nose at him, but the effect was ruined because she was sitting down and her nose had swollen to twice its usual size. Ross was shocked at how bad she looked. Her eyelids were swollen and turning black, while the cut on her forehead had been cleaned and white paper strips applied to the wound. With her cropped hair and flat chest, Danny Lawton looked more like a teenage boy than a woman. She looked vulnerable and in no condition for the conversation they were about to have. Ross wished he could walk away and come back again another time.

Vanessa seemed reluctant to leave Danny alone with him, studying Ross suspiciously as if she suspected he might be concealing an axe under his clothes.

'You'd better get back to the triage desk, Van,' Danny finally said.

'Oh for chrissakes!' he snapped. 'I left my machete and ice pick at home with my ski mask!'

A smothered snort of laughter came from Danny's direction, but when he checked she was poker-faced and staring at the top of the desk.

'Haven't you got some poor sap due for a hypodermic or an enema?' Ross asked Vanessa.

Her eyes narrowed to slits. 'If you upset her, so help me I'll find a way to give *you* an enema *with* a hypodermic needle,' she said over her shoulder as she left the room.

His lips twitched and Danny frowned. She didn't want him turning human on her.

Ross took his time looking about the office. Two computers stood on a narrow bench at one end of the room. Kids' drawings were taped on the wall behind two of the desks, alongside various charts and flyers advertising courses and study days. He read the messages on several of the mugs discarded around the room.

Super Nurse.

Is It Time For Your Medication Or Mine?

The one on Danny's desk had written on it in black letters: *How Many Times Do I Have To Flush Before You Go Away?* A notice on the wall behind her read *Sarcasm Is Just One More Service We Offer.* Ross spied a dog-eared copy of one of his earliest novels on one of the desks beside her, the place marked with a wooden tongue depressor.

Danny indicated a worn blue chair in front of her desk with a negligent flip of her hand. He sat down and transferred his attention to the two-tiered tray on her desk, which had a piece of white cardboard attached to it with her name crossed out and reprinted several times in felt pen, each time in different handwriting. Ross read *Duh-Nika, Nika* and finally *Knickers*.

She jerked the basket and its telltale sign around to face her. 'Why are you still here?'

Ross settled back into the chair and folded his arms across his chest, his relaxed attitude telling Danny, I have all the time in the world and I'm used to getting what I want. 'Did you honestly think I would leave after I'd spent so long trying to run you to ground?'

Danny leaned back and crossed her arms over her uniform tunic. Her body language semaphored back *News Flash — me too.* 'Having finally set eyes on you, I think my instincts were excellent.'

Ross fixed her with his most intimidating stare. 'The way I look is hardly relevant, Ms Lawton.'

Danny raised her brows in disbelief, and the white strips made a little hill on her forehead. *'Hardly relevant?* Have you looked in a mirror recently? You look like a mad axe-murderer.'

'Hilarious.'

'Not from where I'm sitting.'

Ross was intrigued. It had been a long, *long* time since he'd locked horns with somebody who didn't give a damn that he was RF O'Rourke celebrated novelist, and even longer since he'd lost an argument. Family arguments didn't count; his family regarded his increasing moodiness as a free pass to interfere in his life. It occurred to Ross that somewhere along the line he might have turned into that nightmare creature, the celebrity prima donna. He dismissed the idea; he wasn't the type.

'For your information, Ms Lawton, I got off a plane from the States at five-thirty this morning.'

'It's two o'clock in the afternoon. Plenty of time to tidy yourself up, unless of course you had something else on the agenda? Serial Killer Conference? Mad Axe-murderer Convention?'

Danny Lawton might have a screw loose, but she was an entertaining screwball. 'You think I need to worry about creating a good first impression? This, from a woman who crashes a truck into a pile of concrete blocks?'

'We've explained all that,' she said stiffly.

A brief knock on the door heralded Vanessa carrying a stethoscope, blood-pressure cuff, small torch and chart. 'Time for your neuro obs, Danny.'

'Shouldn't you be lying down somewhere?' Ross asked Danny.

She pushed up her sleeve so that Vanessa could wrap the cuff around her arm. 'Shouldn't you be in America somewhere?'

He glowered at her.

When Vanessa had gone, Danny asked, '*What* exactly do you want?'

When he said, 'To see my niece and nephew', Ross thought he glimpsed fear in her eyes.

'Why?' she demanded.

'Why what?'

'*Why*, after all these years, do you suddenly want to get to know

Matt and Mia? They've never received so much as a birthday card from the Fabellos, so why the sudden interest? What is it?' Her look was scathing. 'Guilt?'

Ross stiffened. 'We didn't know about them until we went through Pat's things after he died.'

Danny's contemptuous expression told Ross exactly what she thought of him and his family. 'Why should I let you get to know them? If you're anything like their father, you'll disappear after a couple of weeks and only reappear at yearly intervals.'

Anger and resentment left a sour taste in his mouth. So Pat had played the same fast and loose game with his children as he had with the rest of the family. He'd done more than his fair share of sweeping up in the wake of his brother's catastrophic, selfish actions.

'The children are part of the Fabello family,' Ross said coldly. 'And we are keen — no,' he leaned forward and fixed Danny with an implacable black stare, 'let me rephrase that: we're determined to get to know them better. My brother is dead, and his children are all we have left of him. They have grandparents, aunts, uncles and cousins.'

Danny looked down at the desk.

Ross waited. She was starting to crack.

'Crikey, you mean there are more of you?'

He gritted his teeth. 'Don't push it, Ms Lawton.'

Danny leaned towards him, her eyes blazing. 'Don't threaten me, Mr Fabello! My *sister* — Matt and Mia's *mother* — is dead, and their so-called father never even knew because he couldn't be bothered to keep in touch. He didn't even know she was sick, because she didn't want to worry him. So you can take your big happy family and shove it right up your arse.' Abruptly she stopped talking and sat back.

They'd both lost siblings in recent months, but the Lawton

sisters' relationship had obviously been much closer than the one he'd shared with his brother. He'd seen tears in Danny's eyes before she'd looked away.

'How did she die?' he asked quietly.

'Breast cancer.'

Ross clasped the back of his neck and stared up at the ceiling. He wished again that he hadn't pulled the short straw and been dispatched to deal with this particular item of family business. Deirdre would have known what to say to Danny; Ross didn't have a clue. What could anybody say that would be right under the circumstances? He could imagine that Daniella Lawton's death had been far different to Pat's drunken fall from a luxury yacht.

Ross dragged his eyes from the ceiling to Danny. 'I'm sorry.'

She shrugged and stared at the desk.

'How long ago?'

'Six months.'

'You were . . .' he probed carefully, 'close?'

Pain and grief washed across Danny's bruised and battered face.

Ross squeezed the back of his neck to keep from reaching across the desk to touch her.

'We were twins,' she said softly.

He had twin sisters and knew just how strong the bond between Danny and her sister would've been. He couldn't imagine Aoife or Annie without the other one. Marriage, kids and moving a couple of hours apart hadn't made any difference to the deep, intrinsic bond they shared. They were like two halves of a whole — if you hurt one, you hurt the other.

Ross could tell Danny was uncomfortable about revealing so much of herself, and wasn't surprised when she went on the offensive — in her shoes, he would've done the same.

'What proof do I have that you're Patrick's brother? I didn't even know he had a brother.'

She was noticeably paler. Ross was anxious to wind up the meeting so that Danny could get some rest and he could put some distance between himself and all that raw emotion. For some reason Daniella Lawton's death felt far more real to him than Pat's. He pointed at the paperback on the other desk. 'That's me.'

Danny looked at the book. 'What is?'

'I'm the writer.'

She stared. 'You're trying to tell me you're RF O'Rourke?'

He felt like an ass. 'Yes.'

Danny touched the book. 'You wrote this book?'

'Yes. If you look on the back there's probably a photograph.'

She turned the book over and studied the photograph. It was a black-and-white shot of a man in a battered black leather jacket with the collar turned up staring unsmilingly at the camera, as cars streaked behind him. Danny held it up. 'You're trying to tell me that this is you?'

OK, so the photograph was a few years old, but Ross hated publicity shots — it wasn't as if he *wanted* to be recognized. Her incredulous disbelief was beginning to annoy him. *'It is me.'*

'Uh huh,' she nodded slowly. 'Either this has been airbrushed to hell or they used George Clooney as your stand-in, because it doesn't look anything like you.' Danny tapped the photo. 'This man looks human.' She almost added: *This man has a regular-sized nose.*

'It's an old photo. I wrote that book years ago.'

'Of course you did,' she said patronizingly. 'But even if you are RF O'Rourke, it doesn't make you Ross Fabello, does it?'

'It's a pen name! O'Rourke is my mother's maiden name; the RF stands for Ross Fabello. I'll give you the number of my agent; she'll back up what I'm telling you.'

'D'you think I came down with the last spring shower? It'll probably be your sister or the Cocker Spaniel's girlfriend on the other end of the line.'

'Are you calling me a liar?'

Her brows rose and the little hill reappeared on her forehead. 'You expect me to take you at your word? A complete stranger? Who wants access to Mia and Matt?'

She had a point. Ross changed the subject. 'Why do you keep calling Jeff a cocker spaniel?'

'Because he's got beautiful brown eyes.' '

As opposed to a serial killer's eyes?'

That aggravating upper lip curled.

'Yes.'

'Which are?' Ross demanded.

'Black, bloodshot and unhinged.'

Danny suddenly gripped the edge of the desk and closed her eyes.

'What's wrong?' Ross was halfway out of his chair when Vanessa walked in.

She hurried to Danny's side. 'Danny, you look like crap.'

Danny took deep breaths. 'Thanks.'

'It's time you went,' Vanessa told Ross in a don't-mess-with-me voice.

He felt torn between concern for Danny and fear of losing her again. 'We haven't finished.'

'Yes, we have,' Danny said faintly.

'Yes, you have!' Vanessa insisted.

'I'll be in touch again *soon*,' Ross said firmly.

As Vanessa shut the door behind him, Ross heard Danny say feebly, 'Get knotted, Fabello.'

When Jeff phoned with an invitation to dinner, Ross told him that Danny thought he looked like a cocker spaniel.

'She does? Why?'

'She thinks you've got beautiful brown eyes.'

Jeff chuckled. 'How do you think I got Christine to marry me? What does she think you look like?'

'None of your damned business.' 'That bad, huh?'

Ross grunted. 'What does "Get knotted" mean?'

'Did Danny Lawton tell you to get knotted?'

'Uh huh. Am I right in thinking she wasn't offering to teach me rope tricks?'

'You got it.'

Chapter 3

Danny hunched over the laptop and gently tapped the keyboard. It was 4 a.m. and she was researching the enemy. If — when — Vanessa discovered her missing, Danny knew Kommandant Cooper would march her straight back to bed. Danny didn't mind, it was nice having somebody take charge for a change. She'd given up trying to sleep after Vanessa woke her for the second time to check she hadn't lapsed into unconsciousness.

'How'd you feel?' She asked.

'My head hurts.'

Vanessa yawned. 'I know that, but do you know where you are?'

'I'm in hell, and I don't belong here. Ross bloody Fabello does, but I don't.'

'Nothing wrong with you.' Vanessa lay down and went back to sleep.

Danny watched her from the other side of her double bed, wishing she could do the same. Eventually she gave up trying. The gyrations and contortions required to slide from the bed without disturbing Vanessa alerted Danny to what to expect in the morning. Bruises seemed to have blossomed all over her body.

She shuffled past Matt and Mia's bedrooms to the kitchen and booted up the miniscule, shiny, grey laptop that Patrick had bought on his last visit — or at least, semi-bought: Danny had taken over the repayments when Nella died. When she first saw the size of the tiny machine, Danny was worried Patrick had bought himself a make-up case to go with all his hair products.

The light from the laptop lit up the dark interior of the kitchen. Danny squinted at the screen, her head tilted sideways; one side of her nose was more swollen than the other, and it was the only way she could see over it.

Several things concerned her about Ross Fabello: foremost that he was here, but also that he didn't seem to be anything like his brother, and had a presence that Patrick had lacked. Patrick might have got the looks, but it was obvious that his big brother had got the brains. Danny was a good judge of character and trusted her instincts. One look from those penetrating black eyes had alerted her that Ross couldn't be manipulated like his brother. Danny had run rings around Patrick in a verbal argument — although, in fairness, Mother Nature had also contributed by making Patrick a doofus. Danny's conversation with Ross after the accident had revealed him to be shrewd and — even more worrying — just as thick-skinned and rude as she was. By stealing her best weapons, he'd done more than wrong-foot her; he'd knocked Danny flat on her bum. She needed to regroup and quickly come up with a different plan of action. Sticking her head in the sand and hoping he'd go away hadn't worked.

Danny briefly considered employing Nella's tactics, but discarded the idea. She'd never pull it off; she didn't find arrogant men with bloodshot eyes and big noses attractive, and she knew Ross wasn't attracted to her either. Unlike her mother and sister, Danny was a lousy actress. While they were growing up, it was Nella who had the boys falling at her feet, Nella who fell in and out of love, Nella who was always getting her heart broken — sometimes it even lasted an entire week. Danny was choosy about who she went out with, and was always the one who broke things off. The more she liked a guy, the sooner she exited the relationship; and she had enough insight to recognize that she got rid of them before they could abandon her the way her father had. She also understood that Nella's relationship with Patrick Fabello was a carbon copy of their mother and father's. Mike Lawton was an English-born seaman who'd settled in New Zealand in the 'seventies. He never married Rose Smith, and spent weeks at a time away from home, working the coastal routes up and down New Zealand and returning to England at least once a year for a prolonged visit. He never took Rose or the twins with him, saying it was too expensive. Danny was convinced he'd had a wife and family they knew nothing about and who knew nothing about them.

'You're tough, Danny,' Mike had told her before he departed for England the last time, supposedly to see his sick mother. 'You're not like your mother or your sister. While I'm gone, you're in charge.'

Danny was much closer to her father than to her mother. It was Mike who encouraged her tomboyish tendencies and shortened her name to Danny instead of the more feminine *Dani*. She missed Mike much more than Nella did when he was away, and was his shadow when he returned.

'You're like me, Danny. You're ruled by your head, not your heart,' he always said.

Danny wondered if her apparent toughness had made it easier for him to walk away from them. The letters Rose sent to the address in England that Mike had given them came back marked *Wrong Address*, and she was told that the telephone number was disconnected. The day Danny finally admitted that her father wouldn't be coming home, she'd cropped her hair and painted it with pink and green hair mascara. It was the only show of rebellion she allowed herself. She was now the head of the family, and if she didn't keep her act together her mother would disintegrate completely.

Four years later, Rose died from breast cancer. She'd fallen out with her family before the twins were born, so the girls had never met their maternal relatives. They were nineteen and alone. While Danny got tougher, Nella grew more dependent, and was content to let Danny call the shots until Patrick Fabello arrived on the scene. It didn't take long for Danny to figure out that Patrick wasn't offering her sister a lifetime commitment. When Matt and then Mia arrived, Danny took on responsibility for them, too.

She googled *RF O'Rourke* and watched as pages of information came up on the screen. He had a website, but Danny wasn't interested in reading about how old Ross was when he was toilet-trained and lost his first tooth. She wanted to look at photos of RF O'Rourke so that she could compare them with the face of the Serial Killer, and she wanted dirt — the filthier, the better.

There were plenty of photos. And they were all of Ross Fabello, admittedly a tidier, smoother-looking Ross Fabello, but there was no mistaking that surly expression and those intense, dark eyes. Until a couple of years ago he'd lived with the ballerina Simone Marchant — even Danny had heard of her. She studied a photo of Ross wearing a tuxedo at some red-carpet do with Simone draped on his arm. Simone was a doe-eyed, raven-haired beauty with a radiant smile, and the graceful, upright posture and toned body of a dancer. She was wearing a Vera Wang original and looked nice — way too nice for Ross, who looked about as cheery as a turkey at Yuletide. Although Danny had to admit he did clean up OK, but then what man wouldn't look good in Armani? The only reason Danny knew Ross was wearing Armani and Simone was wearing Vera Wang was because it said so beneath the photo.

If Simone was representative of the kind of woman who attracted Ross, Danny had been bang on the mark about him not being attracted to her. Her interest and knowledge of designer clothes was about as extensive as a plumber's, her hair was short and blue (at the moment), and her breasts were so small she didn't bother buying bras. Danny peered over her swollen nose at Ross Fabello's most prominent feature — there wasn't a tuxedo made that'd be able to shrink *that* honker to normal proportions.

His split from Simone hadn't been amicable; she'd tried to take him to court, claiming mental cruelty and loss of earnings, because she'd sacrificed her career while living with Ross. Danny snorted, and winced at the pain. Simone Marchant was an idiot if it had taken her three years to figure out what had taken Danny just a few hours: Ross Fabello was a ruthless bastard. She clicked in and out of a few more sites — a *very wealthy* ruthless bastard. All his books had made the *New York Times* bestseller list, and one of them, *John Doe*, was about to be released as a movie with Kevin Spacey and Marisa Tomei in the lead roles.

'So why is he so miserable?' Danny muttered. 'He's got money coming out of every orifice, beautiful women dumb enough to live with him, and he has the gall to look unhappy. The man deserves a slap.'

'Who are you talking to?'

Danny started. Vanessa was standing in the doorway glowering at her. 'Don't do that!'

'What are you doing out of bed? You're supposed to be resting.'

'I couldn't sleep.'

Vanessa pointed towards the bedroom. 'Get to bed!'

Danny began closing down the laptop.

'What were you looking at?' Vanessa asked.

'Ross bloody Fabello, or at least RF O'Rourke Ross bloody Fabello.'

'Really?' Vanessa's slippers almost left scorch marks on the wooden floor. 'You can leave the laptop if you want, I'll close it down. You go back to bed.' She was a sucker for gossip and celebrity pages.

'Don't be fooled by that Armani tux,' Danny warned. 'He's still Darth Vader — he just left his helmet at home.'

Vanessa peered at the screen and squawked, 'He slept with Simone Marchant!'

Danny winced. 'Please, I'm already feeling nauseous. Can you imagine what it'd be like sleeping with him? Like a trip to the Death Star.' She shuffled to the door. 'I'm going to bed.'

'You do that,' Vanessa sat down in front of the laptop. 'He *does* look like George Clooney.' She leaned closer. 'With a bigger nose, of course.'

In the morning, before she left for her shift at the hospital, Vanessa made Danny promise she'd get Deryl, her neighbour, to take the children to school. Overnight, Danny's face had puffed up like a blowfish and turned purple and black.

'You need to take things easy today,' Vanessa said.

'What I need is a hitman to take out Ross Fabello.'

Reading his website had dampened down some of Vanessa's take-no-prisoners attitude to Ross. The guy was loaded and well-connected, whereas Danny was broke and unconnected. 'I checked on his website: RF O'Rourke is thirty-six years old. He has a brother called Patrick and four sisters. He's also got a house with a turret.'

The house was spectacularly beautiful. It was tucked away down an overgrown driveway behind a rusty gate and stood on a cliff overlooking the ocean. The photos had been taken from a boat out in the bay below the white stone house. RF O'Rourke was notoriously reclusive and jealously guarded his privacy. He wasn't the kind of man who'd invite journalists in for tours of his inner sanctum.

'He probably uses the turret to practise pouring boiling oil on his enemies,' Danny sniped. 'Van, will you do me a favour? If I have to murder him, will you help me bury the body?'

Vanessa nodded solemnly. 'Absolutely.' She decided not to mention another thing she'd discovered on the website: that Ross Fabello's birthday was November the seventeenth, the same as Danny's. It was a day Vanessa knew Danny was dreading — her first birthday without her twin.

'So what's an uncle again, Auntie Danny?' Mia asked as Danny crept about the kitchen spilling cereals into bowls and snack bars into lunchboxes.

Danny barely heard her. Her head felt as if it was stuffed with wadding that was swelling and contracting in time with the thud of her heart.

She still wore her nightclothes, a shapeless, over-sized fuchsia-pink T-shirt beneath an orange-and-brown leopard-print dressing gown, and a pair of grey and pink slippers with *Hot Stuff* in faded black writing across the instep. The slippers had seen better days. Canary-yellow socks poked through the holes worn by her big toes, but she refused to buy a new pair because summer was just around the corner. Unfortunately, several days of southerlies and torrential rain were making Danny feel as if spring and winter were having a good old laugh at her puny human expense — one day it was sunny, the next cold and wet. She scrubbed a hand wearily across her hair. In the morning, it always stood up on one side of her head and was flat as a pancake on the other, which meant she looked as bad as she felt.

Mia had cried when she saw Danny's battered face, and Matt had offered to fix breakfast. After sleepless hours spent worrying about Ross bloody Fabello and what she should tell the children, Danny was exhausted.

'Auntie Danny?' Mia asked.

'Mmm?'

'What's an uncle?'

Matt spoke around a mouthful of cereal. 'It's the brother of your mother or father.'

Danny considered telling him not to speak with his mouth full, but couldn't be bothered. She sat at the kitchen table, one eye on the book wedged beneath the table leg closest to him. It was imperative the leg didn't fall off the book — it had taken them ages to find the right-sized book and get it positioned just so.

Matt studied the back of the cereal packet. 'What do you call somebody who poisons cornflakes?'

'I don't know,' Danny replied. 'What do you call somebody who poisons cornflakes?'

'A cereal killer.'

She laughed weakly.

'Mum didn't have any brothers — just Auntie Danny,' Mia said.

Matt rolled his eyes. 'He's *Dad's* brother, stupid!'

That started a row, just as there was a knock on the front door. Danny expected it to be Deryl, the neighbour who looked after the children when she was at work, but when she opened the door she found herself looking up at Ross Fabello. '*Oh shit . . .* ' she mumbled.

He looked rested and almost human in faded denim jeans and a white T-shirt beneath a black leather jacket. Clearly *he* hadn't been awake all night worrying about *her*. Danny eyed the black jacket. It wasn't the kind you found in a cheap chain store. Danny could hear the *ka-ching ka-ching* of a cash register as she stared. With the stubble gone and his eyes no longer tinted red, Danny reluctantly conceded that the photo on the back of the book might not be George Clooney after all. She was upset that his nose appeared to have shrunk, or maybe she was just getting used to it.

It didn't seem to be nearly as big— well, perhaps, large, arrogant, *noteworthy* — but not the epic proportions she recalled from the day before. He also seemed to have got a lot taller. Danny checked his feet to see if he was wearing platforms, and was disgruntled to see a pair of bright white Nikes sparkling up at her.

'Good morning to you, too.' Ross looked her over. Hell, she was a mess. He hoisted a plastic bag. 'I brought breakfast.'

Danny looked at the bag suspiciously. Why was he suddenly being so nice? Whatever was in there was probably laced with arsenic.

'No, it's not poisoned.'

Was she that transparent?

The night before, Jeff had counselled Ross to be nice. 'You'll catch a lot more bees with honey.'

'Does that count for hornets, too?'

Jeff sighed. 'You're doing it again — remember Simone.'

How could Ross forget? He'd been totally upfront with Simone Marchant before she moved in with him. He told her he wasn't looking to get married or have children; that his Irish mother, Italian father, spendthrift brother, four voluble sisters and twelve nieces and nephews were all the family he could handle, and his writing would always come first. Simone insisted she understood how Ross felt about his writing, because she felt the same way about her dancing, and she thought his noisy, intrusive family was wonderful. Simone loved all things Irish, and considered Breda to be a Celtic treasure. Ross kept telling her his mother was a Celtic crock. For her part, Breda was flattered and willing to forgive Simone for not being a Catholic if she got Ross to put a ring on her finger and get her pregnant — in that order.

Aoife looked Simone up and down the first time they met and accused Ross of always hooking up with doormats. 'What you need is a woman who'll kick your ass at least once a day.'

Ross was truly surprised when, three years after she'd moved in, Simone had announced she was leaving him because their relationship was going nowhere.

'I kept thinking you'd fall in love with me, but I don't think you're capable of falling in love with anybody. You're generous with your money and your body, but you never share yourself with me. You built this beautiful, romantic house, and I thought that meant deep down you were romantic, too.'

Ross felt exasperated — and guilty. 'If you were so unhappy, why did you stay?'

'The sex, I guess. You're the best lover I've ever had.' Simone shook her head. 'I don't understand how you always know what I'm feeling and what I want in bed before I even know it myself, but the moment your feet hit the carpet you disappear inside a bubble I can't penetrate.'

He was furious when Simone was reported in a newspaper interview as saying that if Ross hadn't been so hot in bed she would have left him a lot sooner. Findlays, his publishers, had to bring in extra staff to manage the sudden increase in fan mail sent by crazed nymphomaniac women sending him their panties and contact details. When Simone took him to court for mental cruelty and lost earnings, they settled out of court for a figure that was nowhere near what Simone had wanted. For Ross, it wasn't about the money; it was the loss of trust and the seediness of the whole sordid affair that sickened him. He hated having his personal life splashed across the tabloids and magazines, hated being kept a prisoner in his own house by the paparazzi and nutcases camped at the end of his driveway. The only winners were the lawyers.

Ross looked at Danny's blackened eyes and squashed nose and decided she had something in her favour: she'd never want him to fall in love with her, and the only piece of herself she would ever want to give him would be the sharp edge of her tongue or her knee in his groin. He would never make the mistake of trusting her. A sentiment she returned.

Danny pointed at the disposable cup Ross held. 'Is that what I think it is?'

He looked at the coffee. 'What do you think it is?'

She sniffed and gagged.

Ross took a hasty step backwards. 'You're not going to be sick are you?'

Danny looked regretfully at his Nikes. 'Unfortunately not.' She gestured to the cup. 'I hate coffee.'

He stared at her in disbelief. 'You *hate* coffee?'

She nodded. 'I hate coffee.'

'*Everybody* likes coffee.'

'Not this body.' Ross waved the bag and Danny's traitorous nostrils flared. 'What's in there?'

'Freshly baked flaky croissants.' He moved it from side to side like a hypnotist with a watch.

Danny followed it with her eyes, her saliva buds bursting. Ross inched his way towards the door. She backed up a step at a time, her eyes flickering between the bag and the disposable cup of coffee. 'How did you get that? Starbucks isn't open this early in the morning. Is it?'

'Sure it is.'

Ross noted the cracked paintwork and pitted wooden floors in the hallway and tried to decide which looked worse, the house or Danny. She still wore the safety pins in her ears, her blue-tipped hair was squashed flat on one side of her head, and her battered nose slanted in the opposite direction. Her eyelids looked like fat bruised pillows wedged against her eyes. The godawful robe didn't help matters; even his mother owned a more attractive one. It was the first time Ross had seen Danny on her feet. She was average height and as straight up and down as a boy. He eased forward another step. 'How's your head?'

'Fine.' Danny halted her backwards shuffle. 'What are you doing here?'

'Bringing you breakfast.' Ross attempted another step.

She dug in, her holey old slippers toe-to-toe with his Nikes. 'Stop right there!'

He dredged up his best publicity smile; it was so rusty it was a wonder his facial muscles didn't squeak. It was wasted on Danny, who couldn't have cared less that RF O'Rourke was on her doorstep, smiling. She folded her arms beneath her non-existent breasts and said, 'You can't just come bursting into my house uninvited.'

'Auntie Danny? Who's that?'

Ross looked behind Danny and got his first look at Pat's daughter. A variety of emotions swamped him — uppermost disbelief that Pat was partly responsible for this beautiful child. Long, blonde hair hung down her back. She wore pink Barbie pyjamas and carried a faded cloth doll. She'd inherited Pat's blue eyes, and had already mastered the knack of looking at people from beneath her lashes.

'Are you our uncle?' she asked.

Ross looked at Danny. She opened her mouth, but for once nothing came out.

'Yes,' he said.

A boy, a few years older, joined the junior interrogator. Like his sister he wore pyjamas, but his were blue and decorated with Bart Simpson. Ross drew a deep, shuddering breath. Goosebumps pebbled his skin. Here was all the proof he needed that these children were his brother's. The boy was the image of Pat, with the same long, black, curly hair, bright blue eyes and olive skin. 'Who're you?' he asked.

'He's the uncle Auntie Danny told us about,' Mia — Ross remembered their names — told Matt.

Matt wasn't convinced. He had clearer memories of his father, and apart from the curly hair this guy didn't look much like him.

Danny came out of her trance. She grabbed Ross by the wrist to check his watch and nearly upended his coffee over his T-shirt. As Ross cursed, she flapped her hands at the kids. 'Get a move on! You'll be late for school!'

There was a mass exodus, leaving Ross to find his own way to the kitchen and take a seat amongst the breakfast dishes littering the big wooden table, one leg of which had been propped on a worn, red book. He was glad to see it wasn't one of his.

There were cracks in the kitchen ceiling, the walls needed re-plastering, and the plumbing over the sink looked ancient. Blue and white gingham curtains hung around the bottom of the sink bench, and the floorboards were planed from beautiful timber, like the ones in the hallway, but they needed a lot of work to return them to anything approaching their original beauty. Ross saw all the telltale signs of an old house that had been let go.

He carried his coffee over to look out the old double-hung window above the sink, and caught his breath. The view was magnificent. Acres of rolling green pasture with a few clusters of trees swept away to the distant cliffs. It was prime real estate. Whoever had made the decision to buy the place had made a good investment — Ross doubted it would have been Pat.

Behind the house was a roughly fenced back garden with a couple of kids' bikes and a trampoline perched drunkenly on a broken leg. Some tumbledown sheds constructed from red, rusting iron stood beneath large evergreen trees at the back of the garden area. Chickens pecked the ground outside the larger of the sheds, and a couple of fat, fleecy sheep — one black and one white — grazed beneath a washing line full of clothes, revolving slowly in the wind as the long, green grass flattened and tossed in a constant, undulating wave.

Danny reappeared and Ross froze, his coffee cup suspended in midair. Holy crap, what the *hell* was she wearing? Her trousers were baggy and mustard-yellow, her shirt was green and white stripes, topped by a burgundy paisley waistcoat and a long, black, shapeless cardigan that hung to her knees. She had a woollen turquoise scarf wound around her neck, and scuffed brown boots on her feet. Ross stared, his coffee forgotten. She looked like Coco the Clown. The leopard-skin robe and holey slipper thing she'd had going earlier had looked a whole lot better.

Danny searched the counter for the grocery list she'd written the previous day. Clothes didn't interest her much, and with money tight she bought most of her wardrobe from second-hand shops. Each morning Danny pulled on the first thing she found, adding more layers if her first choice wasn't warm enough. The results ranged from highly original to downright appalling. Today was downright appalling.

She went up on tiptoe to reach a stack of letters on top of one of the cupboards, and the hem of her shirt momentarily parted company with the top of her pants to expose a smooth expanse of light olive skin and the indentation of her navel. It wasn't pierced or tattooed, just a cute little belly button. He'd still put money on Her having a tattoo hidden away somewhere, most likely a skull and crossbones.

Danny's search for the list grew more frantic.

Ross lounged against the kitchen counter watching her. He was beginning to recognize the telltale signs of her moods: how her nostrils flared slightly when she was angry, and how she chewed her bottom lip when she was nervous. 'What have you lost?'

'The shopping list.' Ross thought he heard her add, 'And my mind.'

He pointed to the plastic lunchboxes — one burgundy, one green — sitting on the draining board. 'Do the kids need those?'

'What?' She looked at the boxes. 'Oh! Yes!'

'I'll pack the boxes. You find the list.'

Danny muttered, 'Now I know how the Stormtroopers felt.'

Ross shook his head. Strange things went on inside that blue head.

He reached for one of the lunchboxes, and saw the children's names written on them in black permanent marker pen. *MATT FABELLO. MIA FABELLO.* It was unnerving to see Ross to see the Fabello family name; all his other nieces and nephews were his sisters' children.

He scooped up the boxes and squatted to pack them into the backpacks lying on the kitchen floor. When he glanced up Ross saw that Danny was watching him, and was disconcerted by the understanding in her puffy amber eyes. She knew he was upset and why. They abruptly broke eye contact, each of them feeling confused by the silent communication they'd shared.

I can't believe it.

I know, neither can I.

'Why did you turn up so early?' Danny sounded grumpy.

His reply was terse. 'To make sure you hadn't flown the coop.'

'My yacht is in dry dock and I've loaned my private jet to a friend.'

He grabbed the bags and rose. 'You're a regular wise-ass aren't you?'

Danny smiled sweetly. 'One tries.'

During the night she'd decided it would be wrong to prevent Matt and Mia meeting their paternal relatives. If she did, she would be repeating her mother's mistakes and the children would suffer the way she and Nella had. But Danny was determined that the Fabellos were going to earn their right to a place in the children's lives. Ross's obvious impatience to do the job and get home did nothing to allay Danny's fears. She thrust the shopping list into a huge, black bag and nibbled at her bottom lip.

Matt and Mia rushed into the kitchen.

'Have you got a car?' Danny asked Ross.

'No, I flew here.'

'The frightening thing is I can believe that.' She turned to the children. 'Come on, we're going for a ride in Uncle Ross's car.'

'Cooo-ool!' Mia cried and raced after Matt to the front door.

Ross followed Danny, wondering what had prompted her sudden change of heart.

Danny had to bang the warped front door twice to close it. She kept meaning to borrow a wood-planer from Deryl's husband, Lloyd, but never seemed to get around to it, just as she never seemed to get around to fixing the toilet. It had to be flushed by pulling on a shoelace. Thanks to her father, Danny could repair almost anything.

Matt and Mia charged towards the deep green Explorer gleaming in the sunshine on the weed-infested driveway.

Danny walked beside Ross towards the car. 'You do know we drive on the left-hand side of the road here, don't you?'

'Just get in the car, will you?'

As they headed down the narrow country road, Matt and Mia became engrossed in a discussion about the car and acted as if they were taken to school on a cart drawn by oxen each day and not their aunt's perfectly respectable Nissan.

Ross asked, 'Where are you going after this?'

'To give blood. I'd invite you along, but they only take the human kind.' Danny kept her voice down so the children didn't overhear. The moment in the kitchen had unnerved her. She needed to get things back on track.

Ross glanced at her blue hair. '*You're* giving blood? Who do they collect it for? Klingons?'

'You are so not funny.' Danny stared at his nose. 'It must be hell when you get a cold.'

'What's that supposed to mean?'

'I just wondered how you coped; I mean, do you buy industrial-sized tissues or just use towels?'

'Sticks and stones, sticks and stones,' Ross said.

He might not have a pretty-girl nose like Pat's, but it wasn't as bad as his Uncle Carmine's. There was a family joke that Carmine once caused a stampede at the beach when he was floating on his back a few yards offshore and somebody mistook his nose for a dorsal fin and yelled *Shark!*

Danny oozed fake sympathy. 'Hey, I think it's great that even though you've probably got thousands and thousands in the bank—'

Ross stiffened at the mention of money. 'Yes?'

'—you haven't felt the need to get a nose job.'

He was too surprised to answer, wondering what she'd do if he told her he didn't have thousands in the bank, he had millions. He decided he must still be suffering from jet lag. His experience with Simone had taught him to only ever discuss money with his accountant and his agent.

Mia spoke up. 'Auntie Danny, that's not very nice. Uncle Ross can't help having a big nose.'

Uncle Ross glared at Auntie Danny.

'You're right, Mia. If Uncle Ross is comfortable with his nose, that's all that really matters.' She said innocently.

'Have you ever considered getting your vocal cords tied?' he growled.

Mia looked at Matt. 'What does that mean?'

'He's telling Auntie Danny she talks too much,' Matt replied.

Ross studied Matt in the rear-vision mirror. The resemblance to his father was obviously only external: they *really* had to be more careful about what they said in front of the kids.

'What do you call somebody who poisons cornflakes?' Matt asked.

Danny cleared her throat. 'Ah Matt, I think— '

Ross interrupted her. 'I don't know; what do you call somebody who poisons cornflakes?'

'A cereal killer!' Matt and Mia cried together.

'It was *my* joke! *I* get to say the answer!'

'I can too!'

Ross narrowed his eyes at Danny. She sniggered.

When they reached the school, Matt asked, 'Are you picking us up from school?'

'No,' Danny said.

Ross smiled at Matt. 'We'll see.' He sniffed. 'What's that smell?'

Danny looked over her shoulder at Mia, who was hastily sliding from the car, and spotted a wet patch on the seat.

Mia's face crumpled. She began to jiggle from one foot to the other, wailing, 'I couldn't hold on! I didn't mean to!'

Ross spied the wet stain on the pale leather. 'Oh, for chrissakes—' He was stopped by Danny's ferocious glare and Mia's tears. 'OK! OK!' He held up his hands. 'It's . . . *OK!*'

Matt looked disapproving. 'She can't help it.'

Danny grabbed Mia's hand. 'Come on, blossom. Let's get you sorted out.'

Chapter 4

Ross watched them march off towards the school gates like the three musketeers. He'd been caught by surprise, that was all; after all, weren't eight-year-olds supposed to be over all that stuff? Still, he felt like a heel. He'd just finished wiping the seat when Danny returned carrying a plastic bag.

'Is she OK?' Ross asked.

'Yes.' She climbed in the car and slammed the door. 'No thanks to you.'

'I said I was sorry,' he said stiffly. 'Isn't she a little . . . well, old for that kind of thing?' Ross knew he'd said the wrong thing when Danny's nostrils flared.

'Mia was fine until her mother died. Need it spelt out any clearer, Einstein?'

There was a tense silence.

'So where are we going?'

Danny folded her arms and stared out the window. 'You can drop me at the supermarket and then go away.'

He sent her an exasperated look. 'What the hell do you want from me? I'd hang myself from my thumbscrews, but I left them at home with my ski mask and ice pick.'

Her lips trembled. She bit the bottom one to keep from smiling.

'Too late,' Ross said. 'I saw it.'

Danny glowered at him. 'If you're going to drop me at the super- market turn left at the school gates, or are we just going to sit here talking hot air?'

Ross started the engine and drove off. 'Even better, I'll come in with you and drive you home again.'

'That's *better*?' Danny cried. 'Why don't you go sightseeing? Climb the harbour bridge or take a cruise around the gulf? Nobody in their right mind travels thousands of miles to visit a supermarket— Ah! I've just answered my question.'

Ross ignored her. 'I like visiting supermarkets. I love food and cooking.'

Kitchens and what went on in them were Danny's idea of hell. Nella had been the cook in the family. Danny only ventured into the kitchen because she had to eat. 'You cook?'

'Of course I cook, I'm half-Italian.'

'I thought you said your mother was Irish. Turn right up here.'

'She is. My father's Italian.' Ross stopped at the intersection, checked both ways and turned right. 'Didn't Pat tell you anything about his family?'

'I didn't think Patrick had a family. I thought he was the result of a scientific experiment that went horribly wrong.' Danny bit her lip. That was cruel. Patrick was, after all, Ross's brother. 'Er . . . sorry.'

He didn't answer. His reaction, or lack of one, puzzled her. If he'd said something like that about Nella, she'd be kneeling on his lap trying to strangle him with his seat belt. Could it be that Ross hadn't liked Patrick either? Danny felt her animosity towards Ross thaw a little more. 'Irish and Italian, huh?'

'Don't tell me you're going to make some dumb-ass comment about the Mafia or the IRA.'

So he *was* upset. 'I wouldn't be so crass.'

He snorted. 'You're the Queen of Crass. What's your ancestry? Klingon crossed with the Wicked Witch of the East?'

Ross had a soft spot for Captain Kirk's arch-enemy: at fifteen he'd lost his virginity to the eighteen-year-old babysitter while Pat and his sisters watched the *Starship Enterprise* battle it out with the Klingons. The only reason they had a babysitter was because when Breda and Vito left Carmen and Ross in charge of the younger children they fought so badly that the neighbours called the police. Breda thought Ross's acceptance of Trixie the babysitter was a sign of his contrition. Even now, whenever he heard the *Star Trek* theme tune Ross got a pang of nostalgia and a hard-on.

He noticed Danny scowling at him. 'You're wasting your time if you're trying out your mind-meld on me.'

'You think I don't know that?' she snapped. 'If I shouted in your ear, I'd probably hear an echo. And it was Vulcans who did mind-melds, not Klingons.'

Danny was annoyed when Ross laughed. He'd stopped looking like a Serial Killer and begun to look like a pirate. In fact, he'd look right at home with a gold ring in one ear and waving a cutlass as he forced her to walk the plank. Danny pictured herself standing on the edge of the plank, wearing a long dress with a loosely corseted bodice (with a Wonderbra sewn in so she had a cleavage) and flowing white sleeves. Her blue hair spilled over her bare shoulders to her waist (hair extensions). She snarled insults at Ross the Pirate as she stood poised high above the sea.

'. . . *listening to me?*'

Danny blinked. 'Mmm?'

'*I said are you listening to me?*'

She came back to earth with a thud. 'No. Why would I do that?'

'I asked you who your mother and father were.' He sounded impatient, and finally wormed out of Danny that her father was English and her mother was New Zealand Maori.

'I read about them in the in-flight magazine. They're the native people, right?'

She nodded.

'Where's your mother?'

'Dead.'

'And your father?'

She took longer answering. 'Dead.'

Cocka-doodle-doo! Cocka-doodle-doo!

Ross started. 'What the hell is that?'

Danny reached into her bag and pulled out a cellphone. 'The kids picked it. It was that or a frog going *ribbit ribbit.*'

'You've got a *crowing chicken as your ringtone?*'

'Chickens don't crow, city boy,' she sneered. 'It's a rooster.'

When Danny had finished taking the call, she asked, 'What is it about my hair that you find so threatening, Fabello? It's been pink, orange and purple in the past.'

'Why do you colour your hair?'

Ross watched Danny chew on her lip.

'When you're an identical twin and your mother insists on dressing you and your sister in the same clothes and doing your hair the same way, you'd find ways to look different, too. Besides,' she shrugged a shoulder, 'it keeps me entertained.'

He had a feeling there was a whole lot more to it than that.

'It's only hair mascara, not a permanent colour.' Danny didn't know why that was important.

Ross did. 'So you don't commit to anything without leaving yourself a get-out clause.'

Her nostrils flared and her eyes flashed. 'What's that supposed to mean?'

Clearly, he'd hit a nerve. 'Nothing.'

'I did dye it once, green for St Patrick's Day. I bet you've never gone to that much trouble and you're part-Irish.'

'I don't need to create a spectacle of myself to celebrate my heritage.'

'S'pose not, that nose will do it for you every time,' Danny sniped.

'Will you stop making cracks about my nose?'

'Will you stop making cracks about my hair?'

Cocka-doodle-doo! Cocka-doodle-doo!

'Could you turn that damned thing off so we can talk?' Ross demanded when Danny hung up.

'Can I help it if I have friends? It's a concept that's no doubt foreign to you.'

He looked pointedly at her hair and clothes. 'Are they all in the circus, too?'

Her nostrils fluttered and a white line appeared around her mouth.

'I'll make you a deal: I'll stop talking about your hair if you'll stop talking about my nose.'

Danny stuck her nose in the air and stared at the view through the passenger-door window. 'Whatever, it'll be a weight off my mind. I'm sure your nose has got national-monument status back in the States.' She clutched the dashboard as the car suddenly screeched to halt. 'What are you doing?!'

Ross parked at the kerb and unfastened his seat belt. 'I'm going to beat the living daylights out of you.'

'You can't!' Danny cried. 'You'll end up in prison and I'll never get rid of you!'

He stared at her, incredulous. She was serious. His shoulders began to shake. Ross hunched over the steering wheel and gave in to laughter. It was several moments before he had control of himself again.

Danny wished she had a gun.

Ross wiped his eyes with the heel of his hand and fastened his seat belt. It would serve his mother and Deirdre right if he was arrested for murdering a woman with blue hair. It would be a crime of passion.

Other than giving him directions Danny refused to talk to him again, so Ross spent the remainder of the journey taking in his surroundings. Their route took them past beaches that sparkled in the spring sunshine. A few people walked their dogs or strolled along the water's edge, but the beaches were largely deserted. Boats of all shapes and sizes were moored in some of the bays they passed by.

They stopped at a supermarket car park in a small town by yet another beach, which Danny identified as Browns Bay. She pointed down the main street and said, 'There's a Starbucks about halfway up — you'll feel right at home. Thanks for the ride.' She turned and headed into the supermarket.

Ross followed at a leisurely pace. He located Danny in the fresh produce section.

'Go *away!*'

'I can't keep away. It's like *Fatal Attraction.*'

'Keep bugging me, mate, and I'll do more than boil your bunny.'

Ross wandered amongst the fruit and vegetables, keeping one eye on her. She was a careful shopper, checking prices and debating carefully over what to buy. His hunch that Danny was short of cash grew stronger. He'd assumed that the mortgage would have been taken care of by insurance when Patrick and Daniella died. He decided to get his lawyer to check out Danny's financial status.

'What's this?' Ross held up a large, knobby brown vegetable with orange flesh showing at one end.

Danny looked up impatiently from the plastic bag she was filling with carrots. 'A kumara.'

'A . . . what-a-wa?'

'A *koo-mah-rah* — Maori sweet potato.' She headed for a bin of apples.

A pretty, well-preserved brunette wearing a pink dress and high heels stopped her shopping trolley on the other side of the kumara bin and smiled at Ross. Sometimes his fans recognized him from a photo on a dust jacket. The memory of Danny's contemptuous response when he'd tried to convince her that he was RF O'Rourke still stung. It did his battered ego good to have an attractive female look at him the way the brunette was at the moment. He smiled back.

'Excuse me?' she asked. 'Are you who I think you are?'

Danny was examining the apples as if she planned to bestow names on them. Ross wasn't fooled; his internal antennae told him she was paying close attention to what was happening. He upped the wattage on his smile. 'I hope so.'

'I can't believe it!' The woman cried. 'You're even better-looking in real life than you are in your movies!'

Danny sniggered.

His smile slipped. 'Movies?'

'I loved you in *Ocean's Thirteen*! You're much *better* looking than Brad Pitt, by the way.'

Danny hooted.

Ross thought about gagging her with a plastic bag. She'd attracted the brunette's attention, who was now staring at Danny's injured face in horror. He leaned closer and whispered loudly, 'Botched plastic surgery. I've seen it before.'

His would-be fan was so mesmerized by Ross's black, velvety eyes that she completely missed the unholy gleam lurking in their depths. 'Oh, that's terrible . . .' The woman glanced apprehensively at the scowling Danny. She'd been considering getting a brow and eye lift. 'I wonder what she's had done?'

Ross looked at Danny's black-and-blue face thoughtfully. 'Eye and nose job, and maybe a brow lift.'

'Oh.' The brunette touched her forehead nervously.

Danny's hand crept towards the apples.

Ross shook his head regretfully at the woman. 'Turning forty does strange things to some women.' He heard an outraged gasp from Danny's direction.

The brunette didn't look too happy either. 'What's that supposed to mean — *Aahh*!'

Something hard whacked the side of his head.

'Oh my God!' The brunette squeaked. *'She just threw an apple at you!'*

Ross clutched his head and spun towards Danny, his lips thinned and his eyes narrowed to slits. Danny quivered like a terrier straining at the leash, her nostrils flared.

Sensing impending disaster, or at the very least a hailstorm of apples, the brunette fled, her high heels clattering on the polished linoleum.

Ross rounded the kumara bin and shoved the woman's abandoned trolley out of his way. It sailed across the floor and into a pyramid of oranges, which tumbled down and rolled in all directions. He stalked towards Danny, his black eyes glittering, and growled, 'I'm going to strangle you with that godawful scarf and bury you in the kumaras.'

She shoved up her sleeves and snarled, 'Not if I kill you first.'

His steps faltered. She wasn't kidding. She was half his size and covered in bruises, but she was willing to take him on. Ross looked at her in confusion. Where the *hell* had she sprung from?

Danny had never backed down from a fight and wasn't about to start now. She barrelled towards Ross, stepped on an orange and lurched sideways into a bin of tomatoes. There was a squelching sound as she landed face-down in the bin. Tomato juice squirted her in the eye and seeped into her clothes. Danny grabbed the sides of the bin, which was only half-full, and tried to lever herself upwards but fell back in again.

Ross strolled across to watch. 'You remind me of a turtle burying its eggs on a beach.'

'*Get —*' she panted, '*get knotted, Fabello!*'

He perched on the side of the bin. 'Tut, tut, Daneka, you shouldn't go making offers of marriage when we've only just met.' Her black cardigan had fallen over her head. She glared up at him from beneath it. 'You — you —' Danny closed her eyes as nausea suddenly lapped the back of her throat.

Ross noticed her sudden pallor and straightened abruptly. 'Are you OK?'

Her hands were shaking and she was taking big gulps of air. 'Do I look OK?'

He hooked one arm around her waist, stuck a hand down the back of her clown pants and hauled her from the bin. She staggered drunkenly and clutched his leather jacket when he placed her on her feet and held her upright. She felt as insubstantial as a child.

Danny rested her bruised forehead against his white T-shirt and smeared it with tomato juice. 'I hate you.'

He stroked her back soothingly. 'I know.'

Two sets of footsteps hammered the glossy floor, one heavy and deliberate, the other the pitter-patter of stiletto heels.

Ross turned his head. 'The cavalry have arrived.'

The brunette pointed a finger. 'There they are! *He's* telling people he's George Clooney and *she's* a lunatic! *She,*' the woman indicated Danny, 'bombarded *him,*' she pointed to Ross, 'with apples from that bin!'

Danny turned her cheek against Ross's chest and protested weakly: 'That's a lie. It was only one apple.' She felt his chest shake and looked up.

He was laughing.

'Thrown out of the supermarket! I've shopped there *forever*, and the first time I set foot in the place with you *I get thrown out!*'

Ross decided Danny must be feeling better. 'Can you screech that again?'

'*Shut up!*'

They were back in the Explorer and headed towards another supermarket. Danny reached between her bottom and the car seat and plucked at her underwear. Ever since Ross had hauled her from the bin of tomatoes she'd been on a search-and-rescue mission for her thong, which had disappeared deep into territory it usually only skirted, so to speak. Danny couldn't decide what was worse, the rectal examination her underwear was giving her or the smell of tomato juice on her shirt and waistcoat.

'Wedgie?' Ross enquired solicitously.

'You leave my knickers out of this! You only got off so lightly because the produce manager was an RF O'Rourke fan. If you hadn't given him an autograph and paid for the damaged fruit, he'd have called the police!'

Ross guided the Explorer into a parking space. 'You're just pissed you owe me. If I hadn't been able to smooth things over, it would have been you in trouble with the police, not me.'

'For what?' Danny wrenched the car door open and climbed out. 'Assault with a deadly apple?' She slammed the door and stormed away, the ends of her turquoise scarf following behind her like horizontal exclamation marks.

Being fished from a bin full of tomatoes by Patrick's overbearing brother topped even yesterday's debacle. Why had her life suddenly turned into a slapstick movie? What was next? Being tied to railway tracks in front of a fast-approaching train while Ross stood over her twirling a gun and grinning? Dignity — she needed *dignity*. She had to stop acting like a fishwife and throwing things; it was just playing into his hands and, even worse, he seemed to enjoy it.

Danny's dignified silence lasted all of ten minutes after they entered the supermarket, when Ross began dropping expensive food items into the shopping trolley, things Danny couldn't afford and didn't want.

'Put that back!' she cried when he added a tin of anchovies. 'Go and get your own trolley!'

Ross took a jar of artichokes from a shelf and studied the label. 'It's not a trolley, it's a cart, and I already told you I'd pay for it.'

Danny stood between him and the trolley/cart waving her arms. 'No!'

'Oh, for chrissakes . . .' He shook his head in disgust and walked away carrying the artichokes.

Danny seethed. How on earth could anybody mistake him for George Clooney? George didn't have evil black eyes and a demonic smile. They continued the game of Ross putting things into the trolley and Danny attempting to return them to the shelves. It was a very unequal contest; Ross had a longer reach and Danny's energy was flagging. She wanted home and her bed. She wanted Ross the Pirate set adrift in shark-infested waters.

He helped her unload the groceries onto the conveyor belt. Danny studied the mountain of groceries and chewed on her bottom lip. How did she go about separating her stuff from his without looking pedantic or desperate?

'Are you satisfied? Look at all this crap!'

'I can't remember the last time I had so much fun grocery shopping. And it *isn't* crap.' Ross dug his wallet from the pocket of his jeans. 'Stop looking at me like that.'

'Like what?' Danny stared at the wad of bills in his wallet. He was carrying the Bank of New Zealand in his back pocket.

'Like you're picturing my head stuffed and mounted over your fireplace.'

'Don't be disgusting — it would frighten the children. Actually, I was trying to decide which was more fun: grocery shopping with you, or staying at home and cleaning the fridge.' She watched him drop hundred-dollar bills onto the conveyor belt. 'What are you doing?'

'It's a custom we have in the States. We call it paying for our groceries.'

She'd been wrong about the resemblance to a pirate. He almost certainly had three sixes carved on his bum, and if he didn't, well, he ought to. Danny snatched up the money and threw it back. 'Pay for your own stuff! *Not* mine!'

Ross scooped up the bills and shrugged. 'Suit yourself.'

Their argument had attracted the attention of the checkout staff and other customers.

Danny waited anxiously as the food was zapped by the checkout girl who wore a name badge that read *Debbie, here to help*, and a black plastic Alice band in her mousy brown hair. *Please go through! Please go through!* Danny chanted silently and sighed with relief when her bank card was accepted. All the emotional upheaval had left her feeling tired and listless. Ross was like a vampire draining energy from a victim. Come to think of it, what was he doing outside in broad daylight? He should be tucked up in his coffin somewhere, with his fangs in a glass of water and the alarm clock set for sunset. Danny wondered wearily if it was possible to buy sharpened wooden stakes online. 'Or holy water,' she mumbled.

'What did you say?' Ross asked.

'Nothing.'

He smiled at the checkout girl as he paid for his groceries. 'Thanks, Debbie.'

'You're welcome.' She pulled off her headband and fluffed her hair. 'Are you—'

Danny couldn't face a repeat of what had happened with the brunette. 'Yes, he is, Debbie.' She tried to lift one of the shopping bags into the trolley. 'He's a creature of the night.'

Ross muttered something about wicked witches and where he'd like to put their broomsticks, and shouldered Danny aside. He began transferring the bags into the empty trolley three at a time.

Debbie looked blankly at Danny.

'Promise me you'll take home all the garlic you can carry tonight and lock all your doors,' Danny urged.

Debbie drew back. 'Why?'

'To keep yourself safe from dark forces.'

When they reached the house, Ross offered to carry the shopping inside.

'Just go away,' Danny said.

'You think I'm offering because I enjoy your company? After that crack you made at the supermarket?'

'I don't need your help.'

'You need all the help you can get.'

Ross rounded the car and opened the passenger door. He rested an elbow on top of the door and studied her. 'You look like crap.' He sniffed. 'And you smell like tomato ketchup.' He held out his hand. 'Give me your front-door key.'

Danny slumped in the car seat. 'After you've carried the bags inside, do you promise to go?'

'Finding Angelina Jolie and Charlize Theron waiting naked in your kitchen wouldn't keep me.'

'For good?'

'No.'

'Bastard,' she said weakly.

'No, I'm the second of six kids and my parents were married eleven months before my oldest sister, Carmel, arrived.'

He'd unknowingly hit a sore point, although being illegitimate hadn't bothered Danny nearly so much as being abandoned. 'Do I need to carry you inside, too?' Ross asked.

'Touch me again and I'll knee you in the nuts.'

He had to put his shoulder to the front door to get it open. 'Why don't you get the damned thing planed?'

Danny shuffled to the kitchen. 'Why? If I'm lucky you might get a big splinter through your black vampire heart.'

'No self-respecting vampire would take a bite out of you; they'd get blood poisoning.' He put the grocery bags onto the kitchen counter and turned to look at her. 'Who looks after the kids when you're working?'

'My neighbour across the road. I bet you'd love to hear that I leave them alone at night — that would suit your purposes perfectly.'

'Which would be?'

'To get custody.'

Ross stared. Matt and Mia seemed nice-enough kids, but the last thing he wanted was custody. Danny loved Patrick's children, whereas he just felt responsible for them.

His silence worried Danny more than his threats. All she wanted to do right now was take some painkillers and climb into bed, but it was important she set Ross straight on a few things first.

'Listen, *Uncle Ross*, I've been managing just fine. I don't need you or anybody else to suddenly come poking their nose in and upsetting our routine. I mean, do the children look unhappy or neglected?'

'No, they seem like nice kids. But I can smell a rat a mile off when it comes to money,' he said. 'You're in financial trouble.'

Danny was feeling increasingly unwell. 'My finances are none of your business.'

Ross wished she'd give in. She looked terrible. 'You don't look so good.'

Danny stared longingly at the cupboard where she kept the

painkillers as the throb in her head stepped up a gear and began to pound. She clutched the back of a chair. 'Go away and let me die in peace.'

Ross was losing patience. 'Will you quit being so stubborn and go to bed?'

'Go to hell.' She wilted some more.

He crossed the kitchen and yanked Danny into his arms, managing to bang her bruised nose on his chest.

'Ow!' She clutched her nose and hooked an arm and leg around him to keep from falling. 'You're useless at this! Put me down!'

Ross made a grab for the back of Danny's thigh to halt her downward slide, but missed and caught her arse instead; it curved into his hand like a warm, ripe peach.

Danny wriggled frantically against him. 'Are you copping a feel?'

Ross let go of her butt and tried to slide his arm beneath her knees. 'Unhook your leg!'

'Keep your hand off my arse!'

They indulged in some undignified jostling while Danny unhooked her leg and Ross hauled her higher against his chest. She considered telling him to put her down, but decided he deserved to do some work after the way he'd treated her. Danny couldn't remember the last time she had been this close to a healthy male who was conscious. Beneath his clothes, his body felt good.

He carried her into the hallway and paused at the doorway of the first bedroom. 'Is this your room?'

Danny stiffened. 'No! Not in there!'

'OK!' He took one last curious look at the room before turning away. 'Don't burst a blood vessel. Where then?'

'There.' She gestured towards the door at the end of the hallway.

Ross continued down the hallway past two other bedrooms, which looked as if they belonged to Matt and Mia. Matt's bedroom walls were covered with posters of cars and the carpet was hidden beneath piles of clothes, soccer balls and assorted junk.

Danny noticed his stunned expression. 'He's always been untidy,' she said defensively, and wondered why she was making excuses for Matt. Nella had done everything for the children, and Matt expected Danny to carry on picking up after him, something she refused to do. Twelve-hour shifts at the hospital meant time for housework was at a premium. Mia helped out, but Matt was being uncharacteristically stubborn, refusing to pitch in and do his share. The clutter and mess drove Danny mad, but most days she was just too tired to care.

Ross carried Danny into her room and laid her on the bed. He was surprised to see it didn't have black covers and there weren't stolen road signs decorating the walls. The double bed had a carved wooden bedstead and pale turquoise covers with tiny white spots. The walls were painted a startling shade of pale lavender. French doors flanked by long white curtains hanging from a thick, nubby wooden rod overlooked a wooden verandah and the back garden. A white wicker chair with the cane uncurling from the bottom of one of the legs stood in one corner with clothes piled on top, including one of the ugly blue uniforms he'd seen Danny wearing the previous day. There was a battered wooden chest of drawers beside the door, and a mirror with a carved white frame hanging above it. The doors of the wardrobe were half-open and an assortment of clothes and shoes spilled out. Ross wasn't too surprised. What else could he expect from a woman with blue hair?

Danny watched him suspiciously from her pillow. 'What?'

'Were you drunk when you chose the colour scheme?'

'Let me guess,' she said sarcastically, 'your house has white walls and lots of pastels.'

She was half-right: white walls and brilliant splashes of colour, red a particular favourite. Ross secretly thought the colour choices in her room worked, in a weird kind of way.

'You shouldn't be alone,' he said.

Her eyelids drooped. 'Yes, I should.'

'I'll call you later.'

'No, you won't.'

'There's nothing you want me to get you before I go?'

'A Taser.'

'Don't think I won't be back,' Ross warned.

Danny pulled the covers over her head. 'You'll be about as welcome as a dose of herpes.'

Ross smiled. Under different circumstances he could almost like her.

'You know,' he said slowly, 'there was some money left over from Pat's estate. I could let you have some of it.' It was a lie. Pat had died in debt. Ross had made sure his parents didn't find out all of the sordid details and had quietly sorted things out.

Silence. Then Danny spoke through the covers, her voice vibrating with anger. 'That's very sweet of you, but I think it would be better all round if you took your money and shoved it where the sun doesn't shine.'

Well, that made a refreshing change. 'I'll be coming to see the children regularly while I'm in Auckland,' Ross insisted.

'I wouldn't bet on it.'

'You and I both need to get together with the lawyers to settle the issue of just who is their guardian. We need to look at Pat and Daniella's will in more detail.'

Danny lowered the covers. 'What are you talking about? *I'm* Matt and Mia's guardian.'

Ross shook his head. 'Not according to Pat and Daniella's will. He appointed me as their guardian in the event their mother died, and your sister appointed Pat as the children's guardian if she died.'

She gaped. 'They made a *joint* will?

He frowned. 'Didn't you know?'

'Nella would never have made Patrick their guardian! He was too irresponsible. She wanted me to be their guardian. She made a will of her own before she died.'

But Danny couldn't find it.

Ross was sorry he'd brought it up. If she wasn't so pig-headed, he wouldn't have had to. 'We need to get together with our lawyers and look at both wills,' he repeated.

And she couldn't afford a lawyer.

Danny raised the covers and closed her eyes. It was her worst nightmare. She wanted to fall asleep and wake up and find everything had been a bad dream. Exhaustion tugged at her seductively.

Ross felt like a heel. 'Danny?' he prompted. 'Are you sure you don't want me to pick the kids up from school?'

'My neighbour'll do it . . .' she mumbled. Her chest eased into the slow rise and fall of sleep. He leaned forward and lifted a corner of the duvet. Her lips were parted and her swollen eyelids closed. She looked young and harmless and made a snuffling sound through her battered nose as she breathed.

Ross eased the cover down from her face and told himself not to be such a sap. Danny Lawton was about as harmless as an Exocet missile.

Before he left, Ross packed away the groceries and dropped his business card on the kitchen counter, with the number of his apartment at the Viaduct Basin and his cellphone number written on the back of it. He looked at the ancient plumbing and the book propped beneath the old table, and muttered, 'How could you do it, Pat? Couldn't you have put somebody else first for once?'

Hell would freeze over before Danny would call him, but Ross knew now that talk of wills and lawyers would bring her to heel.

It wasn't going to be easy.

But it was certainly going to be interesting.

Chapter 5

'Tread carefully,' Vanessa advised Danny. 'Tread very carefully.' They were snatching a quick break on night shift. With sixty nurses on the ED staff, and Vanessa and Danny amongst the most senior members, their rosters seldom coincided.

Danny was sick of thinking of and talking about Ross Fabello. While she recovered from the accident, she'd spent long hours worrying about him and what the repercussions of crashing the Criterion Construction truck would be at work. But it seemed that his friend, the Cocker Spaniel, who owned Criterion, had sacked the foreman and wasn't going to sue for damages to his truck. Experienced ED nurses with Danny's seniority weren't exactly thick on the ground, which certainly helped her case, but she knew she was skating on extremely thin ice. She couldn't afford to lose her job — it would play right into Ross Fabello's hands — but that didn't stop her from feeling annoyed when Vanessa kept advising caution.

Vanessa fiddled with her coffee mug. 'How's the little old lady?'

Danny had been looking after the wife of an elderly man who'd died not long after arriving in the re-suss rooms. It was one of the first deaths she'd had to deal with since Nella died. Vanessa and the other staff offered to care for Mr Reid and his little wife, but Danny had insisted. She might be only thirty-two, but she knew a lot about loss. It was Danny who took Mrs Reid into the unit as her husband of sixty-five years was worked on by the resus team so that she could see that everything possible was being done for him. It was Danny who thought to slip back the sheet from one of the old man's pale feet so his wife could stroke and touch him one last time while he was still warm and clinging to life. And it was Danny who sat with Mrs Reid, held her hand and passed her tissues while she waited for her son and daughter-in-law to arrive.

'Her whole world has fallen apart.' Danny smiled reassuringly at Vanessa. 'I'm OK, you know.'

'You're sure?'

She nodded. It was another milestone reached, another hill climbed. Every moment of every day took Danny further away from the last time she'd seen Nella. That was what hurt the most, knowing there was no way back — only forwards. Danny imagined Ross Fabello's arrogant, sardonic face and launched into another tirade against him.

'Perhaps you're overreacting a bit,' Vanessa suggested when Danny paused for breath.

'What do you mean, overreacting?' Danny asked indignantly.

'You don't think assaulting a guy with an apple in a supermarket isn't overreacting?'

'I was provoked!'

Vanessa sighed and placed her coffee mug on the scratched staffroom table. 'He hasn't said anything about taking the kids back to the States, has he? I mean for heaven's sake, he's a bachelor. Do you really think he'd want a couple of kids cramping his style?'

Was she the only one who could see through Ross Fabello? 'What about those sisters he keeps mentioning? They might be quite happy to take on Matt and Mia. The way Ross talks about his family, it sounds as if two more wouldn't matter.'

'You're jumping to conclusions,' Vanessa insisted. 'You've got to cool it until you know for sure what his plans are — or if he even has any plans.' Her voice softened. 'It doesn't have to be a bad thing, Danny. Now they've got grandparents and aunts and uncles and cousins.'

She was right. The Fabellos could offer the children so much more than Danny could on her own. They could offer financial and emotional security. Danny was envious of his family.

And then there was the bigger issue, the biggest one of all, like a vulture hovering over Danny and the children. Danny's mother and twin sister had both died of breast cancer at a young age. Once or twice Danny had tried to talk to Vanessa about her fears, but Vanessa went into nurse mode, pointing out that — unlike Rose and Nella — Danny attended all her appointments at the breast-screening clinic.

Vanessa got so upset that Danny eventually gave up talking about it. Instead, she took it out in the early hours of the morning and examined it, staring sightlessly into the darkness, picturing what would happen to her — and what would happen to Mia and Matt. She felt as if she spent her life holding her breath, waiting for the other shoe to drop.

Danny reluctantly changed the subject. 'He really is loaded, isn't he?'

Vanessa prised the lid off the plastic container holding her 2 a.m. meal. 'Loaded. Filthy rich. Stinking, malodorously—'

'Yeah, yeah, I get the picture.'

'*John Doe* is about to be released as a movie. Old RF wrote the screenplay and, according to *Woman's World* magazine, there's talk of him being nominated for an Oscar for best screenplay.'

Danny could never figure out why Vanessa got such a kick out of reading celebrity gossip. She watched her lick a dab of pasta sauce from the corner of her mouth. 'Why don't you try and get on his good side?'

'How?' Danny asked sarcastically.

'Sleep with him. You've got a God-given talent. Beneath those shitty clothes you're a hornbag — once men have sex with you, they're putty in your hands.'

Danny checked to see if the other two nurses taking their breaks had overheard, but they continued to read their magazines and fork food into their mouths. She leaned towards Vanessa and hissed, 'Ssssh! Will you shut up?'

'Have you got a better idea?' Vanessa demanded.

'Perhaps it slipped your notice, *but we hate one another!*'

'All cats are grey in the dark.'

'Not when they're sabre-toothed tigers.'

'I just think it would be wiser to stay on his good side rather than piss him off. Making access to the kids difficult might not be the best way to handle the situation,' Vanessa insisted.

In theory, Danny knew Vanessa was right, but she was worried about Matt and Mia getting to know their uncle and then being hurt yet again when Ross did the infamous Fabello disappearing act. He'd made no bones about the fact that he didn't want to be in New Zealand and couldn't wait to get home.

'Just think about being nice to him,' Vanessa urged. 'OK?'

'OK,'

Danny muttered.

'And Danny?' 'Yes?'

'No more throwing food at the man. Find another way to cope.'

The next time Danny was swamped by homicidal thoughts about Ross Fabello, she plugged into her iPod and danced frenetically while Tim Finn sang 'I See Red'. It was the only therapy she could afford.

Deirdre, his youngest sister, spoke carefully into the telephone. 'She threw an apple at you in the supermarket?'

'Yes.' Ross was stretched out on the big L-shaped leather sofa in the living room of his apartment, nursing a glass of red wine and a whole heap of grievances. 'The woman's a menace to society. Not only does she think it's OK to drive a truck into a wall of concrete blocks, she also attacks people with fruit. I guess I should be thankful there weren't any coconuts nearby.'

'Damn,' Deirdre murmured. 'If you ask me, hanging's too good for her.'

'I might have known you'd find it funny.'

Deirdre was more surprised by her big brother's response than by Danny Lawton's behaviour. He sounded irritated rather than angry. Once upon a time Ross would have thought the episode in the supermarket was funny, but he'd misplaced his sense of humour ever since the Simone Marchant business. Their mother liked to think that Ross's heart had been broken by Simone. His sisters knew that it was more a case of hurt pride, and anger that he'd trusted Simone in the first place. Deirdre was sure that there was something else bothering Ross, too. He lived alone in his beautiful house on the coast, becoming more and more withdrawn and moody with each passing month. Getting him to open up was like trying to break into the Tower of London for an after-hours peek at the Crown Jewels.

'You're wasting your time with the touchy-feely stuff,' Aoife, the outspoken twin, advised. 'If Ross wants to play crab and hide in his shell, the best thing would be to take a hammer to him until he talks.'

'Holy crap, Aoife,' Carmel, the eldest of the sisters, said. 'Are you *sure* you're a woman?'

Annie, Aoife's twin, opened her mouth to speak, but as usual Aoife hadn't finished. 'Don't give me any of that *Ross needs to get in touch with his feminine side* bullshit. The only feminine side Ross wants to get in touch with comes with a nice rack and a pert ass.

And we all know he's never had any trouble getting in touch with that.'

Women had been throwing themselves at Ross and Pat ever since their voices had broken, and Aoife insisted that Ross had been getting it on with their babysitter while the rest of them watched *Star Trek*.

Deirdre listened to her brother's complaints about Danny and decided that he wasn't nearly as pissed by Danny's behaviour as she'd expect him to be. In fact, she couldn't recall the last time she'd heard him sound so animated.

'What's New Zealand like?' she asked.

'Beautiful. If I had the time, I'd spend a few weeks just driving around.'

'Perhaps once everything is settled you can.'

Ross snorted. 'The only way I'd do that is if I knew Danny Lawton was somewhere far away — like Greenland.'

Wow — she'd really touched a nerve. 'How's the writing going?'

Deirdre wondered if she imagined the tiny pause before Ross answered. 'Fine.'

Was Ross having trouble with his writing? The idea had been nagging Deirdre since he'd left, and Annie agreed with her. Aoife and Carmel might pooh-pooh Annie's dreamy, barely-in-touch-with-reality manner, but she had a knack for seeing things that the rest of them missed. Annie shared Ross's creative nature and was herself a successful artist. Writing had always been his passion and solace. Deirdre thought back to the afternoon she and their mother had managed to rope him into the role of family emissary to clean up Pat's last big mess.

They'd been sitting in the living room of their parents' house, a room which would have been spacious if Breda hadn't filled every square inch with her collections and memorabilia. China frogs of all sizes and colours covered every available surface, while a bookcase on one wall held hardback copies of the Reader's Digest and first editions of Ross's novels. A large framed painting of the Virgin Mary gazing out serenely from beneath a blue veil took pride of place above the rose-pink-velour buttoned sofa on which Ross and Deirdre sat. The rest of the wall space was covered by photos of the Fabello children and grandchildren, from naked babies posed on fluffy rugs to their First Communion. There was unanimous agreement that Deirdre and Pat had been the prettiest babies, and Aoife and Annie the ugliest because they were premature. Carmel and Ross fell somewhere in between.

A tea tray with a white china tea service decorated with pink roses sat on top of an overstuffed ottoman in front of Breda. Three cups of tea had been poured and left to go cold. The fact that Ross hated tea was one of the things his mother frequently forgot since Pat's death, and he didn't have the heart to correct her. Like his sisters, he'd increased his visits since Pat had died. It hurt them all to watch Breda and Vito's shock and pain turn to shock and bewilderment in the months following Pat's death as they learned he had two children living in New Zealand that he'd never bothered to tell them about. The bewilderment turned to despair when it became apparent that the auntie who was responsible for Pat's son and daughter was doing everything she could to stop their father's family becoming acquainted with them. It was right about then that Daneka Lawton became public enemy number one for Ross.

'Why won't she answer the letters?' Breda cried for the hundredth time. 'We're their grandparents! They're part of our family!'

Ross and Deirdre avoided looking at each another. They'd asked each other the same question, and had both come up with the same answer. If the aunt was using Pat as a yardstick, it wasn't surprising she was reluctant to meet the rest of the family.

'It doesn't make sense,' Breda insisted. 'We just want to get to know them.'

'Perhaps Pat and the auntie didn't get along, Ma. Perhaps she thinks she's protecting the kids,' Ross said.

Deirdre looked at him sharply. Whilst she and her sisters agreed with Ross, none of them were dumb enough or brave enough to say it out loud, particularly to their mother, who had spoilt Pat rotten. And Ross *definitely* wasn't dumb. Deirdre eyed her mother warily and waited for the explosion.

Breda didn't disappoint.

'And just what is *that* supposed to mean?' The bright blue eyes she'd passed on to Pat and Deirdre emitted sparks.

Ross displayed patience Deirdre didn't know he still possessed. 'It means just what I said: if Daneka Lawton didn't like Pat, she's hardly going to welcome the rest of the family with open arms. Be honest, Ma,' he said gently, 'you know how Pat was.'

Breda looked away. 'He wasn't a bad boy, just a little hasty and thoughtless at times, but then young people are like that.'

Ross and Deirdre didn't point out that the rest of them hadn't indulged in Pat's grandstanding antics, riding into their lives to cause chaos and out again when he'd succeeded in pissing everybody off.

Deirdre poked the toe of her sandal at the stack of old wedding magazines Breda kept on the bottom shelf of the coffee table. One fell off the pile. Deirdre picked it up and began flicking through the pages in an attempt to distract their mother and amuse herself by looking at the outdated bridal wear. Few things captured Breda's interest more than weddings and babies — her children's to be specific. Having gotten Carmel, Aoife and Annie successfully to the altar, she considered Ross and Deirdre long overdue to follow in their footsteps, and was irked that, despite her attempts to introduce them to several likely — and more importantly, *Catholic* — candidates, they refused to cooperate.

'One of us needs to go down there in person so the auntie can see what we're really like,' she announced. 'I think your father and I should go to New Zealand.'

'No!' Ross and Deirdre cried.

Letting their mother loose on Daneka Lawton would be disastrous. Breda made Ross look subtle.

'Why not?' Breda cried indignantly.

'Because you and Dad have been through enough these past few months,' Deirdre said quickly.

'Yes. Somebody else should go.' Ross looked at Deirdre meaningfully.

She narrowed her eyes at him.

'Well, I think—' their mother began.

'Ross should go!' Deirdre interrupted. 'I think Ross should go!'

Ross started. '*What?*'

Breda nodded. 'Just what I was about to say, you took the words right out of my own mouth, Deirdre.'

'What? Why me?' Ross cried. 'I get the awkward, messy jobs, not the emotional stuff!'

Deirdre and Breda exchanged glances. Ross could almost see the wheels spinning around inside their heads. Damned devious women — his family was full of them. He had a horrible feeling he'd been set up.

'I can't go, Ross.' Deirdre's big blue eyes shone with treachery and deception. Suddenly Ross could picture her sitting at the side of the guillotine, knitting.

'*Why?*' His glare promised deadly retribution. Unfortunately, the look guaranteed to reduce most people to quivering wrecks didn't have the same effect on his family.

Deirdre held up the bridal magazine. 'Because I'm getting

married.'

Ross blinked. Breda gasped. He tried to make eye contact with her, but Breda looked away.

He scowled at the Benedict Arnold of the family. 'Surely you don't mean Derek?'

'*Darren*,' Deirdre corrected. 'His name's *Darren*.'

'Who cares what he's called? He can hardly string two sentences together.'

'Ross!' Breda snapped.

He glared at her. 'You said he was an idiot!'

She grabbed the sugar bowl from the tea tray. 'Would you look at that? We're all out of sugar.'

'You can say that again,' Ross snarled.

'You've only met Darren twice!' Deirdre exclaimed.

Ross pointed at Breda. 'Two times too many, according to her.'

'Be *quiet*, Ross!'

'Do you know what it's like meeting our family for the first time?' Deirdre demanded. 'It's like watching *One Flew Over the Cuckoo's Nest,* only suddenly you discover that you're *in it* and *nobody's* acting. Just ask Tom, Pete or Joe if you don't believe me.'

Ross didn't need to speak to his brothers-in-law to know his family was nuts.

Breda, however, was deeply offended. 'We made Damian very welcome!'

'*Darren!* His name is *Darren!*'

'We made Darren very welcome! It's not my fault the man is so awful quiet.' Breda lowered her chin and intoned, 'I've only got one thing to say to you, Deirdre: *do not mistake a goat's beard for a fine stallion's tail.*'

Ross and Deirdre rolled their eyes. Breda's Irish folklore had stopped being funny once they'd reached the age of ten. Breda had been affronted when she overheard Aoife calling it 'Ma's mad

Irish mammy act', but then what else could you expect from a girl who paraded through downtown San Diego bare-breasted and carrying a placard in support of Breast Cancer Awareness? It had been weeks before Breda could show her face at church to do the altar flowers.

Deirdre played her trump cards. 'Darren's willing to convert and he earns seventy-five thousand a year after tax.'

Breda stilled. 'Is he?' she cried rapturously. 'Does he?' She snatched the magazine from Deirdre's lap and began to flick through the pages. 'There's an absolutely beeyootiful dress in here with a wee bustle and a cathedral train that would look a treat on you, Deirdre.'

Deirdre began to look uneasy.

Ross smiled thinly. He hoped she tripped on her cathedral train and fell flat on her bustle.

When Deirdre finished speaking to Ross, she called Carmel to pass on the latest in the Ross Fabello versus Daneka Lawton battle of the sexes. Although the sisters hadn't met the New Zealand auntie, they admired her for not caving in to Ross's steel-trap mind and sarcastic tongue.

Carmel was in the last month of her fifth pregnancy, and had spent the past eight days ensconced on the sofa in the family den watching Jerry Springer and Oprah and complaining. She answered the telephone on the second ring.

'What?'

'And a hello to you, too.'

'If you want sweet and nice, hang up!' Carmel snapped. 'My varicose veins ache, my haemorrhoids throb, and I've got heartburn like you wouldn't believe.'

Deirdre shuddered.

'Four girls I've had,' Carmel continued bitterly. 'Four girls and every single one of them had the good manners to arrive two weeks before their due date. None of them gave me as much trouble as this one, and why is that? Because this time it's a boy, that's why! To think that I actually cooperated with Tom. That I agreed to one last try for a boy and I let him knock me up. I must have been insane!'

More like horny, Deirdre thought.

Carmel wasn't done. 'He's probably lying around in there with a remote control in one hand and a beer in the other watching football re-runs.'

'Are you finished?'

'Don't you use that tone with me, Miss-Single-But-Pretending-To-Get-Married-To-Delbert-The-Lame. Just wait 'til it's your turn.'

'His name's *Darren*. And for your information I don't intend ever letting some guy knock me up, as you so romantically put it.'

'Yeah, yeah.' Carmel rearranged the sofa cushions behind her aching back. 'Just hang onto that virginity and you'll be fine.'

'I am *not* a virgin!'

'Oh yeah, I forgot. There was that one time in college.'

'I've done it more than once!'

'What? You mean you've done it twice?'

'Shut up!' Deirdre snapped. 'That's none of your business!'

She'd had sex three times and hadn't enjoyed it. How did Carmel manage to do this? How did she always manage to bring Deirdre's non-existent sex life into every conversation? And why had she ever confided in her in the first place? Ross would have been a far better choice if Deirdre could have swallowed her pride long enough to ask him what she was doing wrong. After all, he was a guy and Deirdre knew he was no monk. More importantly, Ross could be relied upon to be honest. *Brutally* honest.

'Was this a social call or something more interesting?' Carmel asked.

'Ross called me.'

'He did?' She brightened. 'What's the auntie done to him now?'

'She threw an apple at him in the supermarket. It whacked him in the side of the head.'

'She threw an apple—' Carmel burst out laughing.

'And she keeps telling him he's got a big nose.'

'He has, although not as big as Uncle Carmine's.'

'Nobody has a nose as big as Uncle Carmine's.'

'Oh, I love that woman!' Carmel cried. 'Is Ross certain she isn't Italian?'

'Positive.'

'Irish then?'

'Nope.'

'There's got to be something hidden in the mix somewhere,' Carmel mused. 'She sounds like she's related to us, or at least she should be.'

Deirdre heard the thoughtful note in Carmel's voice. 'Don't even go there. Ross will cause you more grief than your haemorrhoids and varicose veins put together if you start matchmaking. Besides, you're beginning to sound like Ma.'

Carmel gasped. 'That was cruel!'

'I've got to go. Do you want to phone Aoife and Annie, or shall I?'

'Oh, I will! I will!'

Chapter 6

Danny didn't rely on Google to research the enemy. She borrowed Ross's book *Think Twice* from Jane Clifford, an American doctor at the ED who was one of his biggest fans.

'Just make sure I get it back,' she warned. 'I've got everything he's ever written, and I only lend them to people I trust to return them. He's brilliant.'

Danny hadn't explained why she wanted to borrow the book. She wondered what Jane would say if she told her RF O'Rourke was a royal pain in the arse and a stalker to boot.

Think Twice was about the assassination of John F Kennedy. In the book, JFK used a body double on the ill-fated day in Dallas and it was the double who was killed, not the president. The story led the reader through a maze of deceit and deception as the real JFK was fobbed off as being the double by powerful people within the government whose interests were best served by having the young, charismatic president dead. Ross had even slipped in Marilyn Monroe's death by having her murdered for being one of the few people who knew the truth and was willing to speak out.

Danny couldn't put it down. The plot was fast-paced, clever and unpredictable. She suddenly understood why Ross was such a big cheese in the literary world. It was depressing, and frightening.

She thought up lots of ways of getting rid of Ross, but unfortunately they'd all result in prison time. He left messages on the answering machine, asking to arrange a time to visit the children. Danny ignored them, knowing she was only buying time. Ross wasn't a patient man, and it didn't help that the kids kept asking when they were going to see him again. She needed to know he wasn't an emotional lightweight like Patrick; she was equally determined that Ross wouldn't be given the chance to become part of the children's lives and then abruptly disappear.

'Doesn't he want to see us?' Mia asked. 'Is he angry because I wet the car seat?'

'No, of course not, love,' Danny insisted. 'He's come all the way from America to see you and Matt. He's not going to care about a silly little thing like that.'

'He doesn't look much like Dad,' Matt said. He had sensed the hostility between Danny and Ross, and out of loyalty to his aunt was prepared to dislike his new uncle.

Danny felt ashamed. 'He's got hair like yours, only shorter.'

Matt didn't answer. His hair was a sensitive issue. When Danny tentatively broached the subject of getting it cut, Matt had got so upset she'd backed off. She suspected he thought that cutting his hair betrayed his father's memory, and was surprised he wasn't being teased at school.

As the bruises on her face faded and her swollen eyes and nose returned to normal proportions, Danny did something she never thought she'd do. She played possum.

Ross was gunning for Ms Lawton. His attempts to see the children again were getting nowhere. He left messages on Danny's answering machine that were never replied to, and on the one occasion that he managed to speak to her she fobbed him off with a lame excuse. For every call he made to Danny, his mother made two to Ross asking for updates about his progress in getting to know Pat's children — which came to a big fat zero.

'What's wrong, Ross? You haven't fallen out with the auntie, have you?' Breda asked anxiously.

'No,' Ross lied. 'She's just very busy with her job at the hospital.'

'A nurse!' Nurses were high on Breda's list of the good and worthy. A nun would have been better, but a nurse came a close second. 'Pat's children are in good hands if the auntie is a nurse. What's she like?'

Ross wracked his brain for something positive to say about Danny. A cute ass that fit the palm of his hand perfectly wasn't the kind of information Breda was seeking. Even worse, she'd take it as a sign Ross was interested in Danny, which couldn't be further from the truth. Breda was keen to see Ross married and producing more little Fabellos, whilst his sisters were champion stirrers and took great delight in milking any situation that might embarrass him. He finally settled for 'She really loves the kids.'

'Oh, *bless her!*' Breda murmured. 'And how old did you say she was, Ross?'

'I didn't.'

'Pardon?'

'About thirty, I guess.'

'Oh? A sensible age, then.'

A 'sensible age' was Bredaspeak for 'well overdue for marriage and a few kiddies'.

Ross groaned softly.

'What was that? Are you alright, Ross?'

'Yeah, Ma, just fine.' He told her Matt looked just like Pat, which made her cry.

At which point his father came on the line. 'You got things straightened out with the auntie, Ross? You tell her she's part of the family?' Vito shouted.

Ross imagined Danny's reaction if he told her she was now a part of the Fabello family. 'We've been talking about the kids and getting to know one another at the moment, Dad,' he hedged.

'So?' Ross could imagine Vito's expressive shrug and upraised palm. 'Have you asked her if she wants to come and live in America with the kids? It's no good them being down the bottom of the world with no family to take care of them.'

Holy crap! He had to keep his parents away from Danny Lawton. She'd hit the roof if they served up any of this to her. Danny wouldn't understand that his parents were sincere when they said they now considered her part of the family; instead, she would see it as a ploy to get hold of Pat's kids.

'She's a grown woman, Dad. We can't just expect her to up stakes and move halfway across the world because it seems the right thing to us.'

'Hmmm.' The sound was infused with disapproval. 'She's called Danny? What kinda name is that for a girl?'

'It's short for Daneka. The kids' mother was called Daniella. They were twins.'

'Breda! Breda!' Vito yelled. 'You hear that? They got twins in the family just like us!'

Ross jerked the telephone away from his ear.

His mother came back on the line, sniffling. 'You let us know when we can come down and see the children, Ross. Don't keep me waiting too long.'

'I'll try not to, Ma.'

'I love you. God bless.'

'Love you, too, Ma.'

Ross tried one last time to speak to Danny, and when that failed he called his Kiwi lawyer, Allan Nicolls, and repeated the conversation he'd had with Danny about wills and money.

'We need to see the will Daniella Lawton wrote and find out when it was drawn up. If it was written after the joint will she made with your brother, it will take precedence,' Allan said.

That was exactly what Ross was worried about. 'That's if the will actually exists.'

'You think Daneka Lawton is lying?' Allan asked sharply.

'She'll do anything to keep those kids away from my family,' Ross said grimly. 'I think it's strange that she hasn't fronted up with a copy of the will already — either it doesn't exist or she can't find it. Have you spoken to her lawyer recently?'

'The lawyer she named is no longer representing her. I got the feeling it was due to lack of funds on Ms Lawton's part. Daneka Lawton is guarantor for several hire-purchase agreements taken out by Daniella Lawton.' Ross could hear papers being shuffled about. 'A spa pool, a plasma television and a home gym were some of the items. On Daniella's death some of the goods were returned, but there's still a lot of outstanding debt.'

Ross knew who would have bought the spa pool, television and gym. Pat. 'So she's in financial trouble?'

'There's still a substantial amount of outstanding debt, plus her third of the mortgage.'

'What about their life insurance? Where did that go?'

Allan cleared his throat. 'I'm afraid your brother stopped paying the premiums on his and Daniella's life insurance quite some time ago.'

Ross clenched his jaw so hard he thought his molars might crack. There wasn't an obscenity bad enough to describe what he thought of his brother. No wonder the house looked neglected. How was Danny managing to survive? If only she'd work with him instead of against him.

'Mr Fabello? Are you still there?'

'Yes.'

'It will be extremely difficult for a single woman on a nurse's income with children to support to meet the monthly repayments.' Allan paused. 'Is Ms Lawton still obstructing your access to the children?'

'Yes.' Ross almost regretted calling him — he was hearing things he didn't want to know and beginning to feel sympathy for Danny, which was dangerous. Despite the obstacles piled against her, Danny would be holed up in her tumbledown house plotting new ways to thwart Ross. He couldn't allow sentiment to cloud his judgement.

'We could take our case to the Family Court,' Allan suggested.

'That takes time I haven't got,' Ross said. 'What I need is leverage.'

'Use the house,' Allan replied. 'You own two-thirds of it.'

'What do you mean?'

'Daniella Lawton died before your brother. In the joint will, she left her share of the house and custody of the children, Matt and Mia Fabello, to their father, Patrick Fabello. Patrick left his estate and custody of his children to you. Unless Daneka Lawton can come up with a new will that tells us differently, she owns one-third of the house. You own the rest.'

Ross arrived unannounced around four o'clock the following afternoon. It was a rainy, wind-tossed day with sullen grey skies. Danny was out. A tall, weather-beaten woman with brown, wrinkled skin and salt-and-pepper hair struggled to open the door when he knocked. She looked Ross up and down with a pair of sharp brown eyes that reminded Ross of raisins. Dressed in baggy black track pants and a beige hooded sweatshirt with Roadrunner on the front, she obviously shopped at the same place as Danny. Her feet were encased in knitted slippers with bobbles on the toes that Ross just knew she'd made herself. He was tempted to ask whether she told fortunes or juggled.

'Are you the brother?' she asked bluntly.

Ross gave her his best publicity smile. 'Yes. I'm Ross Fabello,

Patrick's brother. You must be the neighbour Danny told me about who looks after the children.'

So maybe he was giving the impression that he and Danny had had a cosy chat about her neighbour and the children. So maybe he was full of shit. So, *sue him.*

The neighbour's scraggly, greying eyebrows slunk downwards. Danny had obviously mentioned Ross, and what she'd had to say hadn't been positive, so he was surprised when she extended a dry, callused hand and shook his vigorously. 'Deryl Snedden. I s'pose you want to come in and see the kids?'

'Yes, if that's OK?'

'Probably not.' Deryl turned and scuffed down the hallway. 'But seeing as you're here, you might as well.'

Mia and Matt were sprawled on the sofa in the living room, Mia watching television and Matt reading a book. Like the kitchen, it was furnished with odds and ends and was dominated by two large, squashy sofas in a shabby green-and-blue print. White stuffing spilled out of several rips in the arms. Two sets of French doors overlooked the garden and were framed by long, calico curtains hung on wooden rods. Large, glossy plants stood either side of a brick fireplace filled with pinecones painted gold. The pale carpet was threadbare in several places.

Mia was delighted to see him. She threw herself at Ross and hugged him. Matt was a lot harder to read. He remained on the floor in front of the television and offered a polite hello but no smile.

Ross took a seat on the bigger of the two sofas, which seemed to be full of lumps. Danny probably kept it to discourage unwelcome visitors. 'Is Auntie Danny at work?'

Mia nodded, lifted her butt over a bump and wriggled closer to Ross.

'Won't be home 'til after ten.' Deryl folded her arms over the

Roadrunner. 'Do you want a cup of tea?'

'Do you have any coffee?'

'No.'

'Tea would be great,' Ross lied.

While Deryl went to make the tea, he looked at the framed photographs scattered about the room. It was unsettling to see Pat's face staring out from some of them. In one photo he and a girl with long, fair hair smiled at the camera, their heads close together. In another, Pat, the blonde girl, a much younger, chubbier Matt and a newborn baby with a red face and black hair were perched together on a hospital bed, smiling.

Pat's secret life.

Anger percolated inside Ross like sour coffee. How could Pat exclude his family from such precious moments?

Deryl marched back into the room bearing two steaming mugs on a tray, which she placed on the scarred wooden coffee table between the sofas. Ross thanked her, screwed up his nose and took a sip. The tea almost tore his throat out and sent him into a fit of coughing.

Deryl pounded him on the back. 'Got bones in it, eh?'

'Are you going to stop breathing?' Matt asked hopefully. 'My teacher told us about the Heimlich manoeuvre. I can show you if you want.'

'I am not going to stop breathing,' Ross rasped and took a discreet sniff of the tea.

It reeked of booze.

'It's got a splash of whisky,' Deryl said. 'I always put a dollop in when the weather's like this.'

Ross looked out the window at the trees tossing against the stormy, gun-metal-coloured sky. Spring in Auckland was proving to be a challenge, with literally four seasons in one day, but he didn't think Deryl could use the weather as an excuse for dosing the tea, and was unimpressed by Danny's choice of caregiver. Deryl seemed to know what he was thinking. There was a nasty gleam in her eye and a hard-edged smile on her crafty face. She knocked back her mug of tea and went to check on dinner.

Under the guise of taking a closer look at the photos on the mantelpiece, Ross emptied his mug into one of the plants by the fireplace. Mia climbed off the sofa and came to join him. She pointed at one of the photographs. 'That's Mummy and Auntie Danny when they were little. They were twins.'

Ross studied the photo of two little blonde girls, about the same age as Mia, wearing identical pink dresses, white frilly ankle socks and shiny black shoes. Each wore a large pink bow in their ponytail. Ross guessed which one was Danny. Daniella posed for the camera, her dress held out at the sides and a big smile on her face, a junior model in the making. Danny was a reluctant participant, her smile polite but bored, her bow askew and her socks drooping around her ankles, her demeanour suggesting she really couldn't see the point. While the girls shared the same fair hair and amber eyes, Daniella was prettier, yet Danny's more angular features and uncompromising stare drew his gaze. She was ready to take on the world and kick its ass.

Matt appeared to be riveted by the book he was reading, but Ross sensed his curiosity. He looked at Matt's shoulder-length black curls and wondered if he was bullied at school for having girl's hair. Ross and Pat had been involved in plenty of fights at school over taunts about their hair until Vito realized what was happening. The first time either of the boys came home from school with a black eye or bloody nose from a fight about their hair, their father took them to the local barber shop and had their glossy black curls shorn.

'I will never forgive you, Vittorio Fabello!' Breda sobbed when Ross came home with his scalp covered in little more than black fuzz. 'How could you cut off my wee boy's crowning glory?'

'Breda, mia cara,' Vito soothed. 'For the girls it is a crowning glory. For the boys it's an excuse to get their asses kicked. Today our Ross won the fight, but tomorrow,' he lifted his palms, 'tomorrow he might not be so lucky.'

Matt suddenly spoke up. 'Auntie Danny said you're a writer.'

'That's right,' Ross agreed cautiously.

'She said you don't use your own name.'

Ross nodded, surprised Danny had talked about him to the children.

'Are you RL Stine?' Matt asked.

'No.'

He looked disappointed. 'Are you KA Applegate?'

'No.'

Matt looked really disappointed.

'So what are RL Stine and KA Applegate so famous for?' Ross asked.

'Writing good books.'

'Never heard of 'em.'

Matt was shocked. 'You've never heard of *It Came From Beneath the Sink?*'

'No.'

'Revenge of the Lawn Gnomes?'

'Nope.'

'The Blob That Ate Everyone?'

'No.' Ross could tell he was rapidly losing all credibility.

'Have you written anything good?'

'Some people think so,' Ross replied.

Matt looked at him dubiously. 'I can lend you something good if you want.' He put down his book and stood up.

'One of my books has just been made into a movie.' Ross wondered why he was trying to impress an eleven-year-old.

Matt paused in the doorway. 'Why would anybody want to do that?' he asked and disappeared.

Ross's jaw dropped.

When Deryl announced that the kids' dinner was ready, he got up to leave, carrying a copy of *It Came From Beneath the Sink*.

Mia hung onto his hand. 'You will come back again soon, won't you, Uncle Ross?'

'Of course — I'll have to bring back Matt's book.'

Matt and Mia followed him to the front door.

'Are you any good at fixing things?' Matt asked.

Ross suspected another test. 'Not bad, why?'

'Can you fix our trampoline?'

'Yeah! Can you fix our trampoline?' Mia chimed in. 'Auntie Danny doesn't have time.'

Like she could fix the damned trampoline, Ross thought. Two pairs of blue eyes just like Pat's stared up at him and a knot formed in his throat, like a piece of bread was stuck there.

'Maybe.' Ross didn't want to get their hopes up. This had been way too easy. God only knew how Danny would react when she discovered he'd paid a visit.

Matt shrugged. 'Whatever,' he said, and walked away.

Ross felt even more useless than he did each time he sat at his laptop and stared at the yawning emptiness of the white page on the screen. The door was swollen from the rain. Ross took his frustration out on it and gave it a vicious yank. 'This freakin' door!'

'That's a naughty word, Uncle Ross,' Mia said disapprovingly.

He wrenched the door open: just what he needed — his mother in T-bar shoes.

Before he left, Deryl showed Ross the business card he'd left with Danny. 'Is this you?'

'Yes.'

'Where're you staying?'

Ross couldn't decide if she was plain nosy or had an ulterior motive. 'I've got an apartment at the Viaduct Basin.'

'Very nice,' Deryl sniffed. 'I s'pose you look a bit like your brother, but you don't act like him. He could never keep his gob shut for more than a few seconds.'

Ross was too astonished to answer.

Deryl gave a satisfied nod. 'I'll let Danny know you came around,' she said and banged the door shut in his face.

Ross stalked to the Explorer. He'd run out of patience with Daneka Lawton and her invisible woman act. Discovering she left the children with the neighbourhood drunk when she was at work was the final straw. He climbed into the Explorer and punched Allan Nicolls's number into his cellphone. When Allan came onto the line, Ross briefly explained the situation.

'Do you know a good private investigator?' he asked.

'Yes. In fact there're a couple I use.'

'Good. I want one of them to watch Daneka Lawton twenty-four/seven for the next couple of weeks. I want to know everything about her right down to the colour toothbrush she uses. Tell them not to dismiss anything as too trivial: I want to know everything.'

Inside the house, Matt told Mia, 'He's not going to stay. He's going to go away like Dad always did.'

'No, he isn't! Uncle Ross is different. He likes us.'

'He doesn't like us. He doesn't even want to fix the trampoline.'

Mia cried, 'Stop it! I hate you! Uncle Ross does like us. I know he does. He is going to fix the trampoline.'

'Bet he doesn't, bet he gets on the plane and goes back to America,' Matt said stubbornly. 'I don't care anyway. I don't want him to come back.'

'Yes, you do!' Mia's bottom lip wobbled right along with her voice. 'That's why you gave him one of your books!'

As Ross had anticipated, Danny erupted when she heard he'd paid a visit while she was at work.

Deryl casually let it drop when Danny went across the road to the Snedden house to drop off the money she owed her for the week's babysitting. Danny was astonished that Ross Fabello had somehow managed to charm Deryl, who was well-known for her generally low tolerance level. Ross would have wasted his time turning on the charm he'd shown the brunette in the supermarket; you only had to look at Deryl's husband, Lloyd, to realize Deryl's ideal man was not to be found among the Brad Pitts or George Clooneys of the world.

'Why did you let him in?' Danny demanded.

Deryl was busy feeding her beloved pigs, which were grunting and squealing with excitement at the sight of the slop bucket in her hand. 'Why shouldn't I let him in?'

Danny waved her arms around. 'Because . . . because he's trying to take the children away from me, that's why! He wants to take them back to the States!'

'Alright, my darling Snout, my pretty girl,' Deryl crooned to the wet and quivering pink nostrils thrust through the metal gate of the pig sty. 'Did he say that?'

'Well — not in so many words, but—' Danny sidestepped to avoid being goosed by Snout, and her foot squelched into something wet and smelly. 'Ah! Shit!'

Deryl glanced at the dark, smelly stuff oozing over the top of Danny's flimsy sandals. 'Told you before to wear your gumboots when you come over here, you stupid girl.' She moved to the next member of her porcine fan club. The smell was appalling. 'What would a young bloke like him want with two little kiddies?'

Danny was annoyed to hear Deryl echo Vanessa. Why was he

charming to everybody but her? Wasn't it in his best interests to get on her right side?

'He doesn't seem to be anything like his brother.' Deryl emptied the bucket into a trough. 'Betty! Betty! How is my little mama?' she cried to a gargantuan pink sow with assorted nipples jiggling in excitement. Innumerable little porkers scampered about her trotters and tripped into the trough alongside their mother's grunting head.

Danny was bewildered. How had a level-headed, dry old stick like Deryl come to such an insane conclusion after just one meeting with Ross? Deryl, who saved all her love and approval for her pigs?

A huge pig hoisted its trotters onto the bars of the gate to get closer to Deryl and her bucket, and squealed excitedly. Perhaps it wasn't such a surprise that Deryl had given Ross Fabello the seal of approval, Danny decided sourly; after all he could be a total pig, too.

Deryl headed back towards the house with two empty buckets swinging from her broad, callused palms. 'He wasn't full of himself like Patrick, and he doesn't approve of drinking in the middle of the day.'

Danny stopped. *'What?'* *Please don't say you put Ross through some sort of initiation ceremony,* she thought desperately. She hurried after Deryl to the back door. 'What did you do?'

'I made him a cup of tea and loaded it up with whisky — wanted to see if he got on the turps in the middle of the day like his worthless brother. He didn't drink it — he tipped it into one of the pot plants.' Deryl set the metal buckets down on the first of three concrete steps leading to the back door with a clang.

'Oh Deryl!' Danny moaned. 'Tell me — did . . . did he think you were drinking in the middle of the afternoon?'

Deryl's wiry eyebrows lowered. 'How could I offer him booze in his tea if I didn't pretend I was having some myself?'

Danny gazed morosely at her filthy sandals. The pig poo seemed like a blessing in comparison to this latest development. Ross would never believe Deryl was a teetotaller, and Patrick's fondness for drink was one of the reasons why Deryl disapproved of him so much. Danny would be wasting her time trying to explain to Deryl how things might look from Ross's perspective. Deryl was Danny's lifeline — without her, Danny couldn't go to work.

Danny told Vanessa the whole sorry story when they met for coffee at a mall a couple of days later. By now Vanessa was resigned to hearing Danny complain about Ross Fabello. She sat opposite, eating a coconut-and-lemon muffin and sipping a cappuccino as she watched Danny attack a chocolate muffin with a fork and let her tea go cold. Neither of them noticed the man dressed in jeans and a khaki-coloured sweater sitting at the next table, apparently engrossed in his newspaper, which was exactly what he intended.

'I don't know why people mistake him for George Clooney.' Danny decapitated the muffin with a vicious swipe of her fork. 'He looks more like Darth Vader.'

'I always fancied Darth Vader,' Vanessa said idly. 'All my friends liked Hans Solo and Luke Skywalker, but I fancied Darth.'

Danny grabbed the knife from Vanessa's plate. 'I bet he's got the kind of chest hair that grows over his shoulders and down his back.'

'Who? Darth Vader?'

'How dare he invade my house?'

'Who? Darth Vader?'

'Van, this is serious!'

Vanessa was getting tired of hearing about Ross Fabello. 'I agree it was pretty dumb of Deryl to pull a stunt like that, but Danny —

this is Deryl we're talking about.'

'She's a teetotaller! She only did it to find out if Ross liked booze as much as Patrick did.'

'And did he?'

'No. He emptied his tea into one of the pot plants.' Danny chewed her bottom lip. 'You know what worries me most of all?'

'What?'

'The effect all this is having on Matt and Mia. Deryl overheard them talking about Ross after he left.' Danny repeated what Deryl had said.

'Oh,' Vanessa sighed. 'That's so sad.' Her expression turned fierce. 'You know what I think you should do?'

Danny looked at her hopefully. 'Rub him out and feed him to Deryl's pigs? It'd be like recycling.'

'Rub him out? What have you been reading? *The Godfather?*' Vanessa asked. '*No.* Hide the kids' passports. If Ross can't get hold of their passports, he can't take them out of the country.'

Anxiety curled like smoke in the pit of Danny's belly. 'Do you really think . . .'

'Why chance it?'

'I don't even know where the kids' passports are, or mine. Nella put them somewhere safe.'

Vanessa sighed again. 'Great. With any luck they'll be in the same place as her will.' Daniella's idea of putting something somewhere safe had always been a hit-and-miss affair. 'Find them and give them to me.' She checked her watch. 'We'd better get going or you'll be late for your shift and I'll miss my bikini wax, though God knows why I bother — I'm the only person who ever gets to see it.' She reached beneath the table and grabbed her bag.

Danny stopped her. 'That's my one.'

They both owned the same black bag, bought on their last holiday abroad to Hong Kong, back in the days when Danny had been fancy-free and solvent. Vanessa's was ripped around the zipper because she always travelled with an emergency supply of everything — insect repellent, safety pins, sewing kit — you name it, Vanessa could whip it out. They exchanged bags and walked towards the escalators in the centre of the mall.

Behind them, the man closed his newspaper, stood and followed them at a discreet distance, making mental notes: *Darth Vader, passports, will, murder, pigs.*

He thought it would be better not to mention the chest hair.

Chapter 7

It was Lloyd Snedden who unwittingly let Ross into their lives. It started at seven-thirty when a stranger awakened Ross from a deep, dreamless sleep by hollering down the telephone line that he needed to come and look after the kiddies because his missus was crook, whatever the hell that meant.

Flat on his back amongst a tangle of bedclothes, Ross cracked an eye open at the ceiling and tried to make sense of the long-winded story. He was fighting a mammoth hangover from the previous night's drinking binge with Jeff at several bars in the Viaduct Basin. His mouth coated with fur and his stomach churning, Ross remembered why he'd given up this kind of stuff when he finished college.

'Fine,' he croaked. 'I'll be there in half an hour.'

Ten minutes in the shower revived him sufficiently to stumble into some clothes. The whites of his eyes were riddled with red, and his beard made him look like a grizzly. Ross ran his electric razor half-heartedly over his jaw and stumbled downstairs to the basement parking. The early morning sun felt like bamboo sticks poked into his eyes.

Mia was ecstatic to see him. Her ear-piercing shrieks grew the bamboo sticks into trees being driven into Ross's skull. Matt looked at him and said, 'Dad used to look like you do in the morning.'

Lloyd Snedden was a bowed, weather-beaten man with bandy legs and faded blue eyes set in a permanent squint from years spent outdoors. His washed-out shorts were belted beneath his paunch and flapped about his skinny legs like sails in the wind. He'd already sent Deryl home to bed, but he seemed dubious about leaving the children in Ross's care. 'You sure you're not crook as well?'

'No,' Ross said. 'Worked late last night, that's all.'

With memories of Deryl's doctoring of his tea still fresh in his mind he wondered if her sudden illness was alcohol-induced, but was hardly in a position to voice his suspicions to her husband, who'd obviously guessed the reason for Ross's less-than-stellar appearance.

'Nice work if you can get it,' Lloyd observed dryly. 'Reckon you'll manage then, son.'

After Lloyd had left, Ross recalled that he hadn't yet spoken to Danny about her sitter. He didn't buy what the PI had heard her say about Deryl Snedden being a teetotaller.

Ross headed to the kitchen to make the blackest cup of coffee he could. Mia and Matt followed him and sat at the table watching while he searched fruitlessly inside the cupboards for coffee.

'Has your aunt got anything to drink besides tea?' Ross asked desperately.

'We've got some Milo,' Mia said.

'Milo? What's Milo? Is it like coffee?'

'No,' Matt replied.

Ross felt his left eye begin to twitch.

'We used to have some when Dad was here,' Matt continued. 'But now Dad's dead, Auntie Danny doesn't buy it. She says it's too expensive, and anyway she doesn't like it.'

Ross's right eye began to twitch. He *needed* a cup of coffee.

'Want to go to Starbucks?'

It probably wasn't the smartest thing to let the kids eat triple chocolate cake at nine in the morning, but Ross really didn't care as he took his first sip of strong black coffee and settled down to peruse the morning paper.

Bad move.

Matt and Mia began to get bored and squabble about two minutes after they finished their chocolate cake. He tried to ignore them by hiding behind the paper.

'Uncle Ross?' Matt said. Ross grunted.

'Uncle Ross, I think Mia needs to go to the toilet.'

'I don't!'

'Yes, you do. You're wriggling around like you always do when you're going to wet your pants—'

The wet-your-pants part got his attention. Mia had her legs clamped together with her hands buried between them. She saw his horrified expression, burst into tears and wet her pants.

'Oh no . . .' Ross groaned, and she cried harder.

'I told you,' Matt said.

Ross took Mia to the bathroom where the three of them did their best to clean her up. There was nothing for it but to head home and change her clothes.

It was then that Ross discovered the *shoelace* dangling from the toilet cistern. 'You use a shoelace to flush the toilet?'

Matt nodded. 'Auntie Danny fixed it. Pretty clever, eh?'

Ross stared at the shoelace. This was a freakin' nuthouse.

'We can't afford a new one!' Mia danced up and down the hallway in a clean pink dress which flapped up to display her bare ass. 'I know all the ABBA songs and I've made up some dances to go with them.'

'Maybe show me later — right now put on some underwear.'

'Oh, yeah! I forgot!' She bounced off down the hallway, her bare bottom flashing with every shimmy and bump.

Ross returned his attention to the toilet. He hated seeing things in a state of disrepair. He looked at Matt. 'Got any tools?'

When Matt showed him Pat's extensive toolkit, Ross smiled wearily. It was so typical of his brother. He'd purchased the most expensive and, in several cases, the most obscure tools money could buy, and they were covered in dust — not grease or dirt. It didn't take Ross long to figure out that the whole toilet had to be replaced.

He called Jeff. 'Any chance of finding me a plumber to do a couple hours' work?'

'You're kidding me. On a Saturday? At short notice?'

'I'll pay him double the going rate.'

A plumber was found, the brother of one of the guys from the hospital construction site. He was a huge Maori guy named Joe.

'You get the new bog, buddy, and I'll start ripping out the old one,' he told Ross after he'd checked out the plumbing and assessed the state of the toilet. 'This plumbing is pretty old, bro.'

Ross nodded. 'What's a bog?' The only bogs he knew of were Irish swamps.

'A dunny — a loo — a *toilet*.'

Ross was unsure about leaving Joe in Danny's house. He could imagine what she'd do if she arrived home unexpectedly and discovered a stranger ripping out her toilet. He was about to head out the door with the kids when Matt suggested it would be a good idea if Mia used the toilet before they left.

She insisted she didn't need to go. Ross insisted she did. Mia reluctantly disappeared into the toilet while Ross, Matt and Joe waited in the hallway. Joe had mentioned he had four kids and had been off work for the past six months since hurting his back. Reading between the lines, Ross guessed money was tight.

'Nothing came out!' Mia shouted.

'Sit longer!' Ross called back.

Silence.

'Nothing!'

'LONGER!'

They were eventually rewarded by the sound of Mia peeing, but his relief was short-lived.

'Doesn't mean anything,' Matt said. 'She often wets her pants ten minutes after she's been.'

Ross checked his watch. It was only eleven. He had hours of this torture left.

They went to the bathroom fixtures supplier that Joe had recommended, and Mia sat on all the toilets.

'You know you can't actually use them, don't you, Mia?'

She rolled her eyes. 'I'm not stupid, Uncle Ross. Can we have a pink one?'

They made one visit to the shop's bathroom after Mia managed to fall inside one of the display models and Ross had to fish her out.

'No more sitting on the damned toilets! OK?'

Her eyes filled with tears. 'Yes, Uncle Ross.'

Matt wore his disapproving face.

Ross wasn't above bribery. 'How about we go get a popsicle?' '

A popsicle?' The tears miraculously dried. 'You mean an ice block?'

'If you say so.' He took Mia's hand. 'Have you ever thought of a career in acting?'

She trotted along beside him. 'Auntie Danny says I belong in Hollywood.'

On the way back to Danny's house, Ross watched the children in the rear-vision mirror. Matt was plugged into his iPod and in a world of his own. Ross thought he was extraordinarily mature for an eleven-year-old boy, unlike Mia who was still like a little girl. Ross hadn't paid attention to music until he was thirteen, and then only because it was something to talk about to the girls he'd suddenly noticed.

'What are you listening to?' he asked.

Matt reluctantly pulled off his headphones. 'Nickelback. You probably don't know them.'

'I know Nickelback,' Ross replied. 'Who else do you like?'

'Coldplay, Gorillaz, Nellie Furtado . . . a whole bunch of stuff.'

'Do you like the Red Hot Chili Peppers?'

Matt was shocked. 'You know them?'

'Calm down, we don't want the shock to blow your iPod.'

'The Chili Peppers are mint! I want to get *Stadium Arcadium*.'

And Matt was off on a complex discussion about his favourite groups, most of whom Ross didn't know but wouldn't admit to. But he only had to nod and say *Uh huh* every so often to keep his end of the conversation going. When Matt began to wind down, Ross told him he'd finished the book that Matt loaned him.

'You read it?' Matt blinked in surprise. 'Really?'

'Yeah, really.'

He looked sceptical. 'What'd you think?'

They launched into a discussion about *It Came From Beneath the Sink,* which Ross had actually enjoyed.

Mia watched the scenery and hummed to herself. 'I still think we should have got a pink one.'

Ross and Matt exchanged puzzled looks in the mirror.

'You mean a pink toilet?' Ross clarified.

She nodded.

Matt pulled a face. 'Ugh! Gross!'

'It is *not* gross!' Mia cried. *'You're gross!'*

'And you're just a stupid girl!'

'I am not!'

'Yes you are, you're— '

'ZIP IT!' Ross bellowed. 'Do you two get an allowance?'

They nodded cautiously.

'Have you ever heard of performance reviews?'

Mia looked at Matt; clearly she was nominating him as the party spokesman.

'No,' he said. 'What's a performance review?'

'It's when the person who pays your wages — or allowance — decides if you've earned what you're being paid. It's when that person decides if you deserve a raise.' Ross paused to allow time for the information to sink in. 'I'm instigating a performance review, starting today.'

'What's that mean?' Mia asked.

'We might not get our pocket money,' Matt said.

'But Auntie Danny pays our pocket money!' Clearly when it came to money Mia wasn't as blonde as she looked.

'There's been a change in fiscal policy,' Ross said. 'From now on I'll be paying it.'

The children exchanged worried looks. 'When are you going to do a performance review?' Matt asked.

Ross smiled. 'Now, that's the best part — I'm not telling you.'

Joe was reading the paper and smoking a cigarette when they got back. 'I had a look at the rest of the plumbing while you were out. You need to do some work around this place, mate.'

'That bad?' Ross asked.

Joe snorted. 'You could say that.'

While Joe got on with changing the old toilet connection for the new, Ross looked at the outside of the house. He'd earned extra money during college working on construction sites and knew enough to see Joe was telling the truth.

Once upon a time the old house had been beautiful, but it had gradually fallen into disrepair. Joe was right about the plumbing, and the wooden window frames were rotten in many places. Closer inspection explained why several parts of the wide wooden verandah were blocked off — it was rotten, too. Restored to its original beauty and with its stupendous view over the Pacific Ocean, the house would be worth a lot of money. Danny might be cash-poor but she was asset-rich.

Ross was planing the front door when Lloyd arrived to check on the kids and mentioned that he owned a welding torch. He eyed Ross speculatively. 'Been meaning to fix that trampoline leg for the kids.'

Matt was sitting on the front step, and Ross sensed his sudden alertness. 'If you lend me the equipment, I'll fix it.'

The kids joined him in the garden to watch the trampoline being repaired.

Matt watched dubiously as Ross donned safety goggles. 'Are you sure you know what you're doing?' His dad had been famous for starting to fix things and either never completing the job or botching it.

'I think I'll manage.' Ross pointed to the verandah. 'Go and sit up there out of the way.' Once the children had done as he'd asked, he lit the welding torch and set to work.

'Can we play on it?' Matt asked as soon as Ross had finished.

'Not just yet.'

Mia pouted. 'I'm hungry.'

He sighed. No rest for the wicked.

They trooped into the kitchen. Ross made the kids chocolate and banana milkshakes, and reluctantly fed them some black gunk sandwiches, after they insisted it was what they wanted. He poked about the kitchen cupboards while the children ate. The contents were hardly inspiring. Danny seemed to buy a lot of oatmeal.

'What sort of things does Auntie Danny like to cook?' Ross asked.

Matt and Mia stopped chewing and gazed at him blankly.

'What's Auntie Danny's favourite recipe?'

They frowned.

'Does she like to cook pasta? Or fish?' Ross prompted. 'Or vegetarian?'

Mia spoke up. 'Auntie Danny says being in the kitchen is like being in a laboratory.'

'A laboratory?'

Matt nodded. 'Sometimes her experiments go wrong.'

'Then what happens?'

'Then we have porridge.' Mia licked a milkshake moustache from her upper lip. 'Auntie Danny makes really yummy porridge.'

Danny couldn't cook.

There was a slight hiccup when Mia asked if she could go to the toilet before they'd finished installing the new one. Ross was watching Joe screw the bolts into the base of the toilet when Mia appeared in the doorway. She jiggled from one foot to the other. 'Uncle Ross! I need to go!'

Matt popped up behind her. 'I've got to go, too, Uncle Ross.'

What was it with these kids? Were they camels in another life?

'Go round back and pick a tree.'

Mia stopped jiggling. 'I don't think Auntie Danny would like us doing wees outside.'

He noticed the distraction lessened her sense of urgency. 'Auntie Danny won't mind when she sees the nice surprise we've got for her.'

'You're sure?'

'I'm sure.'

'Hey, Mia!' Matt headed outside. 'Let's sit in our trees and wee!'

Ross was certain Auntie Danny would disapprove of that one. He sure as hell wouldn't want to be one of the chickens or sheep below.

After the new toilet was installed and Ross had checked that the trampoline was safe for the kids to play on, he decided to take a horseback ride in the sunshine.

'B's not a nice horse,' Matt warned.

'What's the matter with her?'

'She tries to bite Auntie Danny.'

Ross decided he liked the horse. 'What else?'

'She bucks sometimes when she doesn't want Auntie Danny to ride her.'

Ross decided he loved the horse. 'Does she buck Auntie Danny off?'

'Sometimes,' Matt replied. 'Auntie Danny says she's a strong old bitch.'

He kept a straight face. 'She won't buck me off — I'm too heavy.'

B did buck him off. Fortunately it happened at the bottom of the hill, well away from the house and out of sight. It took Ross several minutes to catch her again and remount, and he was filthy, sweaty and cursing by the time he rode her back up the hill.

Danny tried not to work on the weekends so she could be home with the children. It put a dent in her pay, because weekends were some of the most lucrative shifts, but the Saturday after Deryl's tea party she was on duty. When Danny arrived home, Ross's car was parked in the driveway. She sprinted to the house. The first thing she noticed was that she didn't have to shoulder charge the front door — it glided open with a gentle push. The house was ominously silent. She hurried into the kitchen and out onto the verandah, which stretched around three sides of the house.

Matt and Mia were bouncing on the trampoline, which stood squarely on all four legs. They waved when they saw Danny, and Mia shouted, 'Look, Auntie Danny! The trampoline is fixed!'

Danny nodded absently and searched the trees and paddocks beyond the garden for a dark, curly head. 'That's great. Who fixed it?'

Matt pumped his knees and flew high in the air, sending Mia bouncing precariously close to the edge of the canvas matting. Danny opened her mouth to tell him off.

'Matt!' Ross shouted. 'I told you not to do that when Mia is with you!'

Danny watched him amble up the slope of the back paddock on B, their old mare. She could have sworn the crabby horse had a smile on her whiskery muzzle.

Ross stopped the horse at the fence and watched Danny walk towards him across the grass. He tried not to stare. She was wearing a short, flirty blue skirt. It matched her pale blue peasant blouse and the ballet flats on her feet. She had legs — pretty ones with dainty ankles. Ross searched, but there was no sign of a tattoo.

Danny stopped at the fence. 'What are you staring at?'

'I'm searching for cloven hooves.'

'Very funny. What are you doing here?'

B leaned over and made a half-hearted attempt to take a chunk out of Danny's shoulder. Ross pulled the mare's head away. B flattened her ears and flung her head up and down.

'You should be in a can,' Danny said. It was an empty threat, just like B's attempt to bite her. She swiped green-flecked foam from her bare arm and asked again, 'What are you doing here?'

Ross stared at her face. 'Your bruises have gone.'

She bent and wiped her fingers on the grass. 'Well, duh? What did you expect?'

Not what he was seeing. She was still no beauty queen, her face was too angular, her amber gaze too challenging, her jaw line too determined — but put it all together and the result was — Ross searched for the right word — arresting. The recent sunny weather had put pale streaks through her light brown hair. The ends and part of her fringe were painted pink today, instead of blue. Ross supposed it would be too much to expect Danny to get her hair and her clothes to match. The peasant blouse had a scooped, gathered neck and tiny sleeves. It clung to her small breasts and revealed the fragile hollows above her collarbones.

'Did anybody ever tell you it's rude to stare?' Danny asked.

'Can you turn around?' Ross replied.

She eyed him suspiciously. 'Why?'

'I want to see if you've got a tail.'

'Hah! Like I'm the one who's likely to have one of those.'

Ross recalled the report from the private investigator who Allan Nicolls had hired. Allan had been concerned about Danny's plans to rub Ross out and feed him to Deryl's pigs. Ross had kept a straight face while he reassured Allan, but afterwards he'd taken the report back to his apartment, poured himself a glass of Merlot, re-read the contents and laughed. The only part of the report he didn't enjoy was what Danny had told Vanessa about the conversation between Matt and Mia.

As Ross read the report, an idea for a story had begun to take shape. He grabbed a pen and a block of paper and poured his ideas onto the pages as fast he could write them. After months and months of drought, his mind was on fire; his hand could hardly keep up.

'Why aren't you wearing your uniform?' he asked.

'I did some shopping after I finished work,' she propped her hands on her hips. 'Answer my question: what are you doing here, Fabello?'

The afternoon had turned hot. The sun beat down out of a cloudless blue sky, and beyond the green paddocks the Pacific Ocean sparkled in the sunshine. Ross's hair stuck to his brow in tiny curls, and his burgundy shirt clung to his chest. His olive skin had darkened even more since Danny had last seen him, which made his teeth look very white. She guessed that was what happened when you had nothing else to do but laze around sunbathing at your penthouse apartment and bug the crap out of people.

In contrast, Danny felt pale and unattractive. She watched Ross raise an arm to wipe the sweat from his forehead. His shirt parted company with the waistband of his jeans to reveal the lower half of a six-pack bisected by a thin line of black hair. Danny felt cheated. Ross wasn't covered in thick fur as she'd hoped. She felt even more cheated when he lowered his arm and his shirt covered the view.

'Take a guess why I'm here.' He was obviously in the mood to yank her chain.

'To break the news that the Mother Ship has returned, and they're taking you home to remove your anal probe? Just answer the damned question!'

B shifted from one foreleg to the other, shuddering to dislodge a persistent fly. Ross draped his wrists across her withers and smiled mockingly. 'Fixing your trampoline; riding your horse.'

'Don't get smart with me, Fabello! Who let you in and—' Danny frowned. 'Where's Deryl?' She spun around in a circle, searching for her neighbour, her little blue skirt flaring out.

Ross enjoyed the view. 'I murdered her and buried her under the chicken shed.'

'Where's Deryl?'

He sighed and climbed off B. Underneath the short skirt and clinging top, the Wicked Witch was alive and kicking. 'She's sick. Lloyd called me to look after the kids.'

'Lloyd? Called you?' Danny was shocked. 'But . . . but she was fine this morning!'

Ross undid the girth and lifted the saddle from B's back. She shuddered luxuriously. 'Were you away from nursing school the day they explained people can get sick without warning?' He propped the saddle against a fence post. 'I offered to help.'

'The only person you want to help is yourself, Fabello.'

He braced his hands on the mare's glossy back. Danny wondered why B didn't snake her head around and try to bite his arm off. And why did Ross suddenly have thick, curly eyelashes? They weren't as long as Patrick's or Matt's, but that wasn't the point — that wasn't where he was supposed to have excess hair.

'Deryl got sick. Lloyd called me about seven-thirty this morning to say he had to take her to the doctor and he didn't like to call you at work, because it's hard for you to come home when you're in charge.'

Danny took a step backwards, away from the wolfish smile and those evil black eyes. 'Lloyd should have called me.'

'Don't bother saying thank you.'

'Don't push it, Fabello.' She watched him remove B's bridle. He had strong forearms and long, blunt-tipped fingers. There was nothing sensitive or artistic about his hands; they looked as if they'd be equally at home wrapped around the handle of a pneumatic drill — or someone's neck. Danny knew she was stupid to keep baiting him, but it was as if she was set on Self-destruct Mode. 'I'm going to phone Deryl.' The distant sound of her cellphone crowing reached them from inside the house.

'I bet that's her,' Danny said, and took off across the grass.

He watched her smooth legs swing and her cute little butt sway beneath the short blue skirt. If only she was mute, she'd be perfect.

Thanks to the PI's report, Ross knew about the missing passports and Danny's plans to give them to Vanessa. He wanted those passports. Danny might not have any money, but Ross was sure her accomplice Ms Cooper could be persuaded to contribute to the cause if Danny decided to skip the country. The cursory search he'd made of the house hadn't yielded anything. Either he was too late and Danny had found the passports and given them to Vanessa, or they were still lost. If they were lost, it wouldn't be such a bad thing, particularly if Ross reported them missing and filed for new ones. All he needed was copies of the children's birth certificates.

He rubbed down the old mare and gave her the feed Matt had prepared. The PI had provided a lot of background information about Daniella and about Rose Smith, the twins' mother. Mike Lawton had abandoned Rose and his daughters when they were teenagers and returned to his wife and children in England. He never contacted his New Zealand family again, and so didn't know that Rose died from breast cancer a few years after he left. Mike never made any attempt to send money or find out how the twins were; he simply walked out of their lives and never returned.

The parallels between Danny's parents' relationship and Patrick and Nella's were discomforting. Mike wasn't there for Rose when she died. Danny couldn't reach Patrick when Nella needed him. The PI reported that it was Danny who took charge of the family after her father left. Rose and Daniella had been cut from the same cloth — both had been careless about money, lived beyond their means, and avoided anything to do with wills, mortgage agreements and debt repayments. Danny had been the glue that held everything together.

Ross could understand why Danny was so hostile towards him and his family, and why she was so worried about the children building a relationship with their father's relatives. She was trying to protect them from being hurt the way she'd been, and he had to admit she was right to be worried. Matt expected the worst from Ross, and Mia dreamed of the impossible. Ross wasn't father material, never had been. He hadn't made the trip to New Zealand with the intention of stepping into Pat's shoes, although, considering the kind of father Pat had been, Ross couldn't do any worse. He didn't want Matt and Mia thinking in terms of forever, but that hadn't stopped him from finishing the book Matt had lent him and fixing the trampoline.

Inside the house Danny was becoming agitated. Ross had done a lot more than look after the kids and fix the trampoline and front door. He'd fixed the toilet!

When the toilet flush had first broken and Danny had made inquiries about getting it repaired, she was told that that particular model hadn't been made for years. As the cost of a new toilet was beyond her, Danny came up with the ingenious solution of tying a shoelace to the plastic arm which when pulled made the toilet flush. It was cheaper to replace the shoelaces than the broken part.

'You fixed the toilet!' She accused when Ross came inside to wash up.

'I fixed the toilet.' He brushed past her and went into the bathroom.

Danny followed him. 'But it's a whole new toilet!'

Ross bent over the low bathroom vanity and soaped his hands. 'You'd rather have stuck with the shoelace?'

'No . . . but . . .'

'You have a pathological inability to say thank you, don't you? Do you think spending a Saturday morning fixing the john is my idea of relaxation?'

'No, I'm sure it isn't. It's just I could have fixed it myself.'

Ross looked over his shoulder and raised a brow.

'I could!'

'Then why didn't you?'

Danny wouldn't answer him. 'How much do I owe you?'

Ross watched her in the mirror above the bathroom vanity. She looked tense. 'Nothing.' He turned to the towel rail and began to dry his hands. 'I couldn't have put up with that damned shoelace every time I wanted to use the bathroom.'

Danny released the breath she'd been holding. 'Your visit today is a one-off, Fabello.'

He ignored her and inspected the front of his shirt. 'Why did you name your horse after a bee?'

'It's not the insect — it's the letter.'

He tugged the shirt over his head. 'The letter?'

Danny watched the burgundy shirt slide down his arms. There was no hair on his back, just smooth, olive skin stretched over broad shoulders and a long, tapered spine. The shirt dropped to the floor. The view from the front was even better.

Ross braced his hands on his hips. 'Are you ogling me?'

'Of course I'm not!' Looking for excess hair follicles wasn't ogling.

'Are you planning on standing there watching me wash up?'

'No!'

'Then take a hike!' Ross grabbed Danny by the elbows, lifted her into the hallway and shut the bathroom door in her face.

Danny stormed away. The call on her cellphone hadn't been Deryl, and she made a quick call to check on her. The mere fact that Deryl had visited her doctor was worrying — the only time Deryl consulted a health professional was to call the vet for her pigs. When she'd finished talking to Deryl, Danny dragged Patrick's suitcase from beneath Nella's bed and hauled it to the bedroom door. There was no way she was letting Ross wander about the house half-naked. She wouldn't be able to stop herself from searching for signs of abnormal hair growth.

Ross stepped from the bathroom as Danny arrived at the door. As she'd expected, he was bare-chested. He had a towel draped about his neck and his dirty shirt in his hand.

She dropped the bag on his foot. 'Here.'

'Ow!' Ross snatched his foot from beneath the bag. 'What is it now?'

She pointed at the bag. 'These are Patrick's things. Put a shirt on.' Danny headed back down the hallway.

The Louis Vuitton suitcase lay on its side at Ross's feet. He squatted and touched it hesitantly. Ross clasped his hands between his spread knees: he didn't want to touch his brother's things. He shook his head impatiently. He was being stupid; besides, if he didn't sort through Pat's belongings it only meant one of his sisters or his mother and father would have to do it.

The zip whirred softly and the two sides parted. Ross opened the case and took a deep breath. It was a mistake. The smell of Pat's cologne filled his nostrils. It flooded into his bloodstream, coated his nerves and seeped into the pores of his skin. Ross slumped back against the wall, feeling sick and shaken. He clenched his fist and braced an arm on his raised knee as the scent of the cologne seemed to grow stronger.

Danny's blue ballet flats appeared beside him. She briefly touched the bare skin between his hunched shoulders and knelt down to zip the bag closed. 'Stay naked.' She grabbed the case handle and stood up. 'Your chest distracts attention from your nose.'

The ghost of a smile curved his mouth. Even when she was being nice, Danny was a bitch. It had happened again — that connection between them. She'd known how he was feeling and that he didn't want hugs or kind words. Her fleeting touch on his back had been enough, and her smart-assed remark about his nose was just what he needed to break the tension.

Ross watched Danny haul the suitcase back to her sister's bedroom. It was much too heavy for her, she bent sideways and had to use both hands, but Ross didn't offer to help. He knew she didn't want it. He braced his elbows on his knees and dug his fingers into the damp curls springing to attention on his head. There'd only been four years between him and Pat, not that huge a gap, but the gulf between them had nothing to do with age. Pat had always been jealous of Ross. Once, in a fit of anger, he'd shouted, 'I'm always trying to get out from under your shadow! Nobody notices what I achieve!'

The whole family had willed Pat to achieve something, anything that would make him happy. But he never settled, never finished anything he started. He was always chasing something just over the horizon that had never been there in the first place. Ross suspected Pat had made him the children's guardian as a joke. As the second eldest of six kids, Ross had done his time wiping snotty noses and fishing Barbie dolls out of the john. He'd listened to his sisters' sob stories about the guys they were in love with who were in love with their best friend, the guys they didn't like but who were in love with them. On a couple of occasions he'd been called in when some of their boyfriends stepped out of line.

'You don't have to do anything nasty,' Annie had said ingenuously. 'Just be yourself.'

Then there were the weddings — oh sweet Jesus, those weddings!

Three of them.

Ross was sure it took less effort and theatrics to run a presidential campaign than it did to get a Fabello woman to the altar. Breda became demented. The bride cried a lot, yelled a lot, called it off, called it back on, fought with the rest of the family, fought with the bridesmaids, and generally became a pain in the ass for the two years leading up to the big day. Ross had the utmost respect for his brothers-in-law, who'd somehow survived this baptism of fire without turning to alcohol or mood-enhancing drugs. The girls were always warning Ross that someday he'd wind up like them with kids and the obligatory station wagon. The idea made him break out in a cold sweat — he'd get a vasectomy first.

Breda went into orbit. 'Over my dead body, Ross Fabello! No doctor will be fiddling with your . . . bits.'

'They're my bits, Ma.'

'Don't be smart: your father and I made them. I don't know what's got into you. You were raised a good Catholic. Children are

God's gift to us.'

Yeah, but did the Fabellos really need so many? Ross never joked about vasectomies again around his mother, but he took care to ensure that God sent all His gifts his sisters' way.

The irony of his present situation wasn't lost on him. Pat had trussed him up like a turkey. He was stuck at the bottom of the world, legally responsible for two kids, and trying to get along with a razor-tongued harpy who wanted to rub him out and feed him to some pigs.

Before he left, Danny told Ross: 'Thanks for the fixing the toilet, Fabello. I owe you — one.'

Chapter 8

The dam broke. The writing drought was officially over. He started writing a story about identical twins separated at birth who reunite to commit the perfect crime. They could provide one another with an infallible alibi, because nobody knew that the other one existed. It was always a sweet moment when the words began to flow and the characters came to life. The provisional title for the new book was *Double Take*.

Ross bought every book he could find about twins. His favourite was one about dysfunctional twins who exhibited criminal behaviour. Even though he had twin sisters, Ross had never given the subject much thought until he met Danny. Now he was fascinated — particularly about the good twin versus evil twin aspect. When Annie and Aoife had found out that Danny and Nella Lawton were identical twins, they'd reacted as if it was one of them who had died. The news of Danny's singleton status had wiped away any anger the twins had felt about her refusal to give the family access to Pat's children. It was almost as if they thought Danny's behaviour was justified. Ross pestered Annie and Aoife with questions about what it was like to be a twin.

'Why the sudden interest after all these years?' Aoife asked.

'It's for my new book.'

'It's Danny, isn't it? She's got you thinking about twins.'

'No.'

'Catriona! Ronan! Come and put your shoes on. Mommy's

taking you on a march,' Aoife shouted.

'What is it this time, Aoife? You're not going to chain yourself to a tree again, are you?'

Aoife was a political activist from way back. Ross had twice bailed her out of jail for creating a public disturbance when her husband Pete was out of town. Pete was a cop. He'd met Aoife the day he arrested her on her bare-breasted march through the CBD of San Diego in support of breast cancer awareness. Carmen said the fact that Aoife had the best rack in the family must have snared Pete, because it certainly wasn't her sweet nature.

'Aoife,' Ross said, 'do you think you could answer a few questions before you go save the world?'

'OK, but make it quick.'

Ross was certain Aoife and Danny would approve of one another.

The performance reviews turned out to be a stroke of genius. Ross had given Matt his business card with his cellphone number. Matt was so concerned about a cut in his allowance that he started calling Ross in a not-so-subtle attempt to find out what the pass/fail criteria were and when the review might take place.

'I already told you I wouldn't give advance warning, but there is something you can do in the meantime,' Ross said.

'What's that?' Matt asked eagerly.

'I want a list of your chores from each of you.'

'Oh.' Matt's response was lukewarm. 'OK.'

Ross guessed that the reason Danny hadn't called to blast him about the reviews was because the children hadn't told her. He didn't know that Matt's lackadaisical attitude to his chores was a bone of contention between him and his aunt, and that Matt had tried to make Mia swear on the lives of their chickens that she wouldn't tell Danny.

'Why should I?' Mia asked. 'I do mine. You're the one who lazes around on the computer and PlayStation when you're supposed to be mowing the lawn or tidying your room.'

Matt hated it when she was clever. 'We've got to stick together. Swear on the lives of Madonna, Kylie, Beyonce and The Dixie Chicks.' And he hated the names she'd given to the chickens.

Mia narrowed her eyes and pursed her lips. 'I'll think about it.'

How could he have been so dumb? He'd played right into her hands. Matt had hoped that if they kept things between the two of them, Auntie Danny would carry on paying their allowance and Uncle Ross would soon get bored and leave like their father always did. What he hadn't accounted for was that Mia wanted Ross to stay and Ross was nothing like their father. Matt had no choice but to go to Plan B and try to pump Ross for information. 'None of my friends have performance reviews,' he said over the phone.

'They don't?' Ross acted surprised. 'Your cousins in the States all have an annual performance review; it's when they find out if they've got a raise.'

A raise? Matt perked up. That sounded a lot more like it. Still... 'How many cousins have I got?' he asked suspiciously.

'Twelve.'

'Twelve?'

'Yes,' Ross rattled off names. 'Sofia, Sinead, Pasqualina, Sandy, Brad, Nicole, Ronan, Catriona.' He paused to take a breath. 'Desi, Raul, Tonio, Sorcha. And your Auntie Carmel is having another baby soon.'

Matt's mouth hung open. He was related to all those people?

'If you don't believe me about the performance reviews, maybe you should speak to one of your aunts.' Not Annie because she couldn't tell a lie, and not Carmel because she was too hormonal, and definitely not Aoife, because she could be downright scary.

'I'll get Auntie Deirdre to call you. She helps with the reviews as an adjudicator.'

Ross waited. If Matt didn't know what an adjudicator was, Ross would bet money he'd be looking up the meaning the moment he got off the phone. How had Pat produced such a bright kid?

'OK,' Matt said reluctantly.

They settled on a date and a time for Deirdre to call.

'Mia might want to ask her some questions, too,' Ross said.

'As long as I get to speak to Auntie Deirdre first — when Mia starts talking, she never shuts up. Auntie Danny says she was inoculated with a gramophone needle.'

Ross laughed. 'I'll tell Auntie Deirdre to speak to you first. While you're about it, you might want to say hi to Granny Breda and Grandpa Vito.'

'OK.'

Ross disconnected the call. At last: progress.

Since Ross had looked after the children, Danny had become more comfortable with the whole situation. She allowed Matt and Mia to call Ross and let him visit and take photos of the kids for his parents, but it was always when she was at work. He spoke to her occasionally on the phone, but hadn't seen her since the day he fixed the toilet. She was as distant and as warm as the North Pole.

While Danny might have made it easier for Ross to see the children, she'd reinforced the barricades between herself and Ross. Trying to pin her down was like trying to get hold of a jellyfish, she just kept slipping out of his grasp. Ross had thought about telling her he owned two-thirds of the house, but held back. It was his ace in the hole, he kept it tucked away ready to be pulled out if things began to unravel.

He was sitting at his laptop working when the phone rang. The glass doors leading to the deck of the penthouse apartment were folded back, and sunshine and the smell of the sea filled the room. The distant sound of people eating outside the restaurants and bars surrounding the Viaduct Basin drifted upwards. A seagull hovered over the deck, searching for food before dipping a wing and gliding out across the pale jade water.

Ross glanced at the caller ID on his cellphone: it was Wanda Newton, his agent in New York. He picked up the phone from the sofa, put it to his ear and said, 'This had better be good.'

'I'm afraid not.' Wanda's voice was husky from years of chain-smoking. 'Did you know there's an article about you in a New Zealand women's magazine?'

No, but Ross could imagine what the article contained: a few photos and a whole lot of supposition. 'My visit to New Zealand was supposed to have been kept quiet. I'm down here on a family matter, not for publicity. How did the press find out?'

'I have no idea; presumably they've got paparazzi down there, too,' Wanda replied idly.

Ross frowned. There was nothing idle about Wanda; the word wasn't in her vocabulary. He heard the distinctive click of her cigarette lighter. 'Did you know,' Wanda asked oh-so-innocently, 'that Findlays has a New Zealand branch?' Findlays was his New York-based publishers. 'It's very much a fledgling affair, but apparently there's enough New Zealand and South Pacific talent to make it worth their while.' She paused.

Ross tried to figure out what Wanda was leading up to. He listened to her exhale. 'You're sucking on one of those disgusting weeds, aren't you?'

'I love the attention it gets me from all the people trying to reform me,' Wanda drawled. 'Especially you.'

Nothing rattled Wanda. She was at least sixty, a veteran of four marriages and a doyenne of the publishing world. Her face was tanned the colour of tobacco and deeply lined from hours spent at her favourite hobby, sailing. Wanda smoked cigarettes in a tortoiseshell holder and drank her Scotch neat. Ross's sarcasm and moodiness bounced right off her. The more difficult he got, the more she liked it. If the occasion demanded it, Wanda could be every bit as stubborn as Ross. He valued her professionalism, editorial instincts and friendship. She had a knack for seeing what was stopping a good story from becoming a great one. Ross didn't always agree with Wanda — but he did trust her. He'd once asked why Findlays never let him work with one of the new (and extremely attractive) young editors making their way up the ranks of the publishing house.

Wanda laughed throatily. 'Because you'd eat them for breakfast, that's why. Half of them are scared of you and the other half lust after you, which might get you laid but wouldn't get your manuscript edited to your rigid ideas of perfection.'

'I'm not rigid.'

'Of course not.'

'I have standards.'

'Mmmm...'

Ross listened as Wanda took a drag on her cigarette. 'How's the new book going?'

'Good.'

Her voice sharpened. *'Really?'*

'Really.' He told her about the new story.

'When can I see some draft chapters?' she asked eagerly.

It felt good to be able to say 'soon'. And mean it.

'Findlays have been very patient, so I think it would be a good idea to do something nice for them.'

Ross stiffened. He knew he was going to hear something he didn't want to.

'They're having a function next week to preview their summer list, and would love it if you could join them for an hour or two.

There's a beach theme, it should be fun.'

'I don't do publicity for fun, Wanda.' He heard the lighter click again. 'Can't you go without one of those things for a minute?'

'They're my lungs,' she coughed. 'You know it wouldn't hurt you to do this publicity thing for Findlays.'

'Yes, it would,' Ross said. 'Very much.'

'You need to brush up on your good manners. You'll be up to your ears in publicity and appearances as soon as John Doe is released.'

Hollywood had been knocking on his door for the past few years, eager to make one of his books into a movie, and he'd finally agreed — provided he wrote the screenplay. Wanda hadn't been keen. 'Writing for the screen is totally different to writing a novel, Ross.'

Ross didn't tell her he desperately needed a challenge, and that for a brief time being back on the knife edge where all his hard-won success might just come crashing down on his head had made him feel alive again. He'd worked hard to turn *John Doe* into a great screenplay, and from what he'd seen of the daily rushes it was going to be an even greater movie, thanks to Kevin Spacey and Marisa Tomei's performances. The producers were raving and kept sprinkling conversations with the word 'Oscars'.

'Why not take this opportunity to get your tuxedo out of mothballs?' Wanda suggested.

'I thought you said it was a beach theme, and besides, I left my tuxedo at home.'

'I hope you get to meet your doppelganger at the Oscars. You'd like George Clooney. He's a wonderful man and he's got a social conscience, like you.'

His response was unprintable. The subject of George Clooney was a sore point with him at the moment, and he liked to keep the money he donated to community organizations anonymous to discourage the crazies and bloodsuckers.

'I suggest you take a date,' Wanda said. 'To what?'

'The Findlays' beach party.'

'I'm not going to the Findlays' beach party.'

'Hmmm. Just how far away are those draft chapters?'

Ross conceded defeat. Wanda, and Findlays Publishing, had him by the balls. 'I haven't got a date.'

'Then find one. If you arrive with a woman, you'll be less likely to spend the evening being stalked. That is,' Wanda exhaled sharply, 'until you open your mouth and reveal that legendary charm and wit.'

'I'm writing. I don't want to waste time finding a date.'

'Hire a model, hire an actress. I'm sure the fee will be tax-deductible.'

Ross felt offended. He'd never had to pay women for their company and he wasn't about to start.

'Come on now, Ross, remember that nice big advance Findlays paid you? You owe them something.'

It was as if a light bulb went on above his head. Somebody owed him — *one*.

'It's OK, Wanda, I've got a date.'

Ross called Danny to tell her about the Findlays party.

'A party? Why on earth would I want to go to a party with you?'

'Because you owe me.'

Danny soon understood Ross was holding her over a barrel — and his fingers were loosening. If she didn't pretend to be his date at his stupid party, he'd turn up the heat about the missing will and exactly who had guardianship of Matt and Mia. And to think she'd begun to think he was almost human. 'You are an evil bastard!'

Ross sighed. 'You've got to stop accusing my parents of having their children out of wedlock. I'll pick you up at seven o'clock on Friday night.'

'What if I can't get a sitter?'

'Deryl said she's happy to sit with the kids.'

'What?' Danny's shriek nearly perforated his eardrum. 'You asked Deryl *before* you even spoke to me?'

'Now, now, no need to get all riled up,' he needled.

'I'm work—'

'No, you're not. You're not on duty until Monday.'

'How do you know that?'

The PI had provided a list of all her duties for the next four weeks — not that Ross was going to tell her. 'I checked.'

'Are you spying on me?' Danny demanded.

He changed tactics. 'If it makes you feel any better, I don't want to go either.'

'Then don't go!'

If only it were that simple. Ross couldn't remember the last time he'd felt obliged to do something he didn't want to, until he recalled boarding the plane for New Zealand. Anyone would think he had bubonic plague. Why was it that most other women would be falling over themselves to accept, but the one he asked to the damned party used every excuse in the book to get out of it?

'Tell me how you knew I wasn't working,' Danny insisted.

'Deryl told me.' She had, but Ross already knew.

Danny swore.

'Tut, tut, I hope the children didn't hear that, Daneka.'

'Stop *tutting* at me you sanctimonious vampire-pirate-Darth Vadering *pig!*'

'Who says men can't multi-task?'

Before Danny hung up, Ross said, 'It's a beach party. That skirt and top you had on the day I looked after the children was nice.'

'If you want to borrow it you're wasting your time, you'll never fit the top over your big, swollen head,' Danny snarled. She suddenly gasped. 'Oh! *Ohhh!* You're worried about what I'm going to wear, aren't you?'

Ross grimaced. Bad move, Fabello — *very* bad move.

'I'm sure I can do much better than a boring old skirt and top.'

'Oh no, you don't! You're not going dressed as Coco the Clown. I'll get some clothes sent over. Pick something and I'll pay for it.'

'Oh no, you won't,' Danny retorted. 'I'll wear my own clothes.'

'I'm warning you, Danny: if you look like a swamp witch when I come to pick you up, I swear I'll dress you myself.'

'Oh yeah?' the swamp witch sneered. 'You and whose army?' And disconnected.

Danny jammed a CD into Patrick's almost-paid-for music centre and Tim Finn's voice flooded the room. She cranked the volume up as high as it would go and let Dr Tim work his magic.

Vanessa was incredulous when Danny told her what had happened. 'You passed up free clothes? *Expensive* free clothes?'

'Van, I think you're missing the point. I *don't want* to go to his stupid party. I'm being *blackmailed* to go. I've got clothes of my own; some of them are even nice.'

Vanessa loved Danny, but her definition of nice clothes definitely wasn't normal. 'A girl can never have too many nice, expensive clothes.'

'I don't have *any* nice, expensive clothes.'

Vanessa felt a flicker of sympathy for Ross.

Danny did own one nice dress, one she'd picked up in a second-hand shop. Even Nella had approved, christening it the Marilyn Monroe dress. It was similar to the white halter-neck dress Marilyn wore for the famous scene where she posed over air vents in the street. Danny always felt like a flat-chested version of Marilyn when she wore it — flat-chested and *glamorous*. Everybody would be going in sarongs and bikinis and hula skirts; as usual, Danny would buck the trend. She began to feel excited about the party. It had been so long since she'd done anything nice. And when Ross didn't open his mouth and she didn't think about why he was here, he wasn't really that ugly. Or maybe she was getting used to that nose?

'Don't trust him an inch,' Vanessa warned. 'Being good-looking *and* loaded, he'll be used to having women falling all over him.'

'Why are you calling him good-looking? What about that nose?'

'There's nothing wrong with his nose, Danny. He's just not a pretty boy like Patrick.'

Danny only partly agreed.

Ross told Danny she was his insurance policy against women harassing him all night. If she hadn't seen how the woman in the supermarket had behaved, she would have thought his ego was as big as his nose.

'I'm not making it up about women hassling me,' Ross said.

'I believe you. With all your money you could be a metre tall with buck teeth and halitosis and women would still be falling over themselves to have your babies.'

He wouldn't be sidetracked. 'No smart remarks, no painting your hair, and no throwing any fruit.'

'Now you're making me nervous.'

'All you have to do is pretend you're enjoying yourself.'

Danny pursed her lips. 'I want to renegotiate. What you're asking for goes way beyond a new toilet. In fact, I think we're talking a whole new bathroom.'

Ross wasn't the only one trying to lay down the law. Vanessa kept fluttering about like the Fairy Godmother getting Cinderella ready for the ball.

'What are you going to wear?' she asked.

'Doc Martens and fingerless, black leather biker gloves.'

'Dannnneeee!'

'Alright, don't blow your pacemaker! My Marilyn Monroe dress.'

Ross had posted her the party invitation, which said: *An evening at the beach: come cool or come glamorous — the choice is yours.* She'd been tempted to wear her ripped jean shorts and ratty old bikini top.

Vanessa looked relieved. 'What about your hair? You're not going to colour it are you?'

'No, the Vampire Lord has very straight ideas about hair colour — although I don't suppose he could complain about blood-red.'

Danny conceded that her personal grooming had been a little sloppy lately, but she knew how to pull out the stops. Before Nella's illness she'd had a busy social life and plenty of boyfriends. When a taxi arrived with several zippered bags containing clothes for Danny to try on, she thanked the driver and sent him and the clothes away.

Ross was on the phone within the hour, demanding to know what she was up to.

'I told you: I'll wear my own clothes,' Danny said.

'You'd better not turn up wearing your yellow clown pants.'

'What do you mean *my yellow clown pants?*'

'Those things you had on the day at the supermarket. All that was missing was a pair of outsized red shoes and a big red nose.'

'You're wrong; I distinctly remember seeing a big nose.'

He'd walked into that one. 'I meant what I said about dressing you myself if I have to.'

'Listen to me, Fabello, if you lay one finger on me I'll make you sorry. Don't think because you're bigger than me I can't do it. I haven't worked in an Emergency Department all this time without learning how to look after myself. *Do I make myself clear?*'

There was a pause.

'My ears were ringing so bad I didn't hear a thing after *Listen to me, Fabello.*'

He knew the drill and hung up at the same time as Danny.

Ross went into the bathroom and checked his nose from every angle. OK, so it wasn't exactly small, but it still wasn't outsized, it fitted the rest of his face. It was nothing like Carmine's nose. He felt uneasy about Friday night. The last time Ross recalled being this tense about a date was in high school, the first time he took Beth Goodwin out and she told him to bring a pack of condoms. Bless her heart, Beth hadn't disappointed. She lived a couple of blocks from his parents' house, so he still saw her from time to time. Beth was married with three kids, a double chin and love handles, but she still gave Ross the eye whenever they bumped into one another and he always joked he'd been a fool to let her get away. He had a feeling that in her uniquely warped way, Danny wouldn't disappoint him either.

He just hoped he survived the explosion.

Chapter 9

Ross was late. Breda called in tears just as he was about to leave the apartment. She'd received the photographs of the children and, instead of making things better, seeing them seemed to have made things worse.

'Matt is the image of Pat! *When* can we see them, Ross? Can't you bring them over for a wee trip? Or maybe your father and I can come down to New Zealand?'

'No, Ma, that's not a good idea.'

'Why not?'

It took him quite a while to talk Breda out of boarding a flight for New Zealand. She only backed down after she'd extracted a promise from Ross to arrange for Matt and Mia to call them again.

At first Danny didn't care that Ross was late. She was sleep-deprived following night duty, and feeling pleasantly mellow after a couple of glasses of wine. Vanessa hadn't approved, but Danny had insisted she needed something to deaden the pain of an entire evening with Ross.

Vanessa opened her handbag and a mousetrap fell out.

'Van, why have you got a mousetrap in your bag?'

She shoved it back. 'It's for Jane Clifford. Forget about that. I picked up some holiday brochures for Fiji and Rarotonga today. Do you want to have a look?'

Danny gazed at azure water and sand so white and fine that it looked like caster sugar. She sighed wistfully. 'Guess this is the closest I'll get to the islands for a while.'

Vanessa felt guilty. 'I didn't mean to rub it in — I was trying to take your mind off tonight.'

'It's OK.' Danny handed over the brochures and watched Vanessa tuck them into her handbag. 'By the way, guess what I found?' Danny grabbed her own handbag and dug out three little blue books which she waved in the air. *'Ta dah!'*

'The passports!'

'Yes. Now do me a favour and take them home.'

Vanessa put them in her handbag with the holiday brochures. 'You don't really think Ross would kidnap the kids?'

'I wouldn't put anything past that man. He's used to getting his own way.'

Not unlike somebody else Vanessa knew. 'Why are you giving me your passport?'

'So he can't get rid of it to stop me coming after the kids.' Vanessa rolled her eyes.

'If you'd read the magazine article I did at the hairdressers you wouldn't be so dismissive.'

The story had been about children snatched out of the country in a custody battle between their parents. Danny was taken aback when she saw the stupid magazine had an article about Ross in the gossip/celebrity section, with a photo of him climbing into the Explorer, one hand on the door handle and a white plastic bag of groceries dangling from the other. Danny decided he must have been snapped unawares, because he wasn't snarling at the camera. He wore light khaki trousers, a black, red and white checked shirt only half-buttoned up, and a black, rumpled jacket. Somehow that honker of a nose seemed to shrink every time she saw it. The article read: *Imagine our shock when the identity of this gentleman was confirmed as being none other than the notoriously reclusive author, RF O'Rourke. Yes, people — the man does have a face! And a rather scrummy one at that—*

Danny gagged.

'Are you OK?' Brittany the stylist asked.

'Something I read tasted nasty.'

A film based on his bestselling novel John Doe, starring Kevin Spacey, is due for release in November. The multi-talented Mr O'Rourke wrote the screenplay, and the movie rumour-mill is tipping him for an Oscar nomination for best screenplay. His agent, Wanda Newton, had no comment to make when asked for the reason for his visit Down Under, but confirmed that the author is currently working on his next book, which should be ready for release sometime next year.

Danny's heart chugged somewhere in the region of her throat. Ross was *somebody* while she was . . . just plain old Daneka Lawton, broke, overworked and ordinary. The Ross Fabellos of the world held all the aces, while people like her were grateful for the odd pair of twos.

Brittany looked over Danny's shoulder at the magazine. 'Oh, the Yank writer who's over here. Love to bump into him. Hot, isn't he?'

'If you mean he belongs somewhere hot and fiery — yes.'

'Going anywhere nice tonight?'

'No,' Danny sighed. 'Somewhere really awful.'

As the last wisps of blue hair fluttered to the floor, Danny wished she could afford to get it professionally coloured. It would be worth it just to see the look on Ross's face when he came to collect her — with any luck he'd climb in his car and go to the party alone.

Vanessa was taking Matt and Mia home for the night so Danny wouldn't have to rush back from the party. She sent Danny off to get dressed while she fixed the children dinner. At least the kids would be happy, Danny decided as she dug out the only decent thong she owned from her underwear drawer: tonight they'd get something to eat that wasn't burnt or out of a tin. Danny knew she was an indifferent cook. Her speciality and emergency standby was porridge. She was great at porridge, so great that it was only a matter of time before Matt and Mia started speaking with a Scottish brogue.

When Danny walked into the living room, Vanessa breathed a sigh of relief. 'You look awesome!'

Danny knew her Marilyn Monroe dress wasn't a patch on Simone Marchant's Vera Wang original, but she didn't care — the silver-blue dress was her favourite.

'You look beautiful, Auntie Danny,' Mia said.

'Yeah, you look mint,' Matt agreed.

They sat in the living room and tried not to watch the clock as the time Ross had appointed to collect Danny came and went.

Ten minutes late.

'He's probably got stuck in traffic on the harbour bridge,' Vanessa said.

The rush hour was long over. And why was she making excuses for him?

Twenty minutes late.

Vanessa checked her watch. 'I think that clock is fast.'

Danny looked at the tips of her silver stiletto sandals and sipped her wine. Nella had given her the shoes for their last birthday. When Danny had opened the box to get the shoes she'd found the passports tucked in alongside. It was just like Nella to put them into a shoebox for safety and not tell anybody.

There was a knock at the door, but it was Deryl. She bustled into the living room. 'What are you doing here?' she demanded when she saw Danny. 'I thought you'd be gone by now.'

Danny tapped out 'I See Red' on the arm of the chair. 'So did I, but my frog is late.'

'There's probably a good reas— ' Vanessa began.

Danny put down her wine and stood up.

'What are you doing?' Vanessa asked.

'Pleasing myself.' Danny swept from the room.

Vanessa and Deryl looked at one another nervously.

Ross still hadn't arrived when Danny walked back in. 'Bloody hell!' Vanessa exclaimed.

'Oh . . . oh dear,' Deryl murmured.

'Auntie Danny!' Mia cried. 'You look like a rainbow fairy princess!'

Danny's hair was painted silver and blue. She looked as if she'd climbed off the page of a child's storybook — all that was missing was a set of wings, a sparkly crown and a wand. However, the expression on her face wasn't exactly fairy-like. She looked very pissed off.

The sound of a car pulling up to the house at speed reached them. Vanessa rushed to open the front door.

Ross came into the room like a whirlwind, charging the air with energy and impatience. He wore dark grey chinos, a white collarless shirt and a gorgeous pale pistachio-coloured jacket. Tonight he didn't look like a serial killer.

'Sorry I'm late, I had a call—' He saw Danny and ground to a halt.

Her legs were crossed beneath the silvery blue pleated skirt of her dress, and her arms were folded over the deep vee neck of the halter neck bodice. One foot beat an angry tattoo inside a shiny silver sandal that looked as insubstantial as one of Cinderella's glass slippers.

Just as he had been the day he saw Danny crossing the back lawn in the little blue skirt and top, Ross was confused. He couldn't decide what threw him more: that her hair really was silver and blue again or how she looked in her dress — what there was of it. His eyes collided with soft skin, fragile shoulders, a long neck, slender arms and those dainty ankles. Her dress was cut so low Ross was sure it skimmed Danny's bellybutton, and it would take only a tug on the big bow at the back of her neck to bring the whole thing tumbling down around her waist. Her amber eyes glowed with anger, and her full lips were set in a straight line. Ross was outraged. What the hell was she playing at? Dressing up like a — (he borrowed one of his mother's phrases) tart? He'd been prepared for Doc Martens and a boiler suit — *not this*. He was so shaken he didn't even search for the elusive tattoo.

Mia hugged him around the waist. 'Auntie Danny looks like a fairy queen, doesn't she, Uncle Ross?'

'Yeah, like something straight out of *Lord of the Rings*.' If she thought painting her hair blue was going to get her out of coming, she'd thought wrong.

Danny gave Ross a big fake smile. 'What a coincidence: I was thinking of the Orcs.'

'You look lovely, too, Uncle Ross,' Mia said.

'As lovely as a serial killer gets,' Danny muttered.

Deryl arrived bearing a tray with mugs of tea and a plate of biscuits. 'You're late,' she told Ross.

He had the grace to look ashamed. 'I was on the phone to my mother in the States. She was upset.'

'Oh well, that's different. I'm sure she's missing you.' Deryl set the tray on the coffee table. 'Don't s'pose you'll be wanting a cup of tea?'

Ross looked at the tea and said dryly, 'I'll take a rain check.' He turned to Danny. 'You ready?'

She stood and shook out her skirt. The material swirled around her hips and thighs and, just as he had feared, the bodice was slashed to her waist, the shimmery pleats clinging to her small breasts like gossamer.

'Haven't you got a wrap?' he demanded.

'No. I'll be in the car, and the invitation said the party was being held inside.' Her expression clearly asked *What's your beef, Fabello?*

Even Deryl seemed to think Ross was making a fuss.

He decided he'd give Danny his jacket at the earliest possible opportunity. As he followed her from the room, he noticed she seemed to be having trouble walking in the silver sandals. 'Are you sure you should have the training wheels off those?'

Danny turned quickly and took a nosedive into his chest. Ross caught her by the elbows. 'Daneka, tell me the truth, have you been at the teapot?' He grunted as she elbowed him in the ribs.

'Don't make me do something I'll enjoy,' she snapped.

At the front door, there was a delay when Danny realized she'd left her handbag behind.

'I'll get it,' Deryl scurried away as Vanessa stood transfixed by whatever it was that was going on between Danny and Ross.

When Deryl returned with the bag, Ross hustled Danny down the front steps and into his car. 'Come on, the people at Findlays are waiting for us.'

'For *you*, you mean!' Danny waved to the children as they drove away.

'Yes, but I can just imagine how excited they'll be when they see that my date is a blue-haired escapee from Narnia.' Ross turned the car in the direction of the harbour bridge. 'Are you planning on staying pissed at me all night because I was late? I said I was sorry.'

'I'm not *pissed off* at you for being late,' Danny replied. 'I'm *pissed off* you turned up at all.'

'I promise to get you back to the White Witch before midnight,' Ross said solemnly. 'I'd never forgive myself if you turned into a hamster or something.'

She drummed her fingers on the bag.

'Are you giving me the silent treatment? Because if you are, could you do me a favour and keep it up all night?'

'Why don't you go excavate yourself a new rectum, Darth?'

Ross didn't feel like arguing. He didn't know what to make of the Danny beside him. She still wasn't pretty — she was something much better. He sniffed discreetly. Holy Hell! Perfume, too.

'What upset your mother?' Danny suddenly asked.

Ross glanced at her in surprise. 'She saw the photos of Matt and Mia. Matt looks so much like Pat and well . . . I guess it really hit her and Dad that they won't ever see him again.'

She didn't answer.

He debated whether to warn her about what to expect tonight. Ross hated publicity events, hated the small talk and hated the women hitting on him most of all. They dropped notes in his pockets with their numbers and sexually explicit messages, detailing just what they wanted to do with him or to him. They'd also been known to follow him into the men's washroom, and on one memorable occasion one even brought a camera with her and tried to take a photo of his johnson.

Twice he'd been stalked; once by a man named Herschel Swanbeck, and the other time by a woman called Dulcinea Thomas. Somehow Dulcinea had discovered where his parents lived and had arrived at the house with a pillow shoved up her skirt, claiming she was having twins and Ross was the father. Ross had only just stopped paying for round-the-clock security for Breda and Vito. He'd wanted to buy them a new house and move them somewhere safer and with better security, but they'd refused to leave the house where they'd lived for the past forty years and raised their children.

Ross felt sorry for Dulcinea, who like so many others had fallen through the cracks of the mental health system. He'd offered to pay for her rehabilitation, but both Wanda and the authorities advised against it, saying that any further connection with him would make it harder for Dulcinea to recover.

Herschel Swanbeck was a frustrated writer who'd written to Ross just after his first book *Mistaken* became a runaway bestseller. Herschel asked for help and advice on how to go about getting published, and Ross, flushed with success and remembering the rejection letters coming through the post, had been only too glad to provide encouragement and suggestions. Unfortunately, where Ross was talented, Herschel wasn't. Although they never met in person, Herschel began saying he was the real author of *Mistaken*. He went through Ross's garbage for weeks, trying to find proof that Ross had plagiarized him. When Herschel was arrested, Ross knew better than to offer to pay for any help.

The only events Ross attended were his book launches, an occasional interview, and absolutely essential publicity events, and then only if Wanda made the arrangements. That was how he got the reputation for being reclusive and difficult. It was Wanda who'd suggested that one of the best ways to ward off unwanted female attention was to arrive with a date. 'Don't go alone. You're as good as putting a target on your dick.'

Ross usually seconded Deirdre, and if she was out of town he had been known to press-gang Carmel, Annie or Aoife into service, but it wasn't always easy, as at any given time they were either in the early stages of pregnancy and in the john puking, in the late stages of pregnancy and in the john peeing, or breastfeeding and complaining about cracked or leaking nipples.

'Do you have to give me all the gory details?' Ross complained. 'I'm your brother, not your husband.'

'You're a man, which means you can put some poor woman

into the same state of misery,' Carmel retorted.

On one memorable occasion he'd even taken Breda, but he'd never repeated the experience — she'd proven to be even more of a loose cannon with microphones and television network cameras at her disposal. To add insult to injury, there had been a number of articles recently suggesting that RF O'Rourke might be a closet homosexual because the only dates he brought along to public appearances since his split with Simone Marchant were his sisters. Ross had taken real dates, but the women had a nasty habit of reading far too much into the invitation and pointing out engagement rings or asking how he felt about children. So Danny was a godsend. Not that Ross would ever tell her so.

She'd find out for herself soon enough.

Chapter 10

The Findlays' party was being held at a large warehouse near the waterfront at the bottom of town. Danny was impressed by the trouble that had been taken to transform the warehouse into a beach, complete with sand, a volleyball court and a large blue kidney-shaped pool in one corner, shaded by tall potted palm trees. Surfboards were suspended from the iron rafters, and hammocks hung amongst the palm trees, although nobody was brave enough to climb into one and risk a palm tree crashing down on top of them. A DJ pumped out music by the bar, and lights flashed and dipped across the crowd dancing by the pool. Posters on the walls advertised that the party was also a fundraiser for a women's refuge; donation boxes stood on the bar and tables shaded by umbrellas, and people were circulating with raffle tickets.

Danny opened her bag to find her wallet and pulled out a mousetrap. She also found three passports and some holiday brochures: Deryl had given her Vanessa's bag.

Danny felt sick. She hastily rezipped the bag, ripping the stitching around the zipper even further. Ross hadn't noticed, busy shaking hands with Frances Heaton, Findlays' managing director. Danny shoved the bag and its incriminating evidence under her arm and let Ross pull her forward.

'I'm Danny Lawton, his . . .' She just couldn't say it.

Ross slipped an arm about her waist. 'Date.'

Danny hated the dishonesty. 'We're related.'

'Related?' Frances repeated.

Ross cupped her bare shoulder.

She tried to shrug him off. 'By marriage — kind of . . .'

'My brother and Danny's sister were in a de facto relationship,' Ross explained.

'I see,' Frances said.

'They're both dead.'

'Oh, I'm sorry.'

Did he have to be so blunt about it? Danny jabbed the shoulder Ross wasn't holding into his armpit. 'I'm his *sister-in-law*.'

He tightened his hold. 'You're so much more than that, *darling*.'

Frances led them through the crowd, introducing Ross as she went. Everybody wanted to talk to him, to ask about his books and find out when the next one would be hitting the shelves. Danny was surprised at how patient Ross was when he was asked the same questions again and again. He posed for photos and signed autographs; nothing was too much for him. He was utterly charming. Several times Danny tried to detach herself, but Ross kept reclaiming her so she eventually gave up. Besides, leaning on Ross made it a lot easier to stay upright on the silver sandals. *It's a shame he's such an arsehole,* Danny thought, *when his body feels so very promising.*

Ribbit! Ribbit! Ribbit! Ribbit!

Danny froze like a fishfinger at the sound of Vanessa's cellphone ringing in Vanessa's handbag. Vanessa had opted for the frog as her ringtone when Danny had rejected it in favour of the rooster.

Ribbit! Ribbit! Ribbit! Ribbit!

Ross looked at her curiously. 'Did you finally get sick of the rooster?'

'Something like that,' Danny mumbled. She didn't dare risk opening the bag in case he saw the passports.

He scrawled his name across a piece of paper and handed it back to one of the waiting throng. 'Aren't you going to answer it?'

'No.'

He frowned. 'Why not?'

'Because — because I won't be able to hear in all this bloody racket, that's why not!' The frog stopped croaking and Danny heaved a silent sigh of relief.

Ross was looking at her weirdly. 'What if it was something important? What if it was a message about one of the kids?'

Danny was surprised he would think of it. 'If it is, Van will leave a message.' She turned away to indicate the subject was closed, caught her heel in a particularly deep patch of sand and almost pitched onto her nose.

Ross caught her — again. 'Why did you wear those silly shoes?' He was fed up with how good Danny felt plastered against him — the smooth, warm feel of her naked back beneath his palm, her arm looped around his waist, and the way her breast flattened against his chest whenever she stumbled or the crowd jostled them.

'Because they're pretty,' Danny said.

'Pretty?' His brows rose in disbelief. 'Since when have you cared about being pretty?'

Danny looked as if he'd just slapped her. She hooked a finger in his belt and bent down to tug the silver shoes off. *'Here! Take them!'* She thrust them into his hands.

He stared at the shoes. It wasn't Danny's fault she'd made him feel horny and angry. He tucked them into his pockets. 'Danny, I'm sorr—'

She jabbed a finger into his chest. 'Don't you dare say you're sorry! We both know you don't mean it.'

Frances waited a few feet ahead of them, a questioning look on her face. To onlookers Ross and Danny appeared to be having an intimate moment, further reinforced by Danny handing over her shoes to Ross — the kind of thing long-standing couples did. *These shoes are killing me. Can I put them in your jacket pockets? You're hopeless. Give them here.*

Ross watched Danny's smooth, bare back as she stalked towards Frances. Her spine was rigid, her shoulders squared, her posture the equivalent of a raised middle finger. On a scale of one to ten, Ross estimated he'd scored a twenty when it came to screw-ups.

Danny sipped her drink and watched Ross continue to sign autographs. Frances had departed to talk to some of the other Findlays writers, so Danny had nobody to talk to, which was just as well — her nerves were so badly tied in knots that she suspected her nervous system resembled a macramé plant-hanger. When a photographer asked Danny to pose with Ross, her amber eyes spat flames. Ross posed alone, not bothering to explain that the photos might be sold to some of the US tabloids and he wanted his family to see what Danny looked like.

Despite his stony expression, Danny could tell Ross thought he'd hurt her feelings. Perhaps for a nanosecond he had, but she was no green, silly girl, and certainly not one of the simpering women surrounding him. In a lull between autographs and photos, Danny asked, 'What have you done with Ross?'

He got the message: she wasn't going to sulk, just go for his jugular. 'If you make any cracks about number one fans and my ankles being broken, I'll drown you in the pool.'

Danny dredged a finger along the bottom of her cocktail glass and sucked on it. She'd discovered the cocktails being plied by the waiting staff and was feeling a lot calmer, plus Vanessa's phone had remained silent.

Ross wished Danny would stop sucking her finger. 'How many

of those things have you had?'

She licked her lips. 'One Slow Comfortable Screw Up Against The Wall and One Screaming Orgasm.'

He was getting a hard-on. *Danny* was giving him a hard-on. Danny, *the swamp witch*. 'Are you sure you've only had two?'

'Yes, Grandad, I definitely had a Screw before I had an Orgasm.'

He scowled.

'Tell me,' Danny asked. 'Do many women go out on a second date with you?' She looked at the crowded dance floor. 'I don't suppose you want to dance?'

Ross most *definitely* did not want to dance with her. 'I don't dance.'

She sighed. 'I guess that's the price you pay for hanging upside-down when you sleep.'

He clamped his lips together. How did she do it? Make him want to drown her, have sex with her and laugh in the space of a few seconds?

Danny settled down to play her role as arm candy, feeling just as conflicted. Every now and then she saw the sad, weary look on his face that she'd noticed when he arrived at the house. People acted like they owned him. They asked personal questions and expected Ross to answer them. Was he married? They stared at Danny when they asked this. Why not? Did he have any children? Why not?

'I've got twelve nieces and nephews,' Ross said. 'Why do I need kids of my own?'

'He's Italian.' Danny eyeballed the pushy redhead grilling him. 'And Irish. Nobody in the family learned how to say no, which is why he has me.'

Women circled Ross like sharks, rousing Danny's territorial instincts. He was supposed to be her date — she expected the other women to back off and show a little respect.

A waiter approached with a tray of cocktails and a book of raffle tickets.

'How much?' Danny asked.

'Two dollars each.'

She pointed at Ross. 'He'll take a hundred.'

The waiter gaped. *'A hundred?'*

Ross dug his wallet from his jacket pocket. 'What makes you think I've got two hundred dollars in my wallet?' Danny didn't know he'd already donated ten thousand dollars to the women's refuge.

'Of course you've got two hundred dollars in your wallet — you've got the Reserve Bank of New Zealand in your wallet,' Danny insisted. 'In fact, the Governor of the Reserve Bank wants to take a holiday and leave you in charge.'

Ross was glad he'd brought Danny along — she was a combination entertainment service and personal insecticide. Overzealous fans took one look at her slit-eyed stare and opted not to hang around too long. Unfortunately, it didn't stop them from dropping notes in Ross's pockets alongside her shoes.

The cocktails seemed to be catching up with her. She yawned, and Ross remembered she'd been on duty the previous night. He watched Danny snag a cocktail from the waiter's tray, then whipped the glass from her hand and returned it to the tray. They indulged in a brief bout of hand-wrestling, which Ross won. 'Have you got a glass of water or juice?' he asked the waiter.

'Yes, sir, which would you prefer?' The waiter watched Danny bat Ross's hand away.

Ross studied her mulish expression and said, 'Water will be fine.'

The waiter handed him a tall glass of iced water, then turned away.

'Come back here! I don't want a glass of water!' Danny shouted after him. She turned angrily on Ross. 'What was that all about?'

'You're wilting. You didn't get any sleep last night, and it's catching up with you, Cinderella.' He held out the glass.

Danny took it and snapped back, 'What do you mean? Last night is catching up with me?'

A blonde woman wearing a tiny red bikini and red plastic hula skirt stopped beside them. She'd overheard Danny and stared at her enviously; she wouldn't mind a night with RF O'Rourke. She carried a black marker pen in one hand and wore false eyelashes that looked like spiders crawling from her eyes.

Danny thought Spiderilla would have been better off sticking postage stamps on her breasts; they'd have provided more cover than her bikini.

The woman fluttered the spiders at Ross and asked in a low, smoky voice. 'Can I have your autograph, Mr O'Rourke?'

Oh God, Ross thought wearily. She was coming on to him. He took the pen. 'Where do you want me to sign?'

'On my breasts.'

Danny stopped trying to catch the attention of another waiter.

Ross was more interested in the pen than the woman's cleavage.

'Is this a permanent marker?'

Spiderilla looked deep into his eyes and drawled, 'I don't want your name to wash off for a long time.'

Danny was tired of watching women drool all over Ross, brush against his jacket, kiss him and touch his chest. Some of them had asked if he'd sign their arms, legs and bums. He'd signed an arm and a leg but refused to sign anybody's butt.

The woman touched her right breast. 'Could you sign "RF" here?' She pointed to her left breast. 'And "O'Rourke" here?'

Danny sucked noisily on the straw in her glass. 'Sorry to interrupt such a beautiful moment, but do you think that's wise? That pen looks awfully sharp and he might puncture a lung — or something.'

Spiderilla's mouth dropped open. 'I beg your pardon?'

Danny hoped her lashes tangled up so she wouldn't be able to open her eyes properly. 'You weren't to know, but RF is allergic to silicone. It brings him out in hives,' She looked at Ross. 'Doesn't it, Precious?'

His eyes gleamed. 'Bane of my life.'

'These are mine!' Spiderilla insisted huffily.

Of course they are, Danny thought, *and before you got them they belonged to a company supplying medical prosthetics*. 'And aren't we all grateful for that? But just to be safe, perhaps he can autograph your arm instead?'

The glare the woman gave her was toxic, but Ross didn't rate her chances against Danny. He caught the blonde by the shoulders, spun her around and said quickly, 'How about initials on one shoulder blade and surname on the other?'

Spiderilla continued to glare at Danny and lifted her hair — braided, blonde extensions, Danny noted — over her shoulder. 'Some people have no manners,' she said. 'What star sign are you?' she asked Ross.

Watching Ross sign the woman's back set Danny's teeth on edge. 'Does Werewolf count?'

Ross scrawled his name and replied disinterestedly, 'Scorpio.'

Ooh!' Spiderilla shuddered delightedly and the pen bounced off her shoulder blade. 'Secretive, intense and,' she smouldered up at Ross, '*passionate*.'

'Not human.' Danny threw in for good measure.

Ross recapped the pen. 'Tell me,' he asked Spiderilla, 'what star sign are people with big mouths born under?'

Spiderilla was thrilled. If RF's sarcastic tone was anything to go by, things were not all sweetness and light between him and his mouthy date. 'Well, Leos can be very dramatic and Geminis are good communica— '

'What sign was Dracula?' Danny interrupted. 'Or Darth Vader?'

Spiderilla looked confused. 'What are you talking about? Dracula and Darth Vader aren't real people!'

Danny nodded at Ross. 'Neither is he, and for what it's worth: I'm a Scorpio, too.'

He shook his head. 'Can't be, you've got your months mixed up.'

Spiderilla tried to interject. 'Scorpios are born between October twenty-fourth and November— '

'November,' Danny said, 'the seventeenth of November.'

Ross stared. 'That's my birthday.'

'It can't be! It's mine!'

Spiderilla flounced away with only half an autograph and minus her pen.

Ross laughed at Danny's indignation. 'You think you're the only person born on November the seventeenth?' He stopped laughing when Danny flinched. Somebody else had shared her birthday. *Daniella.*

Danny's eyes stung. She blinked furiously. She would not cry in front of Ross bloody Fabello. 'Give me my shoes!'

'What?'

She wrenched her sandals from his pockets and watched as paper notes spilled to the floor like confetti. 'What on earth . . .' Grateful for the distraction, Danny crouched and scooped up a handful.

Ross squatted beside her and tried to grab the notes. 'Don't read those.'

She jerked her hand away. 'This is what you brought me for, remember? To run interference. I'm sure there's plenty more where these came from.' Her gaze snagged on the lipstick mark on the front of his shirt. 'And you've got lipstick on your shirt!'

She leapt to her feet and fled.

Ross watched her go, his expression grim. 'It's yours.'

Danny found a seat at the crowded bar and ordered a cocktail. She was officially off duty; Ross could go screw himself and anything else that caught his fancy. To distract herself, Danny studied the notes.

A buff young Polynesian barman brought her drink. He looked at the notes and asked cheekily, 'Writing a book?'

Danny sipped her drink. 'It'd be X-rated. Do you know a girl called Wendi?' She handed him a slip of paper. 'She spells her name with an *i* and fellatio with a *y*.'

The barman read the piece of paper and grinned. 'No, but I'd like to.' He held out his hand. 'I'm Nathan.'

Danny took it. 'Danny.'

'You came with that American writer, didn't you?'

'Yes.'

Nathan watched her unfold more notes and stack them neatly on the bar.

'What are you going to do with them?' he asked.

'Probably throw them away.'

'That's a waste.' Nathan was only twenty-three and, much as he liked the look of Danny, he wasn't ready for monogamy. He held up Wendi's note. 'Can I have this one?'

Danny considered. 'This is a fundraiser for the women's refuge, right? So how about I sell you the note and we donate the money?'

'Sounds like a deal.' He handed over a ten-dollar note.

'Ten dollars! That's very generous, Nathan.'

'If Wendi can do even half of what she promises, it'll be worth it.'

Danny put the money into one of the collection boxes on the bar and briefly pondered the ethics of selling the notes to strange men, but decided it wasn't an issue, considering the women had put their details into the pocket of a total stranger in the first place.

'Hey, Jase!' Nathan called to the other barman. 'Come have a look at this!'

Before Danny knew it, the lights had been turned up and there was a full-blown auction going on, as guys bid for the notes and the women who'd written them tried to outbid them to win them back, unless they liked the look of the bidder.

The collection boxes filled up fast. Nathan and Jase made Danny sit on the bar and read out the notes while they collected the proceeds, sold drinks and pointed out prospective bidders with loud, theatrical shouts of 'BID!'

From her perch, Danny had a good view of the entire warehouse. She saw the dance floor gradually empty as people joined the crowd at the bar. And she saw when Ross appeared at the back of the crowd, his arms folded across his chest and his face hidden by shadows. Two more cocktails had made it easier to ignore the emptiness inside her, and put a rosy glow on the evening.

When the notes were all sold, the warehouse lights were dimmed again and people drifted back to the dance floor, some with the partners they came with, several more with somebody they'd never set eyes on before. The DJ played a smoochy song usually reserved for the end of the night when couples were draped around one another. Danny stayed on the bar, the skirt of her Marilyn Monroe dress spread about her hips in a silvery blue puddle. She leaned back and braced her weight on her palms, crossed her legs and watched Ross approach.

He stopped and placed a hand either side of Danny on the bar. 'You just couldn't help yourself, could you?'

Danny watched him through a spike of blue hair that had fallen over her eye and gently swung one high heel to and fro. 'Hey, I wasn't the one signing women's legs and bums. I was performing a civic duty.'

'You're shameless.'

It was hard to read his expression in the low light. He sounded more amused than angry. 'Not true, the dim lighting hid my blushes.'

The toe of Danny's stiletto beat a steady rhythm against Ross's thigh. He caught her ankle before she kicked him in the erection that had been plaguing him most of the night. His fingers braceleted her ankle; her skin felt warm and smooth. Ross didn't understand it, he was surrounded by bare breasts and asses but he was turned on by a woman with blue hair, non-existent breasts and a mouth that could blister paint.

'Danny,' he began, 'about the birthday thing—' For a man who had trouble apologizing, he was getting a lot of practice.

Danny pressed the toe of her sandal against his thigh. *'Don't.'*
Don't apologize. Don't remind me.

His flesh felt strong and resilient. Danny wished she was barefoot so she could curl her toes into the muscle in his thigh. Ross tightened his grip around her ankle. She slid her other foot slowly upwards. 'You should thank me for selling those notes.'

Ross caught that ankle, too. 'Oh, really?'

She was trapped, her crossed legs scissored into place by his hands. 'I did you a favour.'

He stroked the insides of her ankles with his thumbs. 'How?'

Danny curled her fingers around the edge of the bar, and said, a little breathlessly, 'Two of them were from men.' She laughed when Ross grimaced. His hair stood up in two points on either side of his head. Danny stroked the silky curls flat. 'Your horns are showing.'

He slid his hands up her calves. 'Are they now?'

Is this how it feels? Danny wondered. Is this how Patrick made Nella feel? How her father had made her mother feel? It was like an earthquake started inside Danny's belly, sending shock waves reverberating outwards, making her nerve endings snap and her skin sizzle.

Danny jumped when Nathan suddenly tapped her on the back. 'Hey, Danny, a guy said he'd pay fifty bucks for a dance with you.'

She blinked at him over her shoulder. 'What?'

Ross dragged out his wallet and emptied it into one of the collection boxes. 'He's been outbid,' he told the barman sharply.

Nathan looked at the bank notes poking from the slot in the top of the box and the look on Ross's face, then shouted down the bar, 'You're out of your league, mate!'

Ross lifted Danny down from the bar. He placed his hands either side of her on the bar top and leaned into her. She could feel he was hard and her heart went haywire. It was a moment before she managed to get out 'I was trying to be good.'

Ross stared at her mouth. 'You do bad better,' he murmured.

And kissed her.

Danny melted across the bar like butter dropped onto a hot stove. Ross was that rare creature, a great kisser. She arched her back, slid her hands across the smooth surface of the bar and kissed him back for all she was worth.

When they finally broke apart, Danny was clutching the lapels of Ross's jacket, he had a handful of her skirt, and her leg was hooked around his calf. They stared at one another, their breath rushing back and forth between their lips like a pair of relay runners.

'Come back to the apartment with me,' Ross said roughly.

Danny nodded.

Nathan tapped her on the shoulder again. 'Er . . . Danny?'

Ross glared at him over her head. *'What now?'*

The barman pushed a black handbag across the bar and stepped backwards with his palms raised. 'Sorry, mate. Somebody found this on the floor. It's got a passport inside with Danny's photo in it.' He disappeared to take an order.

Danny stared stupidly at the bag. Passport? What passport? Reality came roaring back like a locomotive. *The passports!* She made a grab for the bag.

Ross was faster. He unzipped the bag, took out the passports and looked at the names.

Danny made a grab for them, but he eluded her easily. 'I can explain!' she cried.

He replaced them carefully in the bag and looked at her coldly. 'Were you planning on giving them to me?'

'Of course not!'

'You bitch,' Ross said softly.

'Let me explain!'

'Outside.' He grabbed her elbow and marched her through the crowd and out of the warehouse. Neither of them noticed the photographer.

It was drizzling outside. The streetlights wore misty halos, and a cold wind was blowing in from the harbour. Danny was reeling. She'd seen Ross angry, irritated, pissed off before, but never this icy rage.

He unlocked the Explorer and opened the passenger door. 'Get in,' he said coldly.

Danny shook her head and curled her bare toes against the wet tarmac of the car park. Her shoes had fallen off when Ross lifted her from the bar. 'No!'

Ross clenched his jaw and growled, 'Get in the car, Danny!'

The wind gusted and she shivered. 'Only if you'll let me explain.'

He slammed the door. She flinched but stood her ground. 'If you'd rather stand in the rain and tell me why you've got your and the kids' passports and travel brochures in your purse, then go right ahead.'

'It isn't the way it looks! I wasn't planning on taking the kids out of the country.' Danny pushed her wet fringe from her eyes. 'I don't have any money!'

'The implication being that if you did have some money, you would leave the country?'

'No!' She gestured at the bag. 'It's not my bag! Deryl picked up Van's by mistake. I gave Van the passports for safekeeping...' Danny ground to a halt. That didn't sound any better. The rain grew heavier and soaked through her thin dress.

'So that's why you wouldn't answer the phone. It's Vanessa's,' Ross smiled thinly. 'You were keeping them safe from me, weren't you?'

She gestured helplessly. 'Yes and no.' Her teeth began to chatter. 'I w-was worried you'd k-kidnap the k-kids.'

'I see.' He put his hands inside his trouser pockets and balled his fists to keep from shaking her. 'Was fucking me supposed to help lessen my distress when you kidnapped my niece and nephew?'

'No! I wanted to—'

'Fuck me?'

She staggered backwards as if he'd slapped her. The wind changed direction and the rain swirled. The pleats of her silver dress had wilted and turned transparent. Ross watched the material mould itself against her hips, thighs and belly, and wanted to groan when lust ran like wildfire from his belly to his groin. He wanted to roar at her, howl out his rage and disappointment. He'd been a fool.

No more.

Danny crossed her arms and cupped her bare shoulders in her palms. 'I-I wasn't planning on t-taking Matt and M-Mia away! I definitely w-wouldn't borrow money! I'm already up to m-my ears in debt!'

He smiled grimly. 'I know.'

'H*ow?* How do you know?'

Instead of answering her question, Ross pulled out the passports. 'Here's yours. I won't be needing it.' He flipped one of the little blue books at Danny.

It landed in a puddle at her feet. She crouched down and groped for it in the puddle.

Ross opened the passenger door again. 'Now I suggest you get in.'

Danny clasped the passport against her and stared up at him. Rain dripped into her eyes, and goose bumps stood out on her bare skin like bubble wrap. 'G-give me back the bag. I'll f-find my own way home.'

Ross searched the contents of the bag.

'L-Leave that a-alone!'

'There's five bucks, two tampons, a cellphone and—' he pulled out the mousetrap and stared, 'a mousetrap in this bag. How do you intend to get home? Thumb a lift over the harbour bridge?'

Danny stood up. 'N-none of your business; give m-me back the b-bag.'

'Get in the car and I will.'

She headed towards the road.

'*Danny!*' Ross roared. '*Come back here!*'

Danny heard the car engine start and broke into a jog. The Explorer screeched to a halt just ahead of her, and the passenger door was flung open, barring her way. Ross leaned across the seat and snarled, '*Get in!*'

She kicked out at the door, missed and screamed, '*You lunatic! You could have run me over!*'

'If you want to freeze your ass off walking home, then fine, go right ahead! But when you get there, I'll be there waiting for you!'

Danny searched for a way around the car. 'If you set one foot on my property, I'll call the police and have you charged with trespass!'

'It isn't your property.'

She stopped searching and looked at Ross. 'What?'

'Your sister left everything to Pat,' he said with savage satisfaction. 'And Pat left everything to me.'

'No,' Danny whispered. 'Nella would *never* do that!'

'The house is two-thirds mine,' Ross said. 'And I'm moving in.'

He took her back to his apartment at the Viaduct Basin and made her wait while he changed into dry clothes and packed a suitcase. Danny huddled in an armchair in his bedroom. Ross didn't trust her to wait in the lounge. 'Why don't you get out of those wet clothes and put on my bathrobe?' he asked when he could no longer stand watching her shiver.

Danny replied tonelessly, 'Why don't you take your bathrobe and shove it?'

Ross walked into the bathroom next door and returned holding a thick grey and white towel. He held it out to her. 'Do you want to do it yourself? Or do you want me to do it for you?'

'If you touch me, I'll scream the building down.'

'Fine, do it yourself.' Ross dropped the towel in her lap and went back to his packing. He heard the sound of the towel being rubbed against skin and released the breath he'd been holding. The king-sized bed mocked him. What a fool he'd been to think they would finish the night in it together. She was Daneka Lawton. Scarred, battle-hardened, distrustful, *unreachable*.

Danny stared out the floor-length windows at the lights of the boats in the Rangitoto Channel. She was surprised she'd stopped shivering. Inside she felt as if her veins had turned to ice, she imagined them stretching beneath her skin, a frozen white network of icicles. If she got lucky, maybe her nerves would ice up, too, and the pain would go away. She only had herself to blame; she'd brought it on herself by opening up to Ross. Danny was shaken. How had that happened? Men were useful only for sex, and she always decided the *when* and the *where* and remained in the driver's seat throughout any relationship. She wasn't about to become a passenger on an emotional roller-coaster like her sister and mother. So what had happened with Ross tonight? What was different?

He threw some more clothes into the open suitcase and went into the bathroom. Danny's fingers tightened on the velvety towel. She wouldn't accept his bathrobe, but the towel belonged to the apartment. Danny flipped it over her shoulders and felt it catch on something on the table behind her. She turned sharply, thinking she'd knocked the lamp from the table, and saw a brown file and some typed sheets of paper lying on the carpet.

Danny leaned down to pick up the file and papers, and saw a photograph of her in uniform walking across what looked like the hospital car park with her bag tucked beneath her arm and her stethoscope draped around her neck. She slowly reached for the next photograph. This one showed her holding open the door of her blue Nissan while Mia and Matt climbed into the back seat. It was taken outside the school.

Somebody had been taking photographs of her and the children.

Somebody had been following them.
Somebody had been spying on them.

Danny picked up the photos and typed pages and sat back in the chair.

... 15:10hrs — DL collects children from school. 15:21 returns home ...

Her entire life was there on the pages. She flipped through the sheets of paper. There was information about her mother, about Nella. There was even a page about her father. Danny felt violated. Ross had been having her followed. She watched him walk into the bedroom carrying a bag of toiletries.

Ross saw the file on Danny's lap and ground to a halt.

'I was feeling bad about the passports, about not trusting you. And all the time you've been paying somebody to follow me, to invade my privacy.' Her tone was conversational. Danny held up the photograph of her collecting the children from school. 'What were you hoping to find, Ross? That I was the head of a drug ring? Or engaged in a little prostitution to make ends meet while the kids were at school?'

Ross refused to be cast as the baddie in this farce. 'You left me no choice. You wouldn't meet me halfway.'

Danny looked at the big bed with its pristine white linen and thought again about how close she'd come to sleeping with him. She turned away, feeling sick with self-disgust.

Ross knew what she was thinking and wished he could wind back to the beginning of the evening — or even better, back to the day they first met. He wished he wasn't Pat's brother and she wasn't Daniella's sister.

'I don't want it to be like this,' he said quietly.

'You're just sorry you didn't get laid.' She folded one of the sheets of paper in half and then into quarters. 'Thanks, Fabello.'

'What for?'

'For tidying up a loose end.' Danny tucked the piece of paper into Vanessa's bag and got to her feet. 'Now I know what happened to my father. Dead from lung cancer. Mum always warned him the cigarettes would get him in the end.'

Surely she wasn't saying that she didn't know that her father was dead? But when he looked at her again, Ross saw it was true. 'Danny—'

'I want to go home,' she said flatly.

'Danny, we need to talk about this.'

'No, *we don't*. We need to get in your car and drive to our house — I gave Nella and Patrick half the deposit, so you needn't think you're going to do me out of my share.' Danny's eyes flashed. 'You'd better get used to opening that big fat wallet of yours, Fabello, because the place needs a lot of work, and I intend getting my money's worth from the new landlord.'

Chapter 17

Danny barely slept all night. When she finally gave up trying, the dawn chorus was in full voice and her eyes felt as if the sandman had parked his bags in her eyeballs as payment for his thwarted attempt to visit her. It was still raining. The wind had picked up and gusted around the old house, finding its way between cracks and under the rusting roof.

Danny kept reliving the moment Ross told her he owned most of the house. He might as well have said he owned her. Every time she imagined a stranger watching her and the children, recording their every move, her skin crawled. And when she thought about how eager she'd been to sleep with Ross, Danny wanted to curl into a ball and hide. He'd pulled her strings, and she'd reacted like a puppet. Just like her mother and sister, she'd been weak and malleable. She'd always prided herself on being different, but last night had shown Danny she wasn't any different at all. Ross had reduced her to something she despised. It wouldn't happen again.

She lay in her bed in the darkness and felt his presence in the house. It was like an electric current, the atmosphere seemed to pulse and vibrate. Ross was asleep in the living room — if it were indeed possible to get any sleep on the badly sprung couch. Danny remembered the feel of his body and the slow sweep of his tongue against hers. She rolled over restlessly and swept her bare leg across the coolness of the sheet. It was hard enough trying to patch their lives back together without him interfering. There wasn't a pattern or book of instructions Danny could buy to tell her how to repair the hole left behind by Nella's death. She could only follow her instincts and hope for the best. She was flying solo and by the seat of her pants.

They had to find a way to curb their tempers and live together for Matt and Mia's sakes. Danny had to control this . . . *thing* between them. The man she'd kissed was not the real Ross; the *real* Ross was devious and vengeful. She felt even more wretched and guilty as she thought of Matt and Mia being dragged into the ugliness between them.

At six, she gave up trying to sleep and visited the toilet as quietly as possible lest Ross bloody Fabello hear her from his bed on the couch. The morning before, she'd been free to make as much noise as she liked — she could have walked into the bathroom stark-naked and sung the national anthem at the top of her voice. But everything had changed; her home had been invaded by the enemy. She had to get out. Danny decided to go and collect the children early and break the news about Ross moving in. She peeked into the living room as she walked by.

Ross was asleep, one long arm flung above his head, a tuft of black armpit hair and one shoulder showing. Danny doubted he'd had a very comfortable night. The couch had several rogue springs capable of disabling the unwary. The night before, she'd been disappointed by Ross's lack of reaction when she refused to let him sleep in Nella's bed. Instead of arguing, he'd merely begun a search of the hallway cupboard when Danny pointed to it as a possible source of blankets. When he opened the door, a jumble sale's worth of junk came tumbling down on his head. Ross managed to find Matt's old Thomas the Tank Engine quilt and a lumpy pillow. When Nella was alive the household cupboards had been models of tidiness, but now they were like black holes — things went into them and disappeared forever. It took all of his weight against the door to force it shut.

Danny slammed the front door as she left the house, and kicked the wheel of the Explorer as she walked past on her way to the garage. Ross would soon be missing more than the king-sized bed and private elevator at his penthouse apartment.

Vanessa wasn't surprised to see Danny so early. She opened the door wearing a green kimono dressing gown decorated with white cranes and a pair of white towelling slippers. 'Did he find the passports?'

Danny brushed past. 'Yes.'

Mia was watching cartoons in the lounge, while Matt was still asleep in the spare bedroom.

Vanessa waited until they were in the kitchen. 'I didn't realize Deryl had given you my bag until after you'd left. I didn't want to risk calling you until I thought you were at the party and the noise would cover the sound of my cellphone ringing.'

Danny sat on a breakfast stool and nodded. 'I know. I guessed it was you.'

'I'm so sorry, Danny! I should have gone to get your bag. If I had, none of this would have happened. I've been so worried,' Vanessa said miserably. 'What did Ross say when he saw the passports?'

'He's moved in.'

Vanessa frowned. 'What do you mean, he's moved in?'

'Last night — he moved in.'

'Moved in? Why would he move in?' Vanessa hesitated. 'You and he didn't—'

'No!' Danny felt her face heat. 'We did not!'

'OK! Keep your hair on.' She hurriedly closed the kitchen door. 'Perhaps it'd be better if you told me the whole story.'

Danny did, minus the lip-lock she'd shared with Ross by the

bar. 'He's been having you *followed*?'

'Yes. He's got photos and daily reports and everything.'

'And now he says he owns the house? But you gave Daniella *half* the deposit, and you paid most of the monthly repayments!'

Danny rested her elbows on the breakfast bar and dug the heels of her hands into her eyes. 'I feel such a prat. I was so certain Nella had left a will saying all that.'

Vanessa made a sound of disgust. 'You're not to blame. This mess has been caused by Daniella and Patrick.' She raised a hand when Danny opened her mouth to defend her sister. 'I know it's wrong to speak ill of the dead, but honestly, sometimes Nella had the IQ of an amoeba. And Patrick only ever looked out for himself. I'd like to wring both their necks. You've got to see a lawyer.'

'And show him what?' Danny asked bitterly. 'The will I can't find?'

Vanessa sighed. 'Knowing Nella, she probably wrote it on the back of a cereal box and used it to mark where she planted carrots.'

It was a possibility. Danny made a note to check out the garden.

'I know you can't afford to see a lawyer at the moment, but I could lend—'

'*No.*'

'This isn't the time to be stubborn, Daneka.'

'I'm not being stubborn,' Danny said stubbornly.

'What about the children?' Vanessa asked. 'How do you think it's going to be for them watching you two fighting all the time?'

'We'll stop.'

'Do you really think you can?'

'We don't have a choice,' Danny replied wearily. 'We have to.'

Ross was awoken by what sounded like a herd of elephants charging through the house, but turned out to be Mia and Matt returning.

He was sure he'd only managed to get a total of twelve minutes of uninterrupted sleep after spending a tormented night contorted into an unnatural position to avoid the couch springs poking him in his ass, left shoulder blade and right calf. He'd done his best to wind himself around the lumps and bumps, but, never having trained as a contortionist, failed miserably. Halfway through the night he'd started to fantasize about a bed of nails. Each time the spring dug him in the ass, he heard Danny's voice saying, *Why don't you go excavate yourself a new rectum?*

When Mia shrieked 'Uncle Ross!' in his ear, Ross's entire body jerked in response, upsetting the delicate balance he'd established to allow him to fall asleep. The sofa came alive and attempted to skewer his left shoulder blade to his right one.

'Aarghh!' He leapt from the sofa, spilling Matt's Thomas the Tank Engine cover to the floor.

Mia was standing in the middle of the living room, staring at his crotch. Ross's hand shot towards his johnson, his shoulders sagging in relief when he encountered his Calvin Kleins. Usually, he slept in the buff. Considering his state of mind the previous night, it was touch and go whether he'd remembered to keep his underwear on before he climbed onto the sofa.

'They're pretty knickers,' Mia said.

Ross snatched the Thomas the Tank Engine quilt from the floor and wound it around his hips. It didn't seem right to be discussing his underwear with his eight-year-old niece. Danny's muffled voice came through the door leading to the kitchen. 'Mia, come out of there and let Uncle Ross have some privacy.' Ross shuffled over and pushed the door open.

Danny stood at one of the kitchen counters. She looked as bad as he felt; purple crescents marred the skin beneath her eyes. She wore her Coco-The-Clown pants and a T-shirt that read *I Started With Nothing And Still Have Most Of It Left*.

Just looking at the inscription made Ross angry. The springs weren't the only reason he'd spent the night tossing and turning. He kept thinking about Danny reading that her father was dead in the private investigator's report. It was a shitty way to find out something so important. She didn't deserve that.

'Morning,' Ross said.

Danny stared out the window over the sink and replied tonelessly, 'Good morning.' She wished Ross would put some clothes on. Something was wrong with her; a part of her wanted to hit him, while another part wanted to pull the Thomas the Tank Engine cover away and climb all over him.

'Auntie Danny said you're going to be living with us for a while,' Mia said.

Ross shuffled into kitchen en route to the bathroom. Danny flattened herself against the kitchen counter so he didn't brush against her. 'Yes,' he agreed. 'For a while.'

He needed to pee and have some breakfast. He needed a back massage or to be stretched on a rack. Ross had forgotten just how much Mia could talk. She was still gabbing when he shut the bathroom door in her face. When he came out again, she was waiting for him. His eye began twitching. Ross began to understand the enormity of his decision to move in with Pat's kids, certain he could hear his brother laughing in whichever afterlife he'd landed. Ross longed for the peace and quiet of his apartment, a bed with springs on the inside, and the privacy of his own bathroom. He hauled on last night's trousers and a black V-necked sweater, and headed into the kitchen to hunt out breakfast.

Matt was at the table, eating a bowl of cereal. Ross took a seat beside him. Danny stayed by the sink, eating toast thickly smeared with some dark-brown paste. Ross's stomach growled loudly. Danny sank her teeth into the toast with a crunch, took a bite and chewed slowly. Ross knew he'd starve if he waited for her to offer him breakfast. He went to the refrigerator and looked inside. 'Do you have any eggs?'

Danny sipped her tea. 'In the chook house.'

'The chook house?'

'The henhouse.'

Behind her, rain and wind rattled the window panes. Ross opened a cupboard. 'Where's the coffee I bought?'

She pondered. 'I threw it away.'

'You threw it away! Why?'

She munched on her toast. 'Nobody here to drink it.'

Ross dragged his hands slowly down his face. She was going to make him pay — with blood.

Matt helped himself to more cereal.

'Can I have some of that?' Ross asked.

Matt slid the box across the table. Ross shook some cereal into a bowl, added milk and took a mouthful. He gagged on the sugary sweetness.

Mia was shocked. 'Don't you like it? It's our favourite.'

Ross scraped cereal off his tongue with his spoon. He watched as Danny finished her toast and licked her thumb and forefinger. Their gazes locked. Awareness leapt between them like ectoplasm. Danny was the first to look away, and Ross found himself wondering why it was they could read each other's minds when it came to sex but drew a blank when it came to anything else.

An inspection of the kitchen cupboards after breakfast confirmed his suspicions that he would either starve or be poisoned if he didn't do some grocery shopping. The only food Ross found was the kind of processed crap that kids were fond of and enough oatmeal to feed half of Scotland. He grabbed some clean clothes from his suitcase and was headed towards the bathroom for a shower when the front door slammed and a voice warbled '*Coooeee*!'

Deryl Snedden appeared in the hallway. Ross had never seen her so dressed-up, or, to be more accurate, he'd never seen Deryl in a dress. It wasn't a pleasant experience. The dress was long and shapeless and made from a lumpy brown material, with a belt from the same fabric fastened about her waist— except Deryl didn't have a waist. The woman was the same shape from shoulder to hip — long, lanky and flat as a pancake. She wore knee-high pantyhose that ended just below the hem of the godawful dress, and a pair of ugly brown shoes. Her thin, greying hair had been set into small grey sausages across her pink scalp. There was even a smear of orange lipstick on her thin lips.

'What're you doing here so early?' Deryl demanded. 'Has your car been outside all night?'

Danny hurried into the hallway from the kitchen, looking anxious. 'Morning, Dee,' she exclaimed brightly. 'You're dressed up to the nines. Where are you off to?'

Deryl pointed at Ross. 'Did he spend the night here?'

'Er . . . yes.' Danny looked nervous. Ross hadn't realized the old bat's opinion mattered so much to her.

'*Where* did he sleep?'

'On the sofa,' he said curtly.

Deryl pursed her lips so tightly the orange lipstick disappeared. 'I'm very disappointed in you, Daneka.' She jerked her head in Ross's direction. '*Him* I'd expect it from, but not you.'

'Who the hell are—' Ross stopped when Danny threw him a desperate look. 'She *does* know better!' he protested.

Danny seemed surprised to hear Ross defending her. So was Ross.

'She wouldn't be the first girl in this family to be led astray by one of you lot,' Deryl sniffed.

'I have not led Danny astray!' I tried, but I failed. He wondered why even in the twenty-first century men were always the despoiler of innocents, especially when the woman in question had the instincts of a trained assassin.

Danny began to haltingly explain that Ross had moved in.

Ross decided to quit the scene before he gave into the urge to stuff Deryl's shoes in her mouth. Danny might care about her good opinion, but he didn't give a crap. However, he hadn't bargained on Deryl following him into the bathroom. He stopped her at the door. 'Sorry, Deryl: not only do I not force my unwanted attentions on women, I also disapprove of communal bathing. You'll have to go home to take a shower.'

Danny ground her teeth. When it came to Matt and Mia and her, Deryl didn't have a sense of humour.

'You can't just move in!' Deryl raged. 'It's wrong! There are children in the house. What sort of an example are you setting for them?'

Ross pointed a thumb at his chest: 'I'm their uncle.' He turned the thumb on Danny, who was hovering in the hallway behind Deryl. 'She's their aunt.'

'You're sharing a house and you're not married! What sort of message are you sending to Matt and Mia about sex?'

'We're not having sex!' Ross snapped.

Mia pushed through a gap between Danny and Deryl. 'What's sex?'

'Nothing!' the adults shouted.

Mia went into full Hollywood mode, complete with trembling lips and brimming eyes. 'What did I say?'

In frustration Ross thumped the bathroom wall with the heel of his hand. The wall emitted a squelch. He frowned and gave it a gentle tap with his fist.

SQUEEELCH!

'What the—'

The fracas had dragged Matt away from his book. He watched

Ross poke a finger experimentally into the flaking plaster. A large chunk fell to the floor. 'Why's Uncle Ross poking holes in the wall?'

Danny pushed past Deryl and grabbed Ross by the arm. 'Stop that!'

He shrugged her off and continued digging. 'This isn't a wall; it's Swiss cheese.'

Danny hung off his arm like a terrier, dragged onto the tips of her toes as Ross raised his arm and poked at a suspicious damp spot higher on the wall. 'Leave it alone!' she shouted. 'It's *my* Swiss cheese!'

Ross stopped poking and looked down at her through narrowed eyes. '*Whose* Swiss cheese?'

Danny's face contorted with fury. She hooked a leg around one of his, arched her back and heaved on his arm.

'Daneka!' Deryl was aghast. 'Get off him!'

Ross was so surprised that he burst out laughing. This was better than the blank-eyed expression she'd worn in the kitchen.

Danny stiffened, her eyes filling with tears. Ross's smile faded. She abruptly let go of his arm and walked blindly from the bathroom. A few seconds later, her bedroom door closed.

Deryl glowered at Ross. 'I hope you're happy. I'm taking the children home with me. When you and Danny have sorted out your differences, you can come and get them.'

As she herded Matt and Mia along the hallway, Ross heard Mia ask forlornly, 'What's wrong with Auntie Danny? Is she going to be alright?' before the front door closed.

Danny looked at the clock on her bedside table. Two minutes had passed since she'd last checked it. She could hear the sound of the shower running. It had been running for the past fourteen minutes. Ross had been taking a leisurely shower while Danny sat in her room feeling ashamed. He was as much to blame as she was. Deryl was right: they had to sort things out before the kids came home, but Ross seemed unaffected by what had happened.

Danny went into the hallway and tapped on the bathroom door. 'Ross? I need to talk to you.'

The water continued to run. Sixteen minutes.

She knocked louder. 'Ross! Can you hear me?'

No response.

Danny's temper began to simmer. Ross wasn't at his swanky apartment with a limitless supply of hot water — at this rate he'd empty the hot-water tank and run up the electricity bill. The aged plumbing meant it was possible he couldn't hear her knocking, and Danny considered pounding the door with her fist but was terrified she'd lose it and attack him again. She had to think smarter and retain her dignity; it wasn't her fault if that meant Mr Fabello had to sacrifice some of his. In the kitchen she took out the big plastic jug she used to make cordial for the kids and put it in the sink. Danny turned on the cold water.

'Aaarrggh!'

The pipes groaned as the water was hastily shut off.

Danny turned off the tap and waited.

Ross erupted into the kitchen, a towel around his hips and shampoo suds dripping from his head and chest hair. 'You did that on purpose!'

Now wasn't the time to be sidetracked by all that wet skin and muscle. 'You can't take twenty-minute showers.'

'What?' He was wild-eyed. 'Why not?'

'Because it drains the hot-water tank.'

He flinched as shampoo dripped into his eyes. *'What?'*

'We have four-minute showers. There's an egg timer in the bathroom.' His expression told Danny exactly what she could do with her egg timer. 'I did knock, but you mustn't have heard me.'

'Oh yeah!' he snapped. 'I bet you tried real hard to get my attention.' It was entirely possible he hadn't heard her. He'd been so sunk in gloom that a freight train could have roared through the bathroom and he wouldn't have noticed.

'As soon as you're dressed I'd like you to meet me in the henhouse,' Danny said. 'We need to talk.'

Ross looked at the chicken manure clinging to his white Nikes. He was standing opposite Danny in the small, warm confines of the chicken house surrounded by indignant, clucking hens sitting on nesting boxes or perched on the ceiling rafters glaring at him. Ross never knew that chickens could glare. The ceiling was too low for him to stand upright, so he was forced to tilt his head to keep from braining himself on one of the rafters.

'Is this your idea of a joke? To force me out of the shower so I can stand in chicken shit?' he asked.

'I'm sorry about your shower,' Danny said.

Ross blinked. 'Were you smoking something in your room?'

She gritted her teeth. 'No.'

He still harboured suspicions. 'You're sure the real Danny hasn't been kidnapped by aliens and isn't hanging in a cocoon in the bedroom closet?'

She refused to rise to the bait.

Ross was intrigued by this new, calm, reasonable Danny. 'You damn near scalded me to death.'

'So close and yet so far,' she muttered.

That was more like it. He changed the angle of his head to ease the crick in his neck, and got pecked on the ear by one of the hens roosting in the rafters. *'Ow! Shit!'*

'Stay still — Beyonce gets upset if people make any sudden moves.'

'*Beyonce?* You've got a chicken called *Beyonce?*'

'Mia named them.' Danny indicated the other two chickens in the rafters: 'That's Kylie and Madonna, and the three on the nesting boxes are The Dixie Chicks.'

Ross raised his hands in defeat, narrowly missing getting taken out by Kylie. 'Why am I not surprised?'

She ignored him. 'We can't fight in front of Matt and Mia.'

He searched her words for a hidden motive, but couldn't find one. 'I know.'

'We need to act like adults and speak reasonably to one another. Do you think you can do that?' she asked.

'Do you?' he replied.

'It will be hard — *very* hard,' Danny admitted. 'But I can do it for Matt and Mia. We'll both need some sort of a safety valve so we don't snap and murder each other in our beds.'

'Presuming I get any sleep,' Ross said bitterly.

She gave him a syrupy smile. 'There's always that big, soft, *well-sprung* bed waiting for you on the other side of the harbour bridge.'

Ross wondered what kind of a safety valve Danny had in mind. He was warming to the idea: he could think of a perfect way to let off steam. 'Tell me more about this safety valve.'

She gestured at the interior of the chicken house. 'This is it.'

Ross looked around him. 'What is?'

'The chicken house: this is where we sort out our differences — any time we need to have one of our *discussions*, we bring it out here where Matt and Mia can't hear us.'

He searched her face. She was serious. 'Let me get this straight: if I want to have a discussion with you, I have to cross the back yard, dodge a couple of stupid, fat sheep and stand ankle-deep in chicken shit with my head hunched over like the Hunchback of Notre Dame?'

He'd offended her. 'Persil and Charcoal aren't stupid, just a bit overweight.'

'Tell me you're not serious,' Ross said.

'Tell me you're not deaf,' Danny replied.

He was incredulous. 'This is a *chicken house*, not the United Nations!'

She was unmoved. 'You can either accept my terms or develop an ulcer *and* a chronic back problem.'

They locked gazes.

'You really think you can beat me?' Ross asked, wonderingly.

The smell and sound of the clucking, fussing chickens receded. The little wooden henhouse suddenly became a warm and intimate place. Danny licked her lips nervously. 'I mean it, Ross. The house is out of bounds for fighting.'

Ross's eyelids slid to half-mast. He smiled his pirate's smile. 'OK. But out here the gloves are off.'

Danny squared her shoulders. 'Out here, *anything* goes.'

'But — but he can't just move in!'

'Too late, he already has.'

'Yes, but . . .' Deryl fiddled with the covered buttons on her dress. Danny had arrived to collect the children and explain that Ross owned two-thirds of the house, which was why she couldn't kick him out.

'He must know you can't stay there together. You're not married.'

Sometimes Danny wondered which century Deryl inhabited. 'Dee, does Ross Fabello strike you as the sort of person who cares what other people think? He does exactly what he wants to do, when he wants to do it.'

Deryl's sausage curls quivered. 'It's not right! I'll get Lloyd to have a word with him. That'll change his tune.'

Considering Lloyd was the wrong side of seventy with high blood pressure and even higher cholesterol, Danny didn't think that was such a good idea. 'No, Dee, I don't think that would help.'

'No?' Deryl was dismayed. 'Perhaps you and the children should move in here.'

Danny suppressed a shudder. With all those pigs? She thought she was better off coping with just one; after all, Ross smelt a lot better than Deryl's porkers — and looked a lot better, too, she conceded grudgingly. There was no way Danny was handing over her house to Darth Vader. Two could play at his game. The only thing Danny had on her side was time — and the springs in the sofa. 'Thanks for the offer, Dee,' she said, 'but I think it's best that we stay right where we are. I'm sure Ross will be gone soon.'

Deryl still looked unhappy. 'If you should ever need us, you know we're just across the road, don't you, dear?'

Danny smiled. Lloyd and Deryl were the closest thing she had to parents. 'Yes.'

'Any time of the day or night — you and the kiddies come right over to us. Alright?'

Danny nodded.

'Tell him if he's not prepared to make a long-term commitment, he has to go.'

She frowned. 'Long-term commitment?'

'Marriage, of course. We can't let him treat you the way his brother treated Daniella.'

Danny was appalled. 'It's not the same thing, Dee, not the same thing at all!'

She could just imagine Ross laughing himself sick. As for Danny, the very thought of a long-term commitment with Ross Fabello would send her screaming to the nearest cliff.

'Tell him if he's still living in that house with you in another month, I'll start planning the wedding.'

'Waste of time,' Danny said. 'He'll never show up in the photos.'

Chapter 12

All the Fabello children had explosive tempers, an unwanted legacy from their fiery Irish mother and passionate Italian father, but Ross worked hard to keep a leash on his and think before he spoke when he was angry or upset. He hadn't been doing much thinking on the night of the Findlays party; a whole lot of feeling, but not much in the thinking department. Finding the passports and travel brochures had been a wake-up call. Plan A had been the best one all along: it was far better that Ross had an arrangement in place to ensure that Matt and Mia kept in contact and received financial support, then he'd leave the country before the kids got used to him being around. He didn't want to build up their hopes only to disappoint them, like Pat. His parents and sisters would be the ones to become the regular fixtures in their lives. If Danny ever managed to put aside her distrust and prejudices about his family, she would slot right in with his sisters. She might even grow to like them, something that was never going to happen in their own volatile, fiery relationship.

The first rule of any war was to take out the general, but Ross decided subverting the troops was a far easier option and concentrated his efforts on getting to know the kids, figuring once he'd won Matt and Mia over it would be damned difficult for Auntie Danny to kick him out of the nest. There was, however, one slight problem. Despite his army of nieces and nephews, Ross wasn't really sure what interested kids of Matt and Mia's age.

Because as his difficulties with his writing had increased, so had his intolerance. Whereas he'd used to be a regular visitor to his sisters' houses, now an hour in their homes left Ross wondering how on earth they stayed sane amongst all the noise, chaos and constant demands for attention. Ross kept a list of all their kids' birthdays so he didn't miss sending a card and present, but he couldn't remember the last time he'd had any of his nieces and nephews to stay or taken them to a movie. How had that happened? When he needed information for a story Ross contacted experts and did research, so it made sense that what he didn't know about kids he could find out from his sisters.

Carmel, was due to have a baby any day now. The child would be her fifth, and Ross, like the rest of the family, pretty much took it for granted that Carmel would pop out number five as easily as she'd given birth to the others. Danny's lack of a family had made him realize how much he took his own for granted.

'So what's the latest on the auntie?' Carmel asked when Ross called.

'Tell you later. How're you feeling?'

Carmel didn't answer.

'Mel? Are you there?'

'Yes,' she replied slowly, 'I'm still here. Are you OK? Did Danny hit you on the head with something bigger than an apple?'

'No. How are you doing?'

'I'm . . . doing fine. I'm tired, but I'm — you know — *good*.'

Ross detected a quiver in her voice. 'Are you crying?' He was used to his sisters crying when they were pregnant, except for Aoife, who only swore more. Ross knew that the first and last trimesters were the times for an emotional meltdown.

Tom, Carmel's husband, said the middle trimester was like the calm in the middle of a tornado. 'Make the most of it while it lasts,' he recommended.

'Yeah, the sex is always really incredible in my middle trimester,' Aoife once confided.

'Damn, Aoife — do you have to?' Ross complained.

'Is it my fault Pete can't keep his hands off me?' she asked.

Ensconced on her sofa on the other side of the Pacific Ocean, Carmel dabbed her nose with a tissue. Nobody except Tom and her doctor really asked how she was when she was pregnant. But it didn't matter if it was number one, two or *ten*; each pregnancy and birth was still a miracle for her.

'Hayfever.' Carmel blew her nose and wondered why Ross was acting so out of character. 'It's really sweet of you to ask.'

'That's me,' he agreed drily. 'A real candy-ass.'

When he explained his problem, Carmel almost split her sides laughing. 'You mean you've only just realized you're a miserable pain-in-the-butt? Why do you think the kids call you Uncle Grinch?'

'They do not!'

'Yeah, Ross,' Carmel said, *'they do.'*

'I never forget birthday or Christmas presents!'

'We know you get that old witch of a personal assistant to buy your presents.'

'I tell Muriel what to buy.'

'Do you wrap them?'

'Why should I when a gift-wrapping service will do a much better job?'

'That's the point, Ross,' Carmel replied. 'We like getting badly wrapped crappy presents, because it shows some thought went into it. You know what Tonio bought Annie for her birthday this year? A plug for the bath in the en suite bathroom; Tonio knew it was missing and he knew how much his mommy loves the spa bath. *He's* only eight years old.'

'So you want me to buy you a plug for your birthday?'

'Ha ha!'

'OK, Oprah, I get the point.'

'I seriously doubt that,' Carmel said. 'You weren't always like this. I remember when you used to want to spend time with the kids and thought up stupid games to keep them occupied. But you stopped doing that the past year or two. You got boring.'

Ross was deeply offended. He'd gotten *boring?*

Carmel began to laugh. 'I still can't get over the idea of you playing Mr Mom.'

'Have you finished?' he asked sarcastically. 'Or were you planning on tarring and feathering me as well?'

'Touchy, touchy.' She suddenly gasped.

'What's wrong?'

'Just a contraction.'

'Is Tom there? Have you called Tom?' Ross was alarmed. Carmel's labours kept getting shorter; her last baby had arrived in the car en route to the hospital.

'Why would I do that? It isn't anything. Believe me, this kid isn't going anywhere soon. He's already a couch potato. I keep hoping my waters will break on this sofa and then Tom will have to buy me the new one I want.'

'Do you have to give me all the gruesome details? I'm your brother.'

Carmel trotted out her well-worn reply: 'You have a penis, which means you're capable of knocking some poor woman up.'

She had no shame, just like Danny. He'd been right on the money about her fitting in with his family; in fact, Ross suspected they'd like her more than they did him. 'Leave my penis out of this!'

'Your relationship to me in my current condition is totally irrelevant,' Carmel groused. 'You want to get to know Matt and Mia better? Well, here's what you do . . .'

Knowing what a stirrer Carmel could be, and taking into account that she was pregnant and hormonal, Ross called his sister Annie to check if his nieces and nephews truly did think he was a miserable old fart. Annie was a talented artist, sweet and flaky as a croissant. A two-metre-wide abstract she'd painted hung opposite the front door of his house.

'My kids don't call you Uncle Grinch,' she assured him earnestly. 'My kids call you Uncle Squidward.'

'Squidward? Who the hell is Squidward?'

Ross pictured Annie twisting one of her long, red ringlets around her finger nervously.

'He's an octopus.'

'An octopus?' Ross was outraged. 'Your kids think I look like an octopus?'

'No, they think you act like him.'

'Why? What's he like?'

'He's miserable and negative and never joins in when SpongeBob and Patrick are having fun.'

Ross didn't want to know who SpongeBob and Patrick were.

'Ross? Are you still there?'

'Yes, just sitting here with my feet up — all eight of them.'

Ross was not above using bribery to achieve his goal. All his nieces and nephews loved television, particularly cable television. It was obvious from the dish on the roof of the house that at some point Danny and the family had owned cable, so first thing on Monday morning Ross paid an extortionate amount of money to jump the queue and get it reinstalled. When Danny arrived home from work, Matt and Mia were ensconced in the shabby armchairs in the living room while Ross lay on the floor in front of the sofa wielding the remote control. They were watching *SpongeBob*

SquarePants.

'Hi, Auntie Danny,' Mia called, her eyes on the screen. 'Uncle Ross got us Sky TV. Isn't that cool?'

Matt was so engrossed in SpongeBob he hadn't even said hello when Danny walked in, and for some reason Ross was glowering at Squidward.

Danny glowered at Ross. 'Oh, has he?'

The smile he sent her belonged in a toothpaste advert and was just about as authentic. 'I knew you'd approve. The History and Discovery channels are so educational.'

She wanted to drive a stake through his black heart. The way Ross looked at the kids sometimes reminded Danny of somebody trying to figure out the fastest way to complete a Rubik's cube. He didn't seem to understand how vulnerable Matt and Mia were. Danny considered requesting a meeting in the chook house, but she'd gone lukewarm on the idea of being alone with Ross with only a few disgruntled chickens as chaperones. She belatedly noticed the living room was looking remarkably tidy.

'Has somebody dusted and vacuumed?'

Mia and Matt reddened and made odd noises. Sky TV had arrived with a reminder from their uncle about household chores and performance reviews.

Matt seemed to be the only one unaffected by his uncle's dubious charms. He spent most of his time reading or listening to CDs in his bedroom. Danny had given up trying to entice him into a game of cricket or touch rugby because Matt was such a half-hearted participant. He was extremely clever, blitzing his school work and regularly topping the class. Danny was surprised to find Ross shared her concerns.

'Does Matt play any sport?' he asked.

'Only if he has to — he's not the most coordinated kid.'

'He just hasn't learned how to handle his body yet,' Ross said.

The day he moved in, Ross took the kids outside to kick a soccer ball around. He made exaggerated leaps into the air and onto the grass, purposely missing his target. Mia giggled and dived on top of him, and Matt joined in. Whenever Pat had bothered to play soccer with Matt, he had belittled Matt's clumsy efforts and spent the entire time showing off his own skills. Ross was patient. He ignored it when Matt messed up, and offered casual praise when he got it right.

Danny watched them through the kitchen window and pleaded silently, *Don't hurt them, Ross. Please, please don't hurt them.*

After *SpongeBob* ended, Ross changed channels to watch an AC Milan game.

'That's Dad's team,' Matt said. 'He got the new TV so he could watch them.'

Ross kept his tone offhand. 'Your dad and I were brought up watching AC Milan. Grandpa Vito is a big fan. The first time we went to Italy, he took Pat and me to see them play.'

Matt lay on the floor on his stomach with his chin propped in his hands. He stared at the screen. 'Dad was a really good player.'

Ross studied his long, black ringlets. 'Yes, he was.'

'Better than you?'

'Way better. Pat was a natural.'

Matt was silent for several moments. 'Dad said I was useless.'

Ross transferred his gaze to the television screen. In lieu of Pat's neck, he strangled the remote control unit. 'You're not useless. It's just your body is growing so fast that your brain hasn't caught up, so it makes you a bit clumsy. Your dad was just the same at your age.'

Matt looked over his shoulder, his expression sceptical. 'Really?'

'If you don't believe me, ask Grandpa Vito. Have you played

rugby?'

'Yeah.'

'Good. You can teach me.'

'I suck at that, too,' Matt said.

'Not as much as I do.'

Mia *adored* Ross. She followed him everywhere, chattering nonstop. 'Has she got an off switch?' he asked Danny wearily after Mia had woken him at six to give a performance of all of her favourite ABBA hits. Ross wasn't a morning person, and Mia's rendition of 'Dancing Queen' was excruciating.

Danny was in the kitchen trying to catch up on the ironing, another household chore she avoided. 'Mia opens her eyes and her mouth in the morning, and they pretty much stay that way until she goes to bed at night.'

Ross sighed. 'She's got enough energy to power the national grid.' His elbow was hooked under his chin as he tried to dig the kinks from his shoulder blade. The sofa's days were numbered. Ross had picked out a brand-new three-piece suite, including a sofa bed, and paid extra to have the delivery date brought forward. He hadn't got around to telling Danny yet.

Danny had just finished work. Ross realized how tired she must be when she picked up one of his shirts and automatically began to iron it.

'You look like Patrick,' she told him. 'You live in her house. As far as Mia's concerned, you're her father's replacement.'

Ross stopped digging at his shoulder. 'I'm not trying to replace Pat.'

The iron slid across his shirt. 'You should have thought of that before you decided to move in here.'

'I'm her uncle.'

'Uncle — father.' Danny stopped ironing. 'The only difference between you and your brother is you've got money and you don't pretend you're staying.'

'I'm not Pat,' Ross said coolly.

She shook her head impatiently. 'You just don't get it, do you?' The smell of singed fabric rose from the ironing board. She snatched the iron from his shirt and looked at the triangular-shaped scorch mark in dismay.

'You've ruined my shirt.'

Danny lifted her eyes and said fiercely, 'You're not going to ruin my children's lives.'

Jeff had been right: Danny had become Matt and Mia's mother. Living at the house made it impossible for Ross to stay detached, impossible not to feel rage and guilt at Pat's cavalier treatment of his children and Danny's sister. He urgently needed to get the loose ends tied up and get on a plane home, and he needed to find a way into Danny's good graces without being too obvious. She was overloaded by her commitments at the hospital and at home. Ross couldn't do anything about work, but he could do something about things at home.

He arranged for a weekly ironing and cleaning service. 'Don't think this gets you out of household chores,' he warned the children. 'You're still responsible for keeping your bedrooms tidy. I'm sure there are plenty of other jobs Auntie Danny and I can find you to take up the slack.'

Matt and Mia still didn't know Danny wasn't in on the performance reviews. Matt was smarting because he'd only been awarded a three per cent cost-of-living rise, which meant an increase of six cents to his weekly pocket money. Mia had got a whole extra dollar. Ross had taken pity on him and rounded it up to twenty cents, with the proviso that he would review Matt's performance in three months. As soon as he said it, Ross wondered what the hell he was thinking — he wouldn't even be in New Zealand then.

Predictably, Danny objected to the extra help Ross had arranged, but purely for the sake of appearances. Only a fool would turn down a free cleaning and ironing service. 'I don't like the idea of strangers in my house, poking around my things.'

'I told them to stay out of your room,' Ross said. 'To be honest, I think the cleaning lady was relieved.'

She scowled. 'Who said you could send our clothes away to an ironing service?'

'You burnt my shirt. If I leave things to you, I'll be walking around half-naked.'

Danny felt like pointing out his habit of wandering about shirtless anyway, but didn't want to draw attention to the fact that she'd noticed. Ross was attractive when he had his shirt off and his mouth shut, but because she felt the occasional urge to use the facilities didn't mean Danny wanted to sign up for membership. 'Just remember I've got a share in this house, too,' she insisted. 'I'll overlook the ironing—'

'Judging by the pile of clothes in the hallway cupboard, you've been doing that for a while—'

Her voice rose. 'I will overlook the ironing service, but don't go making any other changes without asking me first.'

The next day when Danny returned home from the supermarket she was greeted by the sight of her underwear hanging on the line alongside Ross's Calvin Klein's. Arranging for the house to be cleaned and their clothes to be ironed was one thing, but washing her undies was getting too personal.

Ross was at the kitchen table tapping away on his laptop and wearing the vague expression he got when he was writing. If Danny's killer instinct had been as well honed as she liked to pretend, she would have exploited these times to her advantage.

Instead she was fascinated watching the creative process at work, although she did her best to hide it.

'Who gave you permission to wash my underwear?' she demanded.

Ross tapped in a few more words and looked up. His eyes were like black velvet, soft and unfocused. He blinked slowly and said, 'Believe me, washing your panties doesn't do anything for me on a personal level. The only reason I decided to take over the laundry was that it seemed the safest way to make sure my clothes weren't returned to me in pieces or bright pink.'

Why hadn't she thought of that? Danny looked out the window at the clothes line. 'How did you do that?'

'I put the clothes in the machine, added soap and switched it on.'

'Not that! How did you hang out an entire load of washing with just a dozen clothes pegs?'

'That's all I could find.'

Buying more clothes pegs was another one of the things that Danny had intended to get around to — she'd been drying things indoors on the clothes rack for months.

'Why have you got a pillowcase full of odd socks in the cupboard?'

Danny wished he'd stop poking around in her cupboards. 'Orphan socks.'

He stared. 'Orphan socks?'

'You're trying to tell me you don't own orphan socks?' At last, something Martha Stewart didn't know about. '*Everybody* has got orphan socks. Their partners disappear in the wash to a parallel sock universe never to be seen again.'

'Not if you tie them together.'

'That is the lamest thing I've ever heard. Don't you have a life?'

'I did, but I left it in San Diego, and tying my socks together isn't lame, it's organized. Why weren't there any bras in the hamper? There were plenty of lacy thongs, but no bras.'

Danny coloured hotly. 'None of your damned business!'

She wasn't about to explain she begrudged spending money on an item of clothing that was frankly superfluous given her meagre dimensions. Ross needed to be put in his place. Danny plugged Dr Tim in her ears, sneaked out to the washing line and stole one sock from every pair of his hanging on the line. It was petty and immature, but the no-fighting-in-front-of-the-children rule she'd enforced was driving her nuts.

Ross had his suspicions about where his socks were going, but couldn't prove anything. 'I want to see you in the henhouse, Daneka,' he said, just to see her get all flustered and make excuses. They both knew why she wouldn't go there with him. 'We need to hold a summit meeting about my missing socks.'

'If you think I'm going to waste my valuable time arguing with you about your socks, you've got another think coming, Fabello.'

'Chicken,' he clucked softly. 'You're as chicken as your phone.'

'That is so deep! Why don't you put it in one of your books?'

When Ross, keen to avoid starvation, took over the cooking, Danny only made a token protest. Ross could cook. *Really* cook. Suddenly the kitchen was filled with the smell of olive oil, basil and garlic as Uncle Ross concocted delicious meals from scratch. Danny could hardly wait to get home at night to see what was for dinner, and she began to put on some of the weight she'd lost while Nella was sick.

Ross was flabbergasted when Mia and Matt expressed a preference for Danny's cooking. Mia gazed at her plate dubiously the first time Ross cooked the evening meal. 'What's that?'

'Petti di pollo imbottiti con salsa al pepe verde.'

Danny wasn't sure if it was the smell of the food or the sound of Ross speaking Italian that made her lick her lips.

'What?' Mia asked.

'*Pardon*,' Danny corrected. She pushed the chicken about her plate for at least ten seconds before falling on it and inhaling it.

'Stuffed chicken breasts with green peppercorn sauce,' Ross replied.

Matt frowned at his plate. 'Can't we just have chicken nuggets and chips?'

'No,' he snapped, 'we can't.'

Danny chewed some chicken and nearly groaned in ecstasy as the flavours burst on her tongue.

'Look,' Ross said, 'Auntie Danny's eating it.'

'I don't like to see food going to waste,' she lied.

'You might want to tone things down a bit, Uncle Ross,' Danny suggested when the kids left their untouched plates on the table. 'Stuffed chicken breasts in green peppercorn sauce is a little sophisticated for them.'

Ross scraped the plates into the bin. 'Anything would be sophisticated for them — they live on garbage.'

'They do not!'

'Don't try to defend their diet. The healthiest thing you cooked them was oatmeal.'

It took Danny a moment to figure out he meant porridge. 'They're kids!' she blustered.

'With the arteries of eighty-year-olds.'

'Oatmeal — I mean, porridge — is very healthy,' she said defensively.

He began loading the dishwasher. 'I bet Mia and Matt sleep better at night knowing that.'

Danny stuck out her tongue at his back.

'You're probably in even worse shape.' Ross dropped silverware into the dishwasher basket. 'You think you're going to be around long if you carry on eating garbage?'

Danny didn't like thinking about her longevity. Ross turned and caught sight of her haunted expression, and frowned. Now what was all that about? He preferred it when Danny was abusing him. 'And another thing,' he said.

'What?'

'Stick your tongue out at me again and I'll haul you out to the henhouse.'

'How did you—'

He pointed a spoon at the mirror hanging on the hallway wall opposite the open door.

'Oh yeah? You and whose army?' she sneered and stalked from the kitchen.

That was better.

Ross was writing when the phone rang after the children and Danny had left for the day. When he was working at home he usually disconnected the phone, but he wasn't comfortable doing that here in case the school called to say something had happened to Matt or Mia — or Danny had written off another truck. He snatched up the phone. 'Yes?'

A woman's voice asked, 'Mr Fabello?'

'Yes.'

'Mr *Ross* Fabello?'

'Yes. Who is this?'

'My name is Robyn. I work in the office at Matt and Mia's school.'

'What's wrong?' Ross asked sharply. 'Has something happened?'

'No, they're both fine. I'm calling about the Walking School Bus.'

'The Walking School Bus?' he echoed.

'Yes, your name is on our list of parents volunteering as a regular walker.'

Danny, Ross thought.

'I hope you haven't changed your mind?' Robyn sounded anxious. 'We have the bare minimum number of adults we need.'

'Can you just remind me how many days I volunteered for, Robyn?' Ross asked grimly.

'Five mornings a week, it's very generous of you.'

'Isn't it? How many days has Danny Lawton signed on for?'

'Danny's on our list of people to call on if one of the regular walkers is sick or can't make it. She couldn't commit to a regular day because of her shift work.'

How convenient for her.

Ross cornered Danny as soon as she got home.

'Who gave you permission to sign me up for the Walking School Bus?'

She was more interested in what was cooking in the oven. 'You. I was thinking about what you said about taking responsibility for our health, and when I saw the notice in the school newsletter asking for volunteers I straightaway thought of you. You need the exercise and the school needs helpers.'

'I don't need the exercise! I get plenty of exercise!'

'You call sitting at a laptop all day typing exercise?'

'It's none of your business how I spend my day.'

'I'm only looking out for you and your arteries, Ross,' Danny said piously.

She'd decided to go for broke and bombard him with as much aggravation as possible in the hope that it would wear him down faster. The sofa just wasn't cutting it.

'You might like to invest in a decent waterproof jacket,' Danny suggested. 'You've seen how changeable the weather is this time of year — you might need it.' She widened her eyes. 'What's the weather like at that nice big house of yours this time of year? It's near San Diego, isn't it?'

Ross had never mentioned his house in San Diego, and Danny had certainly never asked him where he lived. 'How do you know about my house?'

'Google is cheaper than a private detective and almost as good,' she said sarcastically. It also supplied a veritable plethora of gossip and photos of the women in Ross's life. They were scattered like train wrecks in his wake, none of them lasting longer than a couple of years.

'First you ogle me and now you google me?'

Danny's smug smile faded. 'I never ogled you! And I only googled you to look at your website.'

'Why?'

'Know thine enemy.'

The Walking School Bus put a serious dent in Ross's lifestyle. He liked to write late and sleep late, but that went out the window because he had get up early to walk Matt and Mia and the other kids to school — not that sleeping in was really an option on the sofa. There was always a minimum of two adults supervising the Walking School Bus, so Ross got to know other parents and the neighbourhood kids as they joined onto the bus when it passed by their door. Because they lived in a semi-rural area, they never had more than a dozen kids walking at any one time. When they reached the end of Danny's road, they had permission to cut across a local farmer's fields and up over the hill to the school on the other side. The smallest children often needed a piggyback up the hill, and Ross frequently had a kid or two clinging to his back while he staggered up the slope. Who needed weight-training?

Mia sang all the way. 'Do you like my singing, Uncle Ross?' she asked after she'd finished blasting him with 'Waterloo'.

'Mia, honey, you're unique.'

It bothered Ross how alone Danny and the kids were — apart from Deryl, Lloyd and Vanessa, Danny had nobody else to call on, and certainly no family so far as he could tell. Trying to worm information out of Danny about anything to do with family, and especially about Pat and Nella, was a waste of time.

It was Lloyd Snedden who filled in the gaps when he started turning up unannounced to help with the repairs on the house. Lloyd told him how Daniella had met Patrick when she was twenty, and their relationship appeared to have followed the same pattern as almost anything Patrick was involved in: long periods of little or no contact, followed by dramatic reunions when his brother got to play the role of the prodigal son — or, in this case, father — to the hilt before boredom or an argument with Danny made him disappear again.

The other thing that bothered Ross was that Danny's mother and twin sister had both died from breast cancer. Lloyd pointed out that Nella was a bit of a scatterbrain, who actively avoided unpleasantness, including cancer checks. She was not a fighter like Danny, but still Ross was worried.

They were repairing some of the rotten verandah. Ross squinted down the length of a piece of wood he'd just run through the saw. 'Does Danny get regular checks?' he asked casually.

Lloyd reddened. 'How the hell would I know?'

Ross banged the wood down in frustration; if he asked Deryl she'd probably accuse him of being a pervert. He had a sudden urge to drag Danny along to the nearest doctor to get her breasts checked, even though he could imagine how she'd react to that. 'Lloyd, I need some advice.'

The older man scratched the back of his neck. 'About what?'

'I don't think I'd be out of line to ask if you knew that Danny inherited some debts when Daniella and my brother died.'

'No, you wouldn't be out of line. That brother of yours was a useless article. And Daniella lived in cloud-cuckoo-land.'

'Yeah.' Ross looked at the piece of wood in his hands. 'I know.'

'So what advice do you want?'

'I want to settle Danny's outstanding debts so that she and the kids are at least on a level playing field. But I don't know how to go about it without losing my balls or kneecaps when she finds out what I've done.'

Lloyd smiled. 'You've got that right. She'd have your guts for garters.'

Ross nodded grimly.

'Stop pussyfooting around and get on with it is my advice, son. If you ask me, you and Danny are too much alike. You're both pig-headed, and neither one of you will back down from a fight. Danny deserves a break, even though she'd chop her own arm off rather than ask for help. So if you're as rich as everybody says you are, stop wasting time and get on with it.'

Ross smiled wryly. 'OK. Just promise me that if you see a fresh grave behind the house you'll dig me up and send my body back to my family in the States.'

'Consider it done, son, consider it done.'

Ross weighed up the pros and cons of his plan. If he backed Danny into a corner, he knew she'd make him regret it. Ross enjoyed fighting with Danny; it kept him on his toes. He loved walking the fine line between pissing her off and pushing her over the edge. Watching Danny's eyes flash and her nostrils flare when she was in a temper was almost as good as Ross imagined having sex with her would be.

Almost.

If something happened to Danny his family would welcome Matt and Mia with open arms, but it would be Ross they would turn to, Ross whose face would be the familiar one amongst so many strangers. For the first time Ross was personally rather than collectively responsible for somebody.

He called Allan Nicolls and arranged for Danny's mortgage and debts to be paid, figuring he had until the end of the month, when the next instalments were due, before Danny would find out what he'd done. The amount of money involved wasn't even pocket change for him, but Ross knew Danny wouldn't see it that way. He also contacted Deirdre and asked her to find out what a woman with a strong family history of breast cancer should do to look after herself.

'Is this research for a new book?' she asked.

'No.'

'Oh. Didn't Matt and Mia's mother die from breast cancer?'

'Yes. And their grandmother.'

'That's terrible!'

'Yes,' Ross agreed, 'it is.'

'You're worried about Danny, aren't you?' Deirdre said slowly.

'Just find out all you can for me will you, Didge?'

'Alright.'

'And keep it to yourself? OK?'

Ross stood by the kitchen window, watching the grass sway in the paddocks and sunshine glitter like tinsel on the distant sea, and brooded.

A good man, concerned about Danny's loss of contact with her maternal relatives, would get a private investigator to find the whereabouts of her family. A good man wouldn't care that finding them would make Danny even less likely to turn to him for help.

Was he that good?

Chapter 13

The arrival of the Saturday-morning paper provided Ross with a far bigger headache than the impending battle over the mortgage.

Things started out well enough. He and Danny managed to sit at the kitchen table and share breakfast without stabbing one another with their cutlery. Ross refrained from making a crack about Danny's decision to paint her hair pink, and Danny didn't turn on the cold water as he took a shower after his morning run. She sat at the table, munching on a triangle of toast and browsing through the paper, half-listening to Mia and Matt's discussion about which toy they could get with the cards they were collecting from the cereal packets.

Suddenly Danny stopped eating, her toast suspended halfway between her mouth and her plate, her eyes riveted to the gossip column. Two photographs of her and Ross at the publishing party were in the centre of the page. One showed her spread-eagled across the bar entwined with Ross — they weren't kissing so much as devouring one another. The other had been taken in the car park, and showed Danny crouched at his feet clutching her passport while he loomed over her.

Danny's vision blurred, and all her good intentions went sailing out the window. Stealing a few socks wouldn't even come close to assuaging the black fury that gripped her. A summit meeting in the chook house would turn into a blood bath.

'Auntie Danny?' Matt asked. 'Are you OK?'

She launched herself to her feet and rushed from the kitchen with the paper crushed in her fist.

'Uh oh,' Mia said.

Ross was luxuriating beneath the soothing, steady, warm flow of water from the ancient shower when the bathroom door crashed against the wall and Danny burst into the room. He blinked at her blurry image through the plastic shower curtain suspended from the rail above the bath.

She waved something at him. *'Have you seen this, Fabello?'*

Ross groped behind him and turned off the water. What the hell was wrong now?

'What are you talking about? Can't it wait until I've finished my shower?'

'NO, IT CAN'T!'

Danny grabbed the curtain and wrenched it aside, sending the plastic rings clattering and skittering along the rusted rail. That Ross was naked and she was stripping away his last bit of cover didn't even register. She was so incensed by what she'd seen in the paper that the only thing that mattered was making him pay for her humiliation.

Ross glowered at her, a large, furious, wet male covered in nothing more than a few sliding soapsuds. His lips barely moved as he ground out, 'What exactly was it you wanted me to see, Daneka?'

Danny's red-hot anger fizzled like a lit fire-cracker held out in the rain. Her gaze slid slowly down his body and snagged on Ground Zero. Her eyes widened as he twitched and lengthened. She had a sudden urge to step into the bathtub and pay a visit to America.

Ross made a sound somewhere between a growl and a snarl, and Danny jerked her eyes back to his face. *'Either get in here with me, or get the hell out!'*

She dropped the newspaper and ran.

Ross counted to ten. Then he counted to thirty. When he hit one hundred, he gave up and turned the cold water on. It was several more minutes before he was in a fit state to climb out of the bath. He picked up the newspaper and sat on the edge of the tub.

Findlays Publishing House gave a Friday-night bash to remember when they turned a downtown warehouse into an indoor beach, complete with surfboards and a lagoon. But the crowning glory was the presence of perhaps the most successful and famous of their stable of international authors, RF O'Rourke — a man renowned for his dislike of the limelight. Imagine the delight of Findlays management upon discovering the delectable Mr O'Rourke right here in Godzone — albeit for 'family business'.

Possibly the only fly in the proverbial ointment was the goldeneyed, gamine lovely on RF's arm who made it clear she wasn't prepared to share him with any of the siliconed lovelies eagerly dropping naughty notes in his pockets. The lady, who called herself Danny and insisted she was RF's sister-in-law, got her revenge by holding an impromptu auction of the notes, which went some way towards raising $6,000 for a local women's refuge. This reporter cannot recall enjoying an evening so much as he watched the notedroppers scramble to buy back their illicit messages or risk being outbid. It was worth watching Ms Danny in action just to see her rout her competition.

RF seemed to agree. He spent the entire night watching her before the pair eventually all but did the horizontal tango on the bar. Intensive behind-the-scenes research by your dedicated reporter has revealed the lady is a senior nurse at a certain busy Emergency Department in our fair city. Unfortunately, what must have seemed a swell evening for the couple degenerated at some point into a slanging match in the car park with Mr O'Rourke clearly getting the upper hand.

Not a man to be crossed — or, as my dear old nana would say, handsome is as handsome does.

Ross looked at the photo of him and Danny kissing and thought he might have to climb back under the shower again. He turned his attention to the photo of them fighting in the car park and winced. Danny was crouched in the rain with her passport, looking like a drowned kitten. She stared up at Ross towering over her, his eyes slitted with anger and his mouth open as he yelled at her.

Ross dug his thumb and forefinger into his eyes. He looked like a bully. He had been a bully. He hated having his privacy invaded, but he'd had several years to get used to it. Danny had no previous experience, and Ross remembered the sense of outrage and invasion the first time it had happened to him.

He pulled on his clothes and went to find her.

She was standing beside the letterbox in front of the house, wearing a pair of baggy old black lycra running shorts, a yellow ribbed tank-top that clashed with her pink hair, and battered running shoes. She was staring at a sheet of white paper in her hand; the torn envelope clutched in the opposite hand.

Danny ran or exercised only when she was upset. When she was happy, she sat on the couch and ate chocolate. The newspaper article had made her drag out her running shoes and shorts. It was habit that made her check the letterbox before she set off down the road. The letter was from the finance company offering her a hefty new personal loan . . . *because she'd repaid her existing one.*

For a moment, Danny wondered if she was concussed again. It was as if her life was a deck of cards that somebody had thrown into the air and she could only watch helplessly as they fell to the ground.

'Danny?'

She turned slowly and looked at Ross.

'By this time next week everyone will have forgotten about the newspaper article.'

It was about the worst thing he could have said. Danny didn't care about everyone. What he'd done made no difference to everyone, but it made a whole world of difference to her. She glared at him, furious.

Ross, who didn't realize the significance of the sheet of paper in her hands, propped his hands on his hips. 'I wanted to apologize, but you don't make it easy. I didn't know the damned photos were being taken!'

She shook the letter at him. *'Yooouuu!'*

He peered at her face. 'Do we need to take this to the henhouse?'

Danny made a strangled sound and flattened the letter face-out against her chest.

Ross caught sight of the name and logo of the finance company and put two and two together. A trip to the henhouse wasn't going to fix it.

Mia and Matt joined them.

Ross hastily checked the surrounding area for any potential weapons, then, with his eyes on Danny, said: 'Could you two go over to Deryl and Lloyd's while Auntie Danny and I talk please, kids?'

Danny hadn't even noticed the children.

'Can't we stay and watch you and Auntie Danny fight?' Mia asked.

'No!' Ross barked. 'Do as I say!'

'Come on, Mia.' Matt grabbed her hand. 'If we stay, they'll only go to the chook house.'

Once the kids were gone, Danny advanced on Ross rattling the letter like a sabre. *'You . . . You!'*

Ross guarded his crotch with his hands. 'Yes and yes to everything.'

'*You paid off my debts!*' She danced on the spot, stopping every few seconds to haul on her drooping lycra shorts.

He noticed a piece of string holding her shoe together and guessed the shoelace had been sacrificed to the late, unlamented toilet. 'Danny, will you calm down and let me explain?'

'Explain?' she shrieked. '*Explain?* Did you think you could *buy* me?'

He stiffened. 'This has nothing to do with buying you. It's about making sure Matt and Mia are financially secure, which is something you sure as hell haven't been able to do.'

Danny stopped her war dance and stared, her eyes full of pain and frustration. She crushed the letter into a ball and fired it at Ross. He tried to duck, but it smacked him between the eyes and bounced onto the grass at his feet. When he looked up again, he saw Danny sprinting down the road.

Ross set off in pursuit. '*Danny!*'

She ignored him.

'*Danny!*'

She put her head down and ran faster.

Ross lengthened his stride. Danny tried to out-sprint him, but Ross was fitter and his legs were longer. 'For chrissakes, stop and listen to me!'

He reached out and snaked an arm around her waist, but their legs tangled and Ross found himself catapulting through the air clutching Danny. He twisted and landed heavily on his back in the long grass at the side of the road with Danny sprawled on top of him, her back against his chest.

'Are — you — OK?' Ross gasped when he got his breath back. He propped himself on one elbow and peered over Danny's shoulder at her face.

She kicked him in the shin.

He grunted. 'Guess that's a yes.'

Ross flinched as Danny wriggled down him, rose on her knees and twisted around to face him. She grabbed his loosely buttoned shirt along with a handful of his chest hair and shook him. 'You have no right to interfere in my personal business!'

'Ow!' He grabbed her wrists. 'That hurts!'

She pulled harder.

Ross lurched onto his knees, sending her tumbling back into the grass. He lost his balance when Danny grabbed him to keep from falling. They landed in a jumble of arms and legs.

He searched for and found the bald spot on his chest. 'That damn well hurt!'

'Good!' She tried unsuccessfully to buck him off. 'Get off me, you big lump!'

Her wriggling made Ross forget all about his chest. The blood rushing to the site of the injury suddenly changed direction and charged off towards his groin.

Danny noticed the change and stilled. She looked up at Ross and said 'Oh.'

He stared down at her and agreed dryly, 'Yeah — *oh*.'

They were distracted by the sound of a car engine, and watched as an ancient, battered Rolls Royce Silver Shadow covered in dust and mud stopped on the road, the driver surveying them disapprovingly through the open window. A tired-looking cloth sunhat with lime green and purple panels was perched on his head like a discarded pancake. His eyes were an indeterminate muddy shade, and he had the worst buck teeth Ross had ever seen. The guy could eat corn on the cob at twenty paces. Ross watched as the apparition put an index finger to the brim of the awful hat and said in a nasal voice, 'Danny.'

She gave Ross a shove and scrambled out from beneath him,

her face glowing like a beacon. 'Hi, Jarvis!'

Caught by surprise, Ross sprawled in the grass and gazed at the car in disbelief. It was a collector's item and would be worth a lot of money if somebody took the time to look after it.

Jarvis pointed at him. 'I thought he was dead.'

Ross thought he'd misheard, but knew he hadn't when Danny squeezed his arm. 'This is Patrick's brother, Ross,' she said quickly.

Jarvis studied Ross suspiciously.

Ross didn't notice. He was preoccupied by Danny's unexpected and surprisingly sweet gesture of comfort. She let go of his arm and jumped up brushing grass from the seat of her saggy shorts. 'I'm so sorry, Jarvis! I didn't even know she'd got out!'

Ross wondered what the hell she was talking about until he spied a large black sheep in the back seat of the Rolls Royce.

It was Charcoal, one of the two lawnmowers that lived in the paddock behind the house.

Jarvis Wainwright was the wealthiest man in the district. He owned the large farm stretching along the cliff top at the end of the road and the hill Ross climbed each morning with the Walking School Bus. It was prime real estate, and property developers had been after Jarvis for years to sell. To his neighbours' relief, Jarvis had refused all offers to develop the area for luxury housing. He was a man of simple needs who just happened to have substantial financial assets. Jarvis's main goal in life was of a far more personal nature.

He was in the market for a wife.

His preference to fill that role had always been pretty, sweet-natured Daniella Lawton. Although she'd been swept off her feet years ago by that Yank larrikin, Jarvis considered every woman was available until a man put a ring on her finger, and the Yank larrikin had never shown any sign of doing so, despite giving her two children. Whenever Patrick Fabello disappeared for months on end, Jarvis got his hopes up and began to visit Nella, but they were always dashed when Patrick returned and Nella tumbled into his arms like a puppy overjoyed to see its owner.

When Daniella died, Jarvis squeezed himself into his one and only suit and placed a handpicked bunch of flowers on her coffin. Danny had been touched, until she realized Jarvis had decided to transfer his attentions to her.

Jarvis wasn't best pleased to find yet another Yank larrikin had got his feet under the kitchen table, and, after releasing Charcoal into the back paddock to a rapturous reunion with Persil, Jarvis accepted a cup of tea, got his feet under Danny's kitchen table, and proceeded to make sure the interloper knew he was poaching on Jarvis's territory.

Ross quickly understood Jarvis's intentions. He poured himself a glass of red wine and sat opposite. Danny hovered, longing to hit Ross over the head with the wine bottle. It was obvious he was out to bait poor old Jarvis. While Jarvis strangled his mug of tea in one meaty fist, his bushy grey and black brows beetling over his bulbous nose, and kept his big, practical feet firmly on the floor, Ross tilted his chair back on two legs, dangled his wineglass carelessly between his spread knees and smiled unpleasantly.

'What d'you do for a living?' Jarvis demanded.

Ross took a sip of wine and rolled it across his tongue. 'As little as possible.'

'Ross is a—' Danny began. She was wasting her time. Neither of them paid her any attention.

Jarvis slurped his tea. 'Where're you staying?'

Ross topped up his wineglass. 'Here.'

Jarvis choked on his tea. *'Here? With Danny?'*

'That's right.'

Danny once again tried to interject. 'The only reason Ross is— '

Jarvis's florid complexion darkened to vermillion. 'Danny's a decent girl — she deserves to be treated with respect.'

'Oh for God's sake!' Danny wished they'd take their pissing contest somewhere besides her kitchen. Ross was enjoying toying with Jarvis, who didn't yet understand he was out of his league.

'Believe me,' Ross smiled lazily, 'I make sure Daneka gets *all* the respect she needs.'

Danny let out a hiss and reached for the wine bottle just as Deryl arrived with the children, who grabbed something to eat and disappeared into the back garden.

Deryl wrinkled her nose when she saw Ross was drinking so early in the day, and smiled at Jarvis. Deryl thought Jarvis was a prime catch, and kept reminding Danny of his good points. She started up again after a scowling Jarvis finally left.

'He's young,' Deryl began.

'He's sixty if he's a day, Dee.' Danny was acutely aware of Ross listening in and helping himself to some more wine watched by a disapproving Deryl. 'Can't you go away?' she demanded.

He smiled and saluted her with his wineglass. 'No.'

'Jarvis Wainwright is in the prime of his life. He's good to his animals.'

Danny sighed. 'Which means?'

'If a man takes care of his animals, he can be relied upon to take care of his wife and kiddies.'

'Dee, I don't want to be taken care of by Jarvis Wainwright.'

'He's a wealthy man. You'd want for nothing.'

'Only my sanity.'

Deryl looked at Ross and sniffed. 'You wouldn't be beholden to anybody.'

Ross gave her a sour look.

After Deryl left, Ross placed a sheaf of papers on the kitchen table. 'You might as well read this.'

Danny eyed the papers as if they were a coiled cobra. 'Why? What else have you done?'

He walked away.

Danny sat down and read the documents. She no longer had a mortgage. She was debt-free. It was all too much to take on board. She felt worn out, emotionally battered. She'd be a liar if she said being debt-free wasn't going to be a huge weight lifted from her shoulders. Ross had put the house in both their names, making them joint owners. It was there on the paper in black ink. *Daneka Aroha Lawton and Ross Igor Padraig Oreste Fabello.* She laughed weakly. What had his mother been thinking?

She tracked Ross down in Matt's bedroom. He was lying on the bed, reading *Revenge of the Lawn Gnomes*. 'Why did you put the house in both our names, Igor?'

Ross sighed. Matt had lent him the book and the bed for a few hours.

'You did it so I'd have to get your approval if I ever wanted to sell my share and move, didn't you?' Danny accused.

Ross put the book on his chest and tucked his hands behind his head. 'If you worked it out, why did you need to ask me?'

'It'd serve you right if I married Jarvis and spiked your guns, Oristo.' Her voice lacked its usual fire.

'Yeah, like that's ever going to happen. And it's *Oreste*,' he corrected her. 'Old Jarvis might be rich, but believe me I'm richer.'

'I googled you, remember? I've seen the list of women you've dumped. You're a real catch, Fabello.'

'I am!'

'I'd rather catch foot-and-mouth disease.' Danny's curiosity was piqued. 'How rich are you? Are we talking billions?'

'Of course not.'

'Only millions?'

Ross eyed her warily. 'What do you mean only millions?'

'How many are we talking about? One million? Two million?' She paused. 'Three?'

Ross was so pissed by her sniffy attitude that he broke one of his golden rules and told her what he was worth.

The colour slowly leached from Danny's face. She swayed.

He leapt up and forced her to sit on the bed. 'Put your head between your knees.'

'That's obscene,' she said faintly. 'What's the point of having all that money? You couldn't spend it in two lifetimes.'

Ross stroked the short, silky pink hair at her nape and noticed how pretty her ears were. From where he stood, he could see the silver butterflies holding her earrings in place. He didn't want to talk about his money, certainly not when it so obviously upset her. Ross thought about the unexpected sweetness of her gesture out on the roadside when Jarvis had spoken so callously about Pat.

He threaded his fingers into her hair and began to massage her scalp. 'What's the deal with your middle name?' he asked, to distract her.

'Aroha?' Danny's eyes drifted closed. She tilted her head to give Ross better access to the sensitive spot behind her left ear. Ross trailed his fingertips across her neck to her ear. Danny sighed. 'It means "love" in Maori.'

He stroked his thumb behind her ear.

Her eyes flew open. What on earth was she doing? She batted his hand away and sprang to her feet. 'This isn't over, Fabello.'

'Tell me something I don't know,' Ross said dryly.

'Leave Jarvis Wainwright alone, d'you hear me? He's my neighbour. I rely on him for help.'

'You can rely on me.'

'Don't be stupid,' Danny scoffed. 'When you get bored with yanking my chain, you'll disappear into the sunset.'

'I'm not Pat.' He was sick of saying it, sick of trying to convince her.

'And you're not Jarvis Wainwright. He wants to marry me; you just want to piss me off.'

Suddenly it no longer seemed imperative that Ross get back to the States asap. *Suddenly* it seemed far more important he stay right where he was.

'While we're on the subject of who's pissing off whom,' Ross snapped, 'the next time you feel the need to catch an eyeful, go rent yourself a blue movie.'

Danny eventually had to do a night shift, which meant leaving Ross in charge of the children overnight. She tried to get Deryl to stay, but she refused, which was probably just as well, because Ross said he'd strangle Deryl with her knee-highs if he had to spend a night with her in the house. Danny knew Ross was angry because she wouldn't trust him with the children, but the truth was Danny didn't want to start relying on him.

'You're just being difficult.'

'Damn right. Now do us a favour and leave us alone.'

'You won't be so cocky at three o'clock in the morning when Mia has a bad dream or wets the bed.'

'Mia will be just fine,' Ross insisted, with more confidence than he felt.

Danny's words came back to haunt him just after midnight. He'd scored himself a night in a real bed by bribing Matt to sleep in Danny's room. Ross felt just as uneasy about using her bed as he did about sleeping in Daniella's old room. He was lying beneath Matt's red-and-black Holden bedcovers, listening to the rain spattering against the window pane and the wind whistling around the old house, reading *How I Got My Shrunken Head* when Mia appeared at the bedroom door. She was rubbing her stomach through her pink Bratz nightdress and looking miserable.

Ross lowered his book. 'What's up, Mia?'

'I've got a tummy ache,' she whimpered.

He climbed from the bed, convinced Mia was just feeling insecure and missing Danny, confident he could handle this minor glitch and show Auntie Danny a thing or three.

'How about I put you back to bed and, before you know it, it'll be morning and Auntie Danny will be home from work?'

Mia shook her head. 'I've got a tummy ache!'

'Honey, if you go back to bed you'll forget all about your tummy ache and soon be asleep.'

She took a deep breath, widened her eyes and threw up all over Ross's feet.

'Aw, shit!' What was it with the females in this family and hurling all over his feet?

Mia burst into noisy tears.

'Sorry, Mia. I wasn't yelling at you, honey.'

Ross's heart sank right along with the puke running down Mia's nightdress and between his toes. He cleaned her up, washed off his feet, and put her to bed with her favourite doll. She promptly sat up and threw up all over the bedcovers, and Ross had to start all over again.

'I — huh — want — Auntie — huh— Danny!' Mia sobbed.

Ross held her on his lap. 'Auntie Danny's at work, sweetheart. I'll take care of you.'

A quick check of the clock revealed it was only 1.15 a.m., which meant Danny wouldn't be home for hours. Ross reminded himself that kids got sick and threw up all the time, but as the night wore on and Mia vomited twice more he decided it wouldn't hurt to call his mother just in case.

It proved to be his second big mistake of the night.

Breda panicked and started talking about appendicitis and food poisoning. Ross couldn't believe what he was hearing. Nothing short of a missing limb had been considered a good enough reason for his mother to allow him or his siblings to stay home from school. The thought of Mia being sick had Breda preparing to donate a kidney.

'Have you phoned a doctor?' she cried.

'No. It's three o'clock in the morning here, Ma. And she's asleep now.'

'Are you sure she's asleep and not unconscious?' Ross heard her yelling, 'Vittorio! Vittorio! Little Mia has appendicitis!'

'I really don't think it's appendicitis, Ma. Just a bug.'

'Have you checked Matt? Is he unconscious?'

Vito came on the line, yelling. 'The kids are unconscious? Call an ambulance, Ross!'

Ross pinched the bridge of his nose between his thumb and fingers and groaned.

'Who groaned then? Was that Mia I heard groaning?' his mother shouted.

'No. That was me.'

'Stop doing that, Ross! Are you trying to give me a heart attack? If you can't call the doctor, then call Danny and get her to come home right away!'

Ross looked at Mia sleeping peacefully in her bed. 'You're fading, Ma. I keep losing you.'

'What? Ross? ROSS, CAN YOU HEAR ME?'

He hung up and called Aoife, who listened impatiently. 'Has she got a fever?'

'I don't know. I haven't got a thermometer.'

'You don't need a thermometer, you idiot. Feel her forehead. Does she feel hot?'

Ross wished he'd called Annie instead. Aoife, like Danny, was the evil twin. 'She doesn't feel hot.'

'What's she doing at the moment?'

'Sleeping.'

'Well leave the poor kid alone! Don't wake her up!'

'You told me to feel her forehead!'

Aoife ignored him. 'When's Danny due home?'

Ross was infuriated by his family's assumption he couldn't manage. 'Not for a few more hours. I can cope with one sick kid, you know.'

Aoife sniffed. 'Just encourage her to drink and keep emptying the bucket.' She hung up.

Ross spent the rest of the night huddled in the cramped little chair beside Mia's bed, sleeping off and on, waking abruptly when his head slipped off his fist or fell backwards and nearly dislocated his neck.

Mia threw up once more, this time managing to hit him right in the face. Ross changed her pyjamas and bedding and himself, and even put on a load of washing in an attempt to keep on top of the towering pyramid collecting in the laundry. He got Mia to take a few sips of water, wiped her mouth and face with a wet washcloth, and counted the minutes until Danny came home.

Matt stopped in the doorway on his way back from the bathroom at around 6 a.m.

'Don't come in here.' Ross tried to ignore the cramping in his stomach. 'Mia's sick.'

'What's wrong with her?'

'She's been throwing up.'

Matt was unsurprised. 'It was that frog you gave us for dinner.'

'I was only joking when I said it was frog,' Ross replied weakly.

'It was chicken.' *Third* big mistake of the night.

Matt was unconvinced. 'I didn't eat any, but you and Mia did.' He peered at Ross. 'You don't look so good.'

'I'm fine,' Ross lied. 'Now, go back to bed.'

He didn't feel fine. He felt like shit. His stomach was clenching and unfurling again like a glove puppet. Sweat had broken out on his forehead from the effort of trying not to throw up.

Mia had just woken up again and was demanding to know where her doll was when Ross heard Danny's car pull up. He was going hot and cold and trying to decide if he could make it to the red bucket by the side of Mia's bed. He heard Matt greet Danny at the front door and announce that Mia was sick because Uncle Ross had fed her frog.

Ross was beyond caring.

Danny appeared in the doorway of the bedroom, dressed in her ugly blue uniform. Her practised gaze took in Mia's pale little face — and Ross's even paler one.

'Busy night?' she asked.

'Uncle Ross fed me frog, Auntie Danny, and I threw up!' Mia cried piteously. 'I threw up all over Dolly and I want her back!'

'It was chicken not frog, and her doll is in the dryer.' Ross gulped and inched forwards on the chair, his eyes glued to the red bucket. Danny snatched it up and shoved it under his face just in time.

Mia nodded. 'Uncle Ross ate the frog, too.'

Chapter 14

There was no choice but to put Ross into Nella's bed. He was so ill that Danny almost carried him there. Despite his best efforts, Ross couldn't make it to the bathroom and had to give in and use the red bucket, which Mia no longer needed.

After Danny had emptied it for the fourth time in as many hours, she entered the bedroom with two white bullets cupped in the palm of her hand. 'Ross?'

He grunted.

'These will make you feel better.'

'I can't.' He looked at the contents of her hand and recoiled. 'If I swallow anything it'll come right back up again.'

'You don't swallow them.'

Ross rolled his head on the pillow and looked at the little wax pellets. Danny held up a sachet of KY gel in her other hand. His eyes widened in horror. 'Nobody's shoving anything up my ass!'

'*Nobody* was offering. You can do it yourself.' Danny placed the gel and suppositories on the bedside table. 'They're painkillers. It's up to you — if you want to be a hero, you're an even bigger idiot than I thought.'

His head fell back against the pillows. 'Your bedside manner sucks, Lawton.'

'My patients usually get better, Fabello.'

'Of course they do,' Ross said weakly. 'How else would they get away from you?' He rolled his head restlessly on the pillows. 'The

Walking School Bus: I can't do it.'

'It's all sorted,' Danny soothed. 'Robyn and the other parents send their best. Now be a good boy and take your medication.'

Ross wasn't a good patient, although he tried his best. He could see how tired Danny was, and having to look after him and Mia had deprived her of some much-needed sleep following her night shift at the hospital. Mia was back to her old self within a day and a half, which made Ross feel even worse. Danny put Mia in bed with him for a brief spell on the first day so she could clean Mia's bedroom.

Mia cuddled her doll and eyed Ross pensively. 'Is your tummy sore?'

'Uh huh.' And his ass, his back, his head and just about everywhere in between, but the suppositories Danny had given him were helping. 'What about you?'

Mia lifted her pyjama top and rubbed her hand across her belly. 'It's all bubbly and gurgly.'

Ross closed his eyes, hoping Mia would take the hint and leave him in peace.

'You look like Daddy.'

He cracked an eyelid at her. 'I do?'

She reached over and rubbed her index finger through the stubble on Ross's cheek. 'Daddy had a hairy face in the morning.' Her eyes drifted to the white T-shirt covering Ross's chest. 'He had a hairy chest, too.' She paused. 'You've got hair on your chest.'

'Yeah, and so does your Grandpa Vito.'

Mia wriggled closer and peered into his face. 'Are you really Daddy's brother?'

Ross watched her through his lashes. 'Yes.'

She looked doubtful. 'But you've got browny black eyes.'

At this rate he'd end up with a complex. If Mia mentioned one word about serial killers or the size of his nose, Ross would rise up out of the bed and clobber her aunt with the goddamned bucket. He had dark brown eyes — women had even called them sexy. But that was hardly the kind of thing he could confess to an eight-year-old girl. 'I've got brown eyes like your Grandpa Vito; your daddy had the same colour eyes as your Granny Breda.'

Mia watched him over the top of her dolly. 'Like mine?'

'Like yours.'

'And Matt's?'

Ross nodded.

Mia wanted to know what colour eyes all of her aunts and cousins had. Like most men, Ross didn't pay an awful lot of attention to eye colour.

Mia was unimpressed. 'You're not very good, are you?'

'I'm doing my best.'

She pressed her warm little body against his side and tucked her feet beneath his leg as if she'd known him for years. Ross frowned at the ceiling, shaken by how trusting Mia was, his lids drifting shut, lulled by the small, warm body curled against him and the unaccustomed weariness of illness.

Mia suddenly whispered, 'This is Mummy's bed.'

Ross's eyes flew open. 'I know.'

'She went to sleep one night and we couldn't wake her up in the morning.'

It felt like his Adam's apple was suddenly forcing its way out of his throat. Ross swallowed convulsively.

'She'd been sick for a long time. We all looked after her — Auntie Danny and me and Matt and Van and Deryl and Lloyd. But the doctors and nurses couldn't make her better.'

Ross nodded and stared hard at the ceiling.

'Auntie Danny used to sleep in here, too, so she was there if Mummy needed anything in the night, but when she woke up that morning Mummy didn't need anything because she'd died.'

Ross could picture it. Danny waking up in this very bed and finding her sister cold and still beside her. He didn't think he could have borne it. How had Danny? How had any of them? He hugged Mia and kissed the top of her silky blonde hair.

She rested her pointed little chin on his chest and stared at Ross with large, serious blue eyes. 'Mummy had cancer.' She wriggled her hand between them and touched her flat little chest. 'In her breast.'

'I know,' Ross said softly.

Mia frowned. 'Did Daddy get cancer, too? Is that why he died?'

'No. He had an accident and fell off a boat.'

It sounded a lot better than saying he got shit-faced drunk, hit his head and drowned. Ross hoped Pat had been unconscious — the alternative gave him nightmares.

Mia regarded him silently for several long moments. 'Men haven't got breasts, only ladies.'

'That's right.' Ross wondered where this was leading.

'Auntie Danny's got breasts.' Mia stared at him with big, frightened eyes.

She couldn't have spelled out her fears any more clearly. Ross's heart felt like a piece of paper being screwed into a ball. 'I'm sure Auntie Danny takes real good care of herself, honey. She's a nurse, so she knows all about that kind of thing.'

Did she? Did she take care of herself?

Ross intended to find out, although how he went about asking a woman about her breasts without being naked in bed with her was going to be a challenge. But considering their recent conversations about suppositories, Ross decided it might not be such an unreasonable question after all.

He wasn't up to thinking about Danny's breasts for the next couple of days, let alone discussing them. As soon as the effect of the suppositories wore off, he felt terrible.

When Mia offered to give a performance of some of the songs from her Destiny's Child CD to help Uncle Ross feel better, Danny suggested she save it for another time. Ross was surprised she'd passed up such a golden opportunity. Mia's performances required several stiff drinks and a set of earplugs to make them bearable — the kid couldn't hold a tune in a bucket.

Ross watched Mia leaping about on the trampoline through the bedroom window. 'Look at her. It isn't fair,' he complained as Danny returned from emptying the bucket. Ross was always at his worst just after he'd been sick, because for a few brief moments he felt marginally better and had the energy to complain.

'She's a kid. They bounce back in no time.'

'I'm not exactly in my dotage.'

'You're an old fart by comparison. Now stop moaning and finish your barley water.'

'What's the point? It'll only come back up again.'

Danny began to lower the bedcovers.

Ross clung to them like a frightened virgin. 'What are you doing?'

She tried to pull the covers from his hands. 'Let me see.'

He tightened his grip. 'You've seen it!'

'Not *that*, you moron, I want to check how dehydrated you are.'

'Looking at my johnson will tell you how dehydrated I am?'

Ross looked so shocked that Danny began to laugh. She flipped down the cover and gently pinched his abdomen between her thumb and forefinger and let it go again. 'No, but that did.' She eyed him thoughtfully. 'If you don't stop vomiting soon you'll need intravenous fluids.'

Ross grabbed his barley water.

Danny smiled approvingly. 'There's a good boy.'

He sipped slowly and grumbled, 'I thought nursing was

supposed to be the caring profession.'

Ross was awakened a while later by the sound of air brakes outside the house then a knock on the front door. A few moments later Danny stalked past the doorway followed by two men, each holding an end of the plastic-wrapped sofa bed that Ross had forgotten to tell her about. Two armchairs and an ottoman joined it in the living room. When the delivery men had departed, Danny came to stand at the foot of the bed with her arms folded and her lips pursed. 'I don't recall asking you to buy any furniture.'

'It was a surprise,' Ross said.

'Try again, Ross.'

'I wasn't spending another night on that sorry excuse for a sofa.'

Danny narrowed her eyes. 'Have you bought anything else?'

'No,' he lied.

'Are you sure about that? Because now wouldn't be a good time to get on my wrong side, Fabello.'

'You'd kick a man when he's down?'

'Not just any man: *you*.' Danny tapped her fingers on her arm and hummed a few bars of music. 'I'm waiting.'

Ross was starting to recognize the tune. It was a danger sign. 'Joe is coming on Wednesday to help me rip out the bathroom,' he blurted.

'Oh, is he?'

'You said you wanted the place repaired. It's OK, I asked Lloyd and Deryl and we can use their bathroom until everything's up and running again.'

Ross decided to close his eyes and play dead before she killed him. Concerned about the memories he might have stirred up for Danny by looking after another sick person in her sister's old bedroom, he had decided that now probably wasn't a good time to ask about breast checks. She was a darned sight better to have around than his mother or his sisters, who fussed and compared the symptoms of friends or acquaintances who'd usually died from whatever it was he had. Ross recalled arguing with his mother that nobody died from an ingrown toenail.

'As God is my witness, Una Docherty most certainly did,' Breda declared. *'No matter how often a pitcher goes to the water, it's broken in the end.'*

What Danny lacked in sympathy she made up for in quiet, no-nonsense efficiency. She had the unique ability to know when to help and when to leave him alone. Ross enjoyed the touch of her cool, practised hands, and soon got over his embarrassment about her emptying his bucket. Danny didn't have any cryptic, moronic insights to offer up. She dealt in fact and was blunt to the point of rudeness.

'Don't be stupid, Fabello,' she told Ross witheringly when he wanted to walk to the toilet the first day he was ill. 'You'll fall flat on your face and then I'll have to lift your sorry carcass off the floor. Do me a favour and puke in the bucket.'

He continued to draw the line at her giving him the suppositories. 'You seen one bum, you seen 'em all.'

Ross felt his face heat. 'Not this bum.'

'My God! Did you just *blush*?'

He *did* blush when Danny gave him a bed bath.

'What's that for?' Ross asked when she carried a bowl, soap and towels into the bedroom after dropping the kids at school.

'Everything I need to make a nuclear bomb. What does it look like?' she asked sarcastically. 'You need a wash.'

'No, I don't.'

'Yes, you do. You stink, Ross.'

Ross sniffed beneath the sheet. She had a point. 'I'll have a shower.' He attempted to sit up, but his head swam and he fell back again.

'Exactly.' Danny went to fill the bowl with water.

Ross suffered through the bed bath in tortured silence; first, because he was embarrassed by how helpless he was, and later because he got hard. He couldn't understand it. How come his dick was feeling so chipper when the rest of him was dying? Why wasn't that dehydrated, too? Danny's touch felt like a caress, winding his nerves and groin tighter and tighter. Under normal circumstances Ross would have known exactly how to deal with the situation, but these weren't normal circumstances. This was *Danny*. He must be misreading the signals she seemed to be sending, but Ross was adept at reading those kinds of signals. He cleared his throat uneasily. 'I can do the rest.'

'It's OK.' She soaped the cloth and began to wash his abdomen.

Ross pushed her hand away. 'I said I'll do it.'

'I'm not offering to wash that, I was just going to do your abdo—' Danny's eyes snagged on the tent pole lifting the sheet from his hips. 'Oh.'

Ross watched her through his lashes. 'Now who's blushing?'

Danny felt like tipping the water over her head. *What* was she doing? This was Ross, who barged into her life, turned it upside-down, and drove her mad. She dropped the soapy cloth into the washbowl and stood up.

'What's the matter? Seen one penis, you've seen 'em all.'

All the moisture seemed to disappear from Danny's mouth and reappear between her legs.

Her silence shamed him. 'Don't take it personally.'

Danny was furious. Don't take it personally! What was she? A troll? When she'd been sandwiched between him and a bar not so long ago Ross had wanted her to take it very personally. She left him to it and hurried from the room. Patrick used to be able to make Nella melt into a puddle with just a look; they'd disappear into the bedroom for the rest of the day. Danny had been part-disgusted and part-envious. What was it like to feel the passion and hunger she'd glimpsed on Nella and Patrick's faces before they disappeared behind the bedroom door? But allowing a man to become that important had weakened her mother and her sister. She'd never allow it to happen to her.

Matt was convinced that Ross's illness could be blamed on him eating frog. When he felt up to arguing that he hadn't cooked frog for dinner, Ross decided he'd improved enough to get out of bed and make contact with the outside world. Unfortunately, Danny had confiscated his laptop and only gave back his mobile phone when she began to receive calls from his family requesting progress reports.

She came to change the sheets on the bed and complain. 'Your family are all mad. Some old lady called this morning asking for Rory — I could hardly understand a word she was saying. It took me a while to realize she was asking for you, and when I asked if she wanted to speak to Ross she just kept shouting *"Rory! Rory! Rory!"* in the thickest Irish accent I've ever heard, and complaining to somebody called Fintan that she'd got the wrong number and they didn't speak English.'

Ross was sitting in the bentwood rocking chair beside the bed. Danny had been at the hair mascara again (lavender and violet today), she had a hole in the seat of her cut-off pants (orange with purple flowers), and, as usual, she was bra-less beneath her crop top (once turquoise, but now a sickly pale blue).

'That would be Granny O'Rourke. If you hadn't taken my phone away in the first place, you wouldn't have to speak to any of them.' He sifted through the debris of crumpled tissues, water glasses, two of Mia's felt-pen drawings, and one of Matt's books on the bedside table. 'I can't find the lead.'

Danny retrieved the lead, plugged the phone in, and began stripping the sheets from the bed. 'Why does Granny O'Rourke call you "Rory"?'

Ross stared at the hole in Danny's pants as she leaned across the bed. She was wearing white panties. 'It's a long story.' He looked up as she shook out a sheet and sent it floating across the mattress.

'I've got all day.'

And I could spend all day watching your breasts move when you do that.

He let her worm out of him that his mother and grandmother had had a violent disagreement about his name when he was born. Breda Fabello had been reading the Poldark novels and wanted to name him Ross. Concepta O'Rourke declared Rory was better and refused to call her new grandson anything else. The ongoing battle between Breda and her mother was just another page in the bizarre family history of the Fabellos and the O'Rourkes.

'Don't you get confused?' Danny asked.

'My Irish relatives call me Rory, and besides,' he shrugged, 'I don't like to hurt the old girl's feelings.'

Ross didn't know why watching Danny make his bed made him feel so horny. Whenever they were home together, he knew pretty much where she was, as if he had a sensing device beneath his skin attuned to her presence. Ross knew he needed to get out more, and after the episode with the bed bath he told himself he needed to get laid.

Ross recalled Jeff's offer to fix him up with one of Christine's cousins when Jeff and Christine and their little boy, JJ, paid a surprise visit the following day. Danny showed them out to where Ross was sitting in the sunshine in one of two Cape Cod chairs on the part of the verandah he'd repaired. He was wearing an old pair of khaki shorts, a faded blue Nirvana T-shirt, and a white cap with *San Diego Chargers* written on it in blue pulled low on his forehead. His feet were bare, his chin covered in stubble, and he looked totally relaxed.

Ross was so engrossed in his writing that it was several moments before he realized he had visitors. He grinned and set his laptop on the wooden deck. 'What are you doing here?' he asked, climbing to his feet.

'We've come to view the remains,' Jeff said.

Christine swatted him on the arm. 'Don't be so horrible.' She leaned up to kiss Ross, but he stopped her.

'Much as it pains me to turn down kisses from a beautiful woman, you'd better not, Chris. I only stopped being sick yesterday, and Florence Nightingale here is still treating me as if I've got the plague.' Ross offered his chair, but Chris sat on the faded sun lounger, with JJ in her lap.

Danny discreetly checked out Jeff Roseman's wife.

She was a slim, dark-haired Maori woman in her early thirties, with large brown eyes, beautiful olive skin and sweeping dark hair. She looked fresh and lovely in a simple melon-coloured shift and delicate gold sandals. Danny felt like a heifer beside her in an old pair of tobacco-brown Capri pants, a shapeless orange T-shirt with *I Make This Look Good* on the front, and bare feet.

Ross made the introductions.

Christine admired Danny's hair. 'Is it a colour?'

'Hair mascara,' Ross said. 'Although in an emergency you can't go past a Magic Marker.'

Danny ignored him. 'Would you like a coffee? A glass of wine? Or a beer?'

'A coffee would be lovely.' Christine handed JJ to Jeff. 'I'll help.'

'There's really no need,' Danny said.

'No, I want to.'

Jeff bounced his drooling son on his knee and smiled warmly at Danny. 'I'll have a beer, please, Danny.'

Ross looked at him sharply. There was something about the way Jeff spoke to Danny that indicated familiarity, which was strange considering they hadn't set eyes on one another since she'd trashed the truck at the hospital. 'I'll have a beer, too, please?'

'No, you won't,' Danny replied, as she headed into the house with Christine. 'See if you can keep down lunch first.'

Ross sat down scowling.

Jeff laughed. 'So has being sick got you off the sofa?'

'For the time being.' He eyed Jeff curiously. 'Who told you I'd been sick?'

'Danny.'

Ross stared. 'Danny?'

Jeff changed the subject to the San Diego Chargers. He held JJ's sticky little hands as JJ levered himself to his feet and bounced up and down on his father's thighs. JJ looked across at Ross and beamed.

Ross smiled and winked at him.

Danny saw him do it as she and Christine returned carrying two trays, with coffees, Jeff's beer, a plate of cheese and crackers, and a bowl containing Ross's lunch. Christine burst out laughing when she saw what Danny had made him. Danny handed around the food and drinks and sat down on the sun lounger beside Chris.

Ross stared into his bowl. It looked like the stuff his sisters fed their babies when they started eating solids. He watched JJ gumming away on a piece of cheese and wondered if there'd been a mistake. 'What's this?'

'Semolina,' Danny replied. 'It's my speciality — aside from porridge, of course.'

Ross eyed her sourly and gestured to the cheese and crackers.

'Why can't I have those?'

'Perhaps for dinner, once we know you can keep the semolina down.'

If she added 'there's a good boy', Ross vowed Danny would be wearing the semolina.

The distant sound of the phone ringing within the house brought Danny to her feet, and she excused herself to answer it.

Ross couldn't work it out. Considering she had totalled one of Jeff's trucks, he'd expected Danny to be uncomfortable around Jeff, but she was all sweetness and light. He looked at Jeff. 'Since when have you two been friends?'

Jeff sat JJ on his lap to retie his tiny shoe. 'Since I offered her a job.'

The baby clasped his father's forearms in his little hands and watched with fascination.

'You did what?'

'I offered Danny a job.'

'Why?'

'Things aren't progressing as smoothly at the hospital as I'd like. I approached the hospital management and we agreed it's in everyone's best interests to set up a project management team made up of the site foreman, one of my engineers, and one of the senior members of the Emergency Department staff to coordinate things. Danny is ideal.'

Christine took JJ from Jeff. 'I wish I could say I felt the same way about Lance Ashburn.'

Jeff looked annoyed. 'He made a mistake, Christine. It's time to move on. He's a damned good engineer.'

'Who's Lance Ashburn?' Ross demanded. 'And what do you mean he made a mistake?'

'He got drunk at last year's Christmas party and things got a little out of hand,' Jeff said briskly. 'Do you think you'll be up and about—'

'Out of hand!' Christine cried. 'You call having sex with the wife of one of our biggest clients in the scoop of a digger a little out of hand?'

Ross's black eyes skewered Jeff. 'Tell me she's kidding.'

He shrugged and pulled a face.

'We were lucky her husband didn't find out. Everyone else saw Lance's bare backside and her legs in the air,' Christine said in disgust. 'He can't keep his pants on at the best of times, so do you really think he's the best choice for a hospital with all those nurses to distract him?'

'He's a damned good engineer!' Jeff repeated.

Christine snorted.

Ross didn't know what bothered him more, his friend offering Danny a job, or Danny accepting and working with this Lance guy. 'I don't want Danny working for you. Find somebody else.'

'Whatever's going on between you and Danny is your business, but it's my business to ensure the hospital upgrade is completed on budget and on schedule and that's what I'm going to do.'

'Thanks a lot. Buddy.'

'It's nothing personal, Ross.'

'Knowing Danny, she'll turn you down flat.'

'Too late, she's already accepted.'

Danny was thrilled about her new job. When the call came summoning her to a meeting with hospital management, she was terrified she was going to be sacked because she'd taken more time off to look after Ross and Mia. It was just as well she was sitting down when the hospital manager explained Jeff Roseman's proposal, otherwise she'd probably have collapsed. It meant regular nine-to-five hours until the building work was completed.

When Danny expressed concern about losing the extra money that working afternoon and night shifts earned her, she was told this had already been addressed and she wouldn't be out of pocket.

'The manager of the Emergency Department would appreciate it if you'd be available to work the occasional shift, but only if it doesn't conflict with the hours you'll be contracted to work with the construction engineer and site foreman.'

Danny could live with that.

She could *definitely* live with that. What she couldn't figure out was why Jeff Roseman had specifically asked for her. He was Ross's friend and Danny had written off one of his company vehicles. The old adage don't look a gift horse in the mouth kept springing to mind — and it was about time some good luck came her and the kids' way.

Danny met with John Miller, the new site foreman, and Lance Ashburn, the engineer in charge of the development.

She liked Miller and his abrupt manner and lack of small talk. *He* would never leave a truck blocking the entrance to the ambulance bay.

Lance Ashburn was an entirely different story. He was tall, buff, blond and blue-eyed, and wore immaculately laundered jeans with a knife-edge crease. The crease alone made Danny's brows rise, but it was Ashburn's casual assumption that every woman he met thought he was God's gift that really irritated her.

She'd taken the opportunity to interrogate Christine Roseman when they were in the kitchen, and Christine had reassured her Lance had two saving graces: he was good at his job, and he didn't have a nasty bone in his body.

'He seems a bit of a doofus,' Danny said.

Christine shrugged. 'He is when it comes to women, but anything to do with construction and the man is a wizard. You'll just have to pull him into line whenever his mind wanders, and believe me it will with all those nurses to distract him. The good news is that John Miller and Lance are absolute perfectionists about their work, and if you have any problems you can always call Jeff.'

Danny thought about what Christine had said when she recalled her first meeting with Lance.

'Would you like to go out to dinner?' he asked, as soon as the meeting concluded.

Danny regarded him with surprise. 'No.'

Lance's confident smile slipped. 'No?' He was bewildered. 'Why not?'

'Because I don't want to.'

Lance stared at Danny as if he expected her to change her mind. 'You mean you really don't want to go out with me?'

'I really, really don't want to go out with you.'

'Oh.'

Danny hadn't been home long when Jeff and Christine arrived to see Ross, and so she hadn't had time to tell Ross about her new job and was disappointed when Jeff stole her thunder. She called Vanessa to tell her about the job and Lance and his amazing ego, hoping it might make her laugh and go some way towards repairing the rift in their relationship since the photos of her and Ross had come out.

'You played *that* very close to your chest, Daneka,' Vanessa said when she saw them. 'Didn't you think you could trust me to keep a secret?'

'There was no secret to keep!' Danny protested. 'I kissed him! I was drunk!'

Vanessa didn't buy her explanation. 'You didn't have a hangover when you came to pick up the kids. Is he really sleeping on the sofa?'

Vanessa wasn't the only one who thought Danny was sleeping

with Ross. Jane Clifford was pea-green with envy. 'You are so lucky! Do you think you could get him to autograph my books?'

'Jane, I know you're a big fan and all that,' Danny picked up a patient file from the walking-wounded stack, 'but he's just like every other man. He leaves the toilet seat up, scratches his balls when he gets up in the morning, and has a thing about socks going missing in the wash.'

'Who *cares* about the toilet seat?' Jane retorted. 'He's *RF O'Rourke!*' She stepped closer to Danny. 'Is he as hot as he looks?'

Danny flushed. 'How would I know? He's my brother-in-law.'

'You know he scratches his balls in the morning,' Jane pointed out.

'He doesn't! I was only joking when I said that!'

Gabby Morgan, a pretty young nurse who was new to the department, said, 'I've got a brother-in-law, but I've never snogged him. What's this about a sock fetish?'

Danny regretted saying anything. It had taken the arrival of photographers with telephoto lenses outside the house to make her understand the lengths people would go to get photos and information about Ross. There was money to be made out of RF O'Rourke.

'He doesn't have a sock fetish. He just ties his socks together before he washes them.'

'RF O'Rourke does *laundry*?' Gabby asked incredulously.

Danny didn't dare mention the cooking.

Chapter 15

After he'd recovered, Ross didn't offer to move out of Nella's room and Danny didn't ask. She secretly preferred seeing the room looking messy and lived-in again — Ross's presence helped erase some of the bad memories it held for her and the children.

Sleeping in Nella's room surrounded by her possessions fed Ross's current obsession about twins.

Wanda couldn't wait for Ross to send her more chapters of the draft manuscript. 'I don't think I've ever seen you write so well from the female perspective, Ross. You've gotten right under the skin of the two sisters. There are some interesting photos circulating of you and a girl with blue hair at the Findlays party,' she added. If Wanda had seen the photos, the odds were his mother and sisters soon would. 'What were you thinking? I couldn't believe what I was seeing.'

Wanda had seen before a side of Ross he kept tucked away from public view. When her fourth husband had died unexpectedly a few years ago, Ross had supported Wanda through the difficult days that followed. Louis had been the love of her life, the only one of her husbands with whom she'd been truly happy.

'I wasn't thinking at all. When I'm with Danny I don't think, I just react.'

'Ah.' Wanda tactfully changed the subject. 'Don't forget you'll need to be back here at the end of November for the John Doe publicity and premiere.'

Days of back-to-back interviews in a multitude of cities wasn't Ross's idea of fun, but there was no avoiding it. Wanda had also mentioned spots on *Oprah* and *David Letterman*. He'd far rather spend the time arguing with Danny and fixing the roof of her house. Ross worried that if he was gone for too long he'd lose any ground he'd gained. Finally, though, he called his parents to let them know he was coming home.

'I've seen those photos in the magazines,' Vito said. 'You seemed to be getting on good in one — not so good in the other. Things better now you've moved into the house?'

'I'm ripping out the bathroom.'

'Good! Good! I told your mother you'd make things right. She's a pretty girl, Ross.'

'Yes,' he agreed cautiously.

'I could tell from those photos you sent to your mother and me.'

'The photos I sent you were of Daniella, the children's mother.'

'I know that, but they're matching twins, aren't they? Like Annie and Aoife?'

Vito never referred to twins as identical but matching.

'Yes, but—'

'So, you seen one you seen the other. Yes, she's a pretty girl,' Vito repeated. 'Blonde, like your mother.'

No, *blue* at the moment.

'Your mother wants to talk to you.'

There was a clatter as the phone was dropped, and Ross could hear his parents arguing.

'She's a lovely-looking wee lass, isn't she, Ross?' Breda said. 'I was only saying to your father when we looked at the photos: "Vito, she's a lovely looking wee lass" I said.'

Ross pressed his thumb and index finger against his eyelids. 'Who?'

'Why little Mia, of course,' Breda replied innocently. 'Who else would I mean?'

There was nothing innocent about his mother. In another life she would have been masterminding bank robberies.

'It was a good idea to move in with Danny.'

'I've moved in with Danny *and* the children.'

'Is she a midwife, too, Ross?'

'Who? Mia?'

'Show a few manners when you're talking to your mother. You won't have me forever, you know.'

If St Peter had any sense he'd lock the Pearly Gates the moment he heard Breda Fabello was shuffling off the mortal coil.

'Are you a midwife?' he asked Danny.

'No. Why?' she asked. 'Are you pregnant?'

Danny seemed to be preoccupied with the new job. A gruff-voiced guy called John and a smooth, oily-sounding jerk who had to be Lance Ashburn sometimes called her at home.

'You should be careful around Ashburn,' Ross said.

She raised her brows. 'Really? Why's that?'

'He's got a reputation.'

'For what?'

'Ask Christine,' Ross replied tersely.

'Maybe I will. Or maybe I'll ask Lance.'

Ross felt like kicking himself for being such an idiot. When had Danny ever listened to anything he said? It was a sure-fire way to make her do the opposite. He was still fuming later that afternoon as he and Joe clambered about the roof assessing the rust. Joe was working for Ross almost fulltime now, and they got along well. Joe saw the funny side of everything and had a skin like a rhino, so Ross's moody growls bounced right off him. Ross enjoyed Joe's sense of humour and the fact he didn't give a rat's ass who Ross was. Joe thought the paparazzi outside the house were a huge joke, and kept asking them if they wanted to take his photo.

'Who're you?' one of the photographers asked.

'The plumber.' Joe grinned cheekily, displaying the wide gap between his upper incisors.

'Can you get me an interview with RF O'Rourke?'

'No. But if you've ever got a blocked toilet, I'm your man.'

'Hey, Ross,' Joe pointed across the rolling green paddocks, 'aren't those your sheep?'

Ross shaded his eyes against the glare from the sun. It was a baking hot day and sweat was dripping from his hair and down his nose. He remained unimpressed with Auckland weather. Today was like the middle of summer, but tomorrow it could be pouring with rain. Ross watched as two woolly shapes, one black, one grey, trotted up a hill in the direction of Jarvis Wainwright's place. A quick check of the garden below revealed that Persil and Charcoal were missing and part of the fence was down.

Ross swore and threw his hammer over the fence and into the paddock.

'Hey, bro?'

'What?' Ross snapped.

Joe nodded at a photographer aiming a telephoto lens at them. 'I think he just got a photo of you chucking that hammer.'

Ross's description of what he was going to do to the photographer when he got hold of him made Joe laugh so hard that he had to climb down from the roof.

The phone was already ringing when Ross stormed into the kitchen to call Jarvis about the sheep.

'Is Danny there?' Jarvis asked.

'No, she's at work.'

'I've got your sheep.'

'I know, I—'

'I promised Danny I'd shear them for her, so I might as well do it while they're here. You be sure to tell her.'

'I will, Jarvis, thanks a lo—'

'Don't need any thanks from you,' Jarvis said brusquely. 'I'm doing it for *her*. You can pick 'em up in half an hour.'

'Pick them up? How?'

'That's your big, fancy four-wheel drive parked outside Danny's house, isn't it? 'Bout time you got some mud on it.'

One of the photographers couldn't believe his luck when he got an even better shot than his colleague, who'd prudently left when RF O'Rourke climbed off the roof with murder in his eyes. Pictures of the reclusive writer clambering about a roof, stripped to the waist, would sell like hotcakes to the women's magazines, but a photograph of RF O'Rourke driving his immaculate dark-green SUV with two sheep sitting on the back seat while their chauffeur cursed a blue streak was priceless. The photographer beat a hasty retreat when O'Rourke launched himself from the driver's seat, snarling.

Ross had had enough of Danny Lawton, her sheep and her demented neighbours. He called Jeff and asked him to arrange a date with Christine's cousin.

'Selena's smart, talented and attractive. She's great company,' Jeff told him.

'Just promise me she's not a stalker, has all her own teeth and hair, and isn't a George Clooney fan,' Ross said.

'Selena's sane and I think her teeth are her own. But I can't answer for George Clooney. Even Chris has got a thing about him. I'll get her to call you with Selena's number.'

After the first week working with Lance Ashburn, Danny knew she'd made a mistake spurning his invitation because it only seemed to encourage him. Chris and Jeff were right: he was a good engineer, which made up for his other shortcomings. If he weren't so good, she'd probably have clobbered Lance with his cylinder of drawings. Danny pointed him in the direction of some of the other nurses in the Emergency Department, but Lance was like a boomerang — he just kept coming back. She even tried to throw him Vanessa's way, but Vanessa insisted she made it a rule never to date anybody who was prettier than she was.

'Did I do something to offend you, Daneka?' Lance kept asking. He never called her Danny.

'No. But if you keep on hounding me I'm going to do something I'll regret, like tripping you into the concrete foundations. What about Gabby, the nurse I introduced you to — she's really nice. Why don't you ask her out?'

'Maybe some other time.' Lance took it for granted that Gabby would be available when he wanted her.

Danny shook her head in disgust. 'You are a piece of work.'

'I am?' he said cautiously.

'Most definitely, Lance.'

Lance was baffled and also fascinated. He'd seen the photos and read the story about Danny and RF O'Rourke in one of the women's magazines, and didn't believe for one second that the guy was just her brother-in-law. Which made Daneka Lawton a challenge, and Lance could never resist one of those . . .

On Saturday night, the children were watching television in the living room and Ross was in his room getting ready to go out when the phone rang.

Danny sat at the kitchen table, reading the newspaper. She'd helped herself to some of Ross's red wine and was pretending she didn't want to know where he was going. She stared at the phone on the kitchen counter as if it were an instrument of the Devil, sipped her wine and waited for Ross to answer it. She avoided speaking to his family, but loved eavesdropping on Ross talking to his father in Italian. It was at times like those that she most wished he wasn't her almost-brother-in-law.

Mia and Matt had long chats with their Fabello relatives. 'Auntie Aoife/Annie/Deirdre/Carmel called,'

Mia would tell Danny. 'She's so funny! She calls herself my *ant-eee* and she laughs when I call *her* my *arntie*!'

'Does she?' Danny tried not to feel jealous. 'She sounds nice.'

'Did you know me and Mia have got twelve cousins and four of them are boys?' Matt asked.

'Mia and I.'

'What?'

'Never mind. Have you?

She was losing them to the Fabellos.

Ross strode into the kitchen, tugging a shirt cuff into place beneath a silky, tobacco-coloured jacket. Danny sniffed as he passed by. He smelt great. He looked better. She knew it — he was going on a date.

'Couldn't you move your butt a few feet to answer it?' he asked.

'Nope.'

He pressed the phone to his ear. 'Hello?'

Pause.

'She has?

Pause.

'Is she OK?'

He grinned and Danny's heart rate picked up.

'And the baby? I bet Tom's over the moon to get a boy.'

Danny picked up her wineglass. Just what the world needed, another *male* Fabello. She guessed his sister Carmel must have had her baby.

Ross frowned.

Danny paused, her wineglass halfway to her lips.

His frown deepened. 'No!'

Danny rose from her seat and moved closer.

'Is there anything they can do? Reconstruction? Or something?' he asked.

She laid a hand on his arm.

Ross was so surprised, he lost the thread of the conversation. 'What, Annie? I missed that.' He finished talking to Annie and replaced the phone.

Danny looked up at him, her golden eyes glowing with concern. 'What is it? Is something wrong with the baby?'

The last time she'd looked at Ross like this was the night of the Findlays' party. Ross watched her mouth move and remembered how she'd tasted.

Danny shook his arm gently. 'Ross? Is everything alright with the baby?'

'Mmm? Yes. I mean — *no* — I mean . . . Annie says he's got Uncle Carmine's nose, and Annie is the last person on earth who would ever criticize — she even called Aoife's newborn daughter Nicole pretty when everybody else thought she looked like she'd been in a train wreck.'

'Nose?' Danny's voice rose in disbelief. 'He's got your Uncle whatever's *nose*? I thought the poor little kid had something *serious!*'

'Uncle Carmine's nose is serious.'

Danny dug her fingers into his arm.

Ross prised them off. 'It's not my fault you got the wrong idea.'

'That was unforgivable! Even for you! You mentioned *reconstruction* for God's sake!' Danny left the kitchen.

'If your kid was born with a honker like that you'd be talking reconstruction!' Ross yelled after her. There was a good chance Kevin Kornecki would be the only baby to ever receive a nose job.

In the living room Mia looked at Matt and said, 'They're at it again.'

'Yeah,' Matt shrugged. 'It's my turn for the remote.'

Before he left, Ross knocked on Danny's bedroom door, something he'd never done before. 'Danny?'

'Yes?' She sounded surprised.

'Can I come in for a moment?'

'I suppose so.'

He opened the door.

Danny was sitting cross-legged on her bed with a photo album propped on her lap. 'Congratulations about the baby,' she said. 'I'm sorry I snapped at you.'

'That's OK. I'm sorry I gave you the wrong impression.' '

Are they both OK?'

'Yes. Although Carmel didn't make it to the hospital: her husband Tom delivered the baby on the dining room floor.'

Danny gasped. 'Is he OK?'

'Oh yeah, he's fine. Tom's getting to be an old hand — their last baby arrived in the car.'

They smiled at each other, and Ross wished he wasn't going out and they could toast his new nephew's birth with a glass of wine. 'Annie said he — the baby — is perfectly normal. Apart from the nose.'

'This nose,' Danny queried, 'it's bigger than yours?'

'I *have not* got Uncle Carmine's nose.'

'Keep your hair on, I just needed something for comparison.'

Ross saw a book on the floor beside the bed. It was his second novel, *Faithless*.

Danny swung her feet over the side and kicked it out of sight with her heel. 'Going somewhere nice?'

'Just dinner.'

The more elusive he was, the more determined Danny was to get an answer. 'Planning an all-nighter?'

'Don't worry, I've got my key.'

'Great,' she said through her teeth. 'Goodnight.'

Danny hugged the photo album to her chest and listened to him drive away. 'Remember to use a condom you oversexed, Italian/ Irish, big-nosed . . . pain in the bum.'

Christine's cousin Selena was lovely.

She reminded Ross of Christine, except that Selena's hips were rounder, her breasts more generous. Selena had warm, chocolate-brown eyes and dark brown hair swept up into an elegant twist. She wore black wide-legged pants with the right leg slit to the middle of her thigh. Her shimmering gold tank top dipped at the front to reveal a hint of her deep cleavage. Selena was warm and witty, interesting and *interested*.

'You like Crazy Frog?' she asked when she spotted the CD in Ross's car.

'It belongs to my nephew,' he said.

'ABBA's Greatest Hits?'

'My niece.'

Ross took her to a restaurant that Christine had recommended, and while they were waiting for their entrées to be served he asked Selena what she did.

'I'm a journalist,' she smiled. 'We already have a lot in common

— I write and earn peanuts, and you write and earn millions.' Seeing Ross's frown, she leaned over and lightly touched his hand. 'It's OK, Ross, I don't have a tape recorder in my handbag or a photographer hidden under the table.'

Ross forced a smile. Jeff wouldn't have arranged the date with Selena if she wasn't totally discreet and reliable. She was easy to talk to, easy on the eye and, judging by the look in *her* eye as the night progressed, she was every bit as pleased with her end of the deal.

They lingered over coffee until Selena stroked her foot up Ross's calf beneath the table, indicating she was done lingering. He thought of Danny pressing her foot against his thigh and moved his leg away. Ross called for the bill and wondered why he didn't feel the hunger and passion that was lighting up Selena's brown eyes. Instead, he kept seeing a pair of snapping, narrowed golden eyes in a face that was all sharp angles and narrow, pointed chin.

When they got in the car, Selena turned towards Ross. He cupped her cheek and kissed her. She was smooth and sensuous, not in too much of a hurry, not too dry and not too wet. Ross didn't feel so much as a flicker of excitement, but deepened the kiss.

Selena moaned and drew back. 'Can we go somewhere? I'm really past the age of making out in the car.'

He could have taken her to his apartment. But he didn't; it seemed too personal. Instead, Ross took her to a good hotel and booked a suite, not because he wanted to impress her, but because she was a nice woman and Christine's cousin. If she hadn't been Christine's cousin, he would have thanked her for the evening and taken her home, but, seeing the arousal in Selena's eyes, Ross felt he owed it to her and to himself to have sex. His inexplicable lack of desire for such an intelligent, attractive woman scared the hell out of him. Selena had made it clear that she wanted him, and

Ross was certain that once they got naked he would want her just as much.

They did get naked in the black marbled bathtub, with a bottle of red wine for company. Ross looked at Selena's lovely breasts, lapped by the scented bubbles. He looked at the long, elegant curve of her neck and the soft dark hair piled on her head. He slid his hand along the smooth, wet curve of her calf where she had her foot propped on his right shoulder — and nothing happened.

Ross had never before encountered this particular problem, and again it scared the shit out of him. When Selena reached over and stroked her hands through the wet hair on his chest, he had to close his eyes and think of Danny giving him a bed bath before his body began to respond.

He relaxed.

That pretty much set the scene for the rest of the night. The only way Ross could perform was by pretending it was Danny, not Selena, beneath him, and because he felt like such a cheat he went out of his way to take his time and make sure she enjoyed herself. Selena finally collapsed on the bed in front of him and looked over her shoulder at him, gasping, 'My God . . . did you . . . take classes in this?'

Ross lay beside her, thinking it was a shame Selena was such a nice lady and he didn't like her more. He was awake most of the night wishing he could go home to Danny and the kids. By seven he was up and dressed. And by nine-thirty he'd forced a couple of croissants and a cup of excellent coffee down his throat over a shared breakfast with Selena in the hotel room and was trying to figure out how to tell her he wouldn't be asking her out again.

Selena already knew, but for the life of her couldn't work out why.

Ross knew why. He just didn't want to admit it.

Danny kept busy.

Keeping busy meant she wouldn't think about Ross staying out all night and wonder what he had been up to. Keeping busy meant she wouldn't have to think about why it upset her so much imagining him making love to some woman in the king-sized bed in his apartment. Whoever she was, Danny loathed her.

Which didn't make sense: Ross was like a weed in her life, Danny told herself firmly as she attacked the weeds in Nella's neglected herb garden. She needed to get rid of him, too. But something had happened when Ross was sick, something so subtle it had slipped under Danny's radar, unnoticed until now. He'd stopped being Ross her enemy and become Ross the man. They still fought, but it had become more like a game because they both enjoyed fighting with one another. It was exciting. It was *addictive*. In fact, their arguments were almost like foreplay. Danny sank back on her heels in the warm, brown earth.

Bloody hell. Just what was she going to do? Snatching up her little green spade, she attacked whatever was growing in front of her, so absorbed in taking her feelings out on the plants that she didn't see Ross until he was beside her.

'That's basil.'

Danny jumped and dropped the spade.

She looked up. Ross was watching her, with Mia swinging on his hand. His clothes were different to the ones he'd gone out in the night before; this morning he was dressed in faded blue jeans and a grey T-shirt with *San Diego Chargers* emblazoned on the front. His dark eyes were sombre. For a man who'd probably just been laid, he didn't look so happy.

For once Danny didn't launch a verbal attack. She looked stupidly at the plant she'd been hacking at. 'Oh.'

Ross stepped over the wooden edge of the raised herb bed and squatted beside her. He took the spade from Danny. 'Move over.'

She scooted sideways and watched as he began to dig around the plants.

He pointed and dug. 'Basil.'

Danny nodded.

'Thyme.'

Nod.

'Marjoram.'

Danny shook her head.

Ross frowned. 'Yes, it is.'

'No, it's *maarjoram*, not *mahjawram*.'

The corners of his mouth curled. 'I stand corrected. Now, listen up: I'm only saying this once.' When he smiled, Danny stopped paying attention to what he was saying about the herbs.

Together they worked their way through the herb bed with some help from Mia and later Matt. Danny sat back and looked at the kids and Ross digging, laughing and squabbling, and blinked back tears. Ross looked up in time to catch her doing it. She braced herself for a sarcastic comment, but he only turned away to rescue a coriander plant from Mia.

This was *way* more serious than she had realized. She was becoming infatuated with Ross Fabello. Danny was so unnerved, so utterly appalled, she was a lot quieter than usual for the rest of the week while she tried to figure out what to do. How did you handle a crush on your not-quite-brother-in-law who also happens to be a wealthy, big-shot bestselling author with designs on your niece and nephew?

Ross was so perplexed by her uncharacteristic silence that he asked if she was sickening for something.

She blushed. 'No.'

'Did you just *blush*?'

'No. It was a hot flush.'

'You're too young for hot flushes.'

'I've always been mature for my age.'

One afternoon after work, Danny took Mia and Matt for a walk on the beach, leaving Ross behind to make homemade pasta. Not the dried stuff or the stuff in the cellophane packages on the refrigerator shelves at the supermarket that ordinary mortals bought and ate — no, he had to make *homemade pasta*, or, as Ross put it, *Anolini al ragu di prosciutto*, carefully omitting to mention the calf brains customarily used for the stuffing, for which he had swapped chicken livers.

'Is that frog?' Matt asked suspiciously when he heard what was for dinner.

'Nope, I checked — no frog.' Danny settled down on the sand to idly thumb through the magazine she'd bought at the petrol station. 'If you two want to go and take a look at the rock pools, you can. Uncle Ross wants us back in an hour.'

Matt and Mia departed for the other end of the beach.

Danny chewed on her lower lip and tried to figure out a way to deal with her current dilemma. Perhaps she needed some other male company? It was worth a try. She flipped through the last few pages of the magazine and was about to close it when she saw a photograph of Ross with a sultry-looking brunette tucked beneath his arm. The woman wore a shimmery gold top that showcased a spectacular set of breasts, and Ross had on the tobacco-brown jacket he'd worn the night he didn't come home. A quick scan of the caption revealed that RF O'Rourke had been seen taking the lovely Selena Harrison, respected current affairs journalist, to dinner at an Auckland restaurant.

Danny closed the magazine.

No prizes for guessing who Ross had spent the night with. Selena what's-her-face had a round, voluptuous figure to go with that sultry face. She was a serious journalist, not one of Ross's airhead fans. She was the real deal.

As soon as Danny got home she phoned Lance Ashburn and told him he could take her out on Friday night.

'I — I can?' Mr Smooth was so astonished he could hardly get the words out, until his normal self-assurance reasserted itself. 'I *knew* you'd come around once you got to know the real me, Daneka.'

'Yeah, something like that.' Danny checked that Ross wasn't in earshot. 'You can take me out to dinner. Don't bother packing any condoms, because you won't be needing them.'

'Danny—' Lance was so shocked that for once he forgot to call her Daneka.

'Just so we know where we both stand,' she continued. 'I'll go out for a meal, but I don't want to have sex. The plus for you is that you'll get to spend enough time with me away from the hospital to realize that you and I are never going to be Yin and Yang, and I get a nice dinner somewhere very expensive.' She paused to let that sink in. 'Can you pick me up at seven-thirty?'

'I . . . I guess so — I mean — yes.'

'Great, that's settled.' Danny was about to hang up when she remembered something. 'Oh, and Lance?'

'Yes?' he asked warily.

'If you mention this to one person at the hospital, I will drug you and while you're semiconscious zap your balls with the defibrillator paddles in the resus room. Do you understand?'

There was a prolonged silence. Danny waited for him to tell her that he'd changed his mind.

'I understand, Daneka.'

Damn. The guy was keen. Or mentally unstable.

Danny's code of silence deal extended only to Lance, not Vanessa.

'You're going out with *Lance Ashburn?*'

'Don't look so amazed. You're the one who's been nagging me about not getting out enough.'

'You're doing it to make Ross jealous, aren't you?' Vanessa cried.

'I am not!'

'You *are*.' Vanessa shook her head. 'Well, I won't be around to see the damage, because I'll be in Rarotonga sunning myself. Lust hasn't made you forget you promised to water the plants and pick up my mail while I'm away, has it?'

'No,' Danny scowled, 'it has not.'

Vanessa smirked.

'I *am not* in lust.'

At least not with Lance Ashburn.

Chapter 16

Lance arrived on the dot of seven-thirty, wearing a cream linen jacket over a white shirt and navy trousers and navy loafers with tassels. Danny decided all he needed was a peaked hat and he'd look like the captain of the *Love Boat*. She had suspicions that Lance's silky, blond hair was highlighted. His blue eyes lit up when she opened the door. 'Daneka, you look breathtaking.'

Danny was looking pretty good. God knows, she'd spent hours in the bathroom exfoliating, shaving and moisturizing all the body parts she'd been ignoring for so long that it was like a reunion with old friends.

It was satisfying to break the news to Ross that she was going out. Danny did it while she made the kids' lunches. 'Can you sit with the kids on Friday night?'

'I guess so.' Ross looked up from the morning paper, his fork suspended over the mushroom and camembert omelette he'd made for their breakfast. 'Why? Are you going out?'

'Yes.' She polished an apple on her T-shirt just above her breast.

Ross watched. When Danny put the apple into Matt's lunchbox, Ross stared at her breast for several moments before he realized the apple was gone. He cleared his throat. 'What is it? Girls' night out with Vanessa?'

'No.' Danny began filling plastic drink bottles. 'Didn't I tell you? Van's off to Rarotonga for a week's holiday today.'

'No, you didn't.'

'Well she is, and I've got the keys to her house.'

Matt and Mia erupted into the kitchen to grab their lunches and schoolbags, and Danny left them to it and headed off to work.

On Friday afternoon she commissioned the newly refurbished bathroom for hours before eventually appearing from her bedroom in a slinky pale-pink knee-length slip. The dress hung from Danny's shoulders on tiny pink straps, skimming the tips of her breasts and the curve of her buttocks.

Ross was annoyed that Danny had managed to colour-coordinate her clothes for her date but didn't give a damn the rest of the time when there was only him to impress. He was sure he could make out the colour of her nipples through the thin fabric. The dress was indecent. In fact it wasn't a dress — it looked more like lingerie. And she had practically nothing on beneath it; certainly no bra, *as usual*. The only thing Ross could detect was the edge of her thong.

'Why don't you just hang a sign around your neck saying *Come and get it?*'

Danny collected her keys from the kitchen counter. 'Why don't you get knotted?'

'I'm surprised you haven't painted your hair pink to go with the dress.'

'He likes me natural.'

So did Ross, but she'd still painted her hair blue and silver. He'd gotten used to seeing her hair all the colours of the rainbow; without any paint, she didn't look like Danny.

They weren't speaking when the door bell rang and Danny went to answer it. Ross expected her to leave. He wanted her to leave so he wouldn't see who she was going out with. But she returned with a big, blond fairy with highlights in his hair. Ross knew all about highlights: his sisters and several old girlfriends set great store by them.

'Lance, this is Ross Fabello, my brother-in-law,' Danny said. 'Ross, this is Lance Ashburn. He works for Criterion.'

Ross was so pissed off by the emphasis she'd placed on his *brother-in-law* status that it took him a moment to realize just who Lance Ashburn was.

Ashburn took exception to the possessive way Ross was looking at his date, and slid an arm around Danny's waist. He nodded coolly. 'Fabello.'

'Ashburn,' Ross replied stonily.

Mia came into the kitchen to look Lance over.

'Hello? Who's this little princess?' Lance teased with a big smile.

She didn't respond. 'Who's he?'

'Mia!' Danny cried. 'Where are your manners?'

Ross looked at Mia and winked. Atta girl!

Danny collected her handbag — a pretty, little pink envelope of a thing, Ross noticed, not the black monstrosity she'd taken on her date with him. How did she think she was going to fight Ashburn off with a silly little purse? She kissed Mia and nodded coolly at Ross. 'Don't wait up.'

Ashburn's eyes flickered with excitement. Ross wanted to plant his fist right in the middle of that perfect, sissy face. Danny had as good as told Ashburn she was giving him the goods tonight. Ross curled his fingers around the edge of the kitchen table to keep from snatching Danny up and locking her in her bedroom.

He followed them to the front door. 'Hey, Ashburn?'

The other man paused. 'Yeah?'

Ross stared at him. 'Don't get any ideas about showing her any construction equipment.'

Lance coloured.

Danny frowned. 'Why would he?'

'Come on.' Lance ushered her down the front steps. 'We'll be late.'

Danny was already bored. She felt guilty about the way she'd blatantly used Lance to annoy Ross; she wasn't proud of herself, but oh boy, had it been worth it! Ross had almost seemed jealous. She tried to concentrate on Lance and be pleasant, but her heart just wasn't in it.

Lance pulled out all the stops. He'd booked a table at a great Italian restaurant, but Danny kept comparing the food with what Ross prepared at home and finding it lacking. Lance even made an effort to not talk about himself, and he only ogled two of the women at nearby tables.

Danny propped her face on her fist and listened to him drone on. If one of the women had been brazen enough to ask for Lance's phone number, she would have happily loaned them a pen. Lance just didn't get it. She could tell by the stubborn, determined look in his blue eyes that he intended to sweep her off her feet with his charm, but he was just too pretty, too smooth and he didn't get her jokes. By the time the main course arrived, Danny knew she wouldn't last through dessert and coffee.

When Lance asked to see the dessert menu, Danny blurted, 'No!'

'No?' he echoed.

'I'm full! I can't eat any more!'

Lance smiled slowly at her and Danny wanted to groan out loud. The idiot thought she was cutting the meal short because she wanted to go to bed with him.

'Can you take me home?'

His smile faltered.

He was subdued on the drive home. Danny was sure this had never happened to him before, and she almost felt sorry for him. When she directed Lance to Vanessa's house, his eyes lit up.

'Down, Bonzo,' Danny said wearily. 'You've got the wrong idea.

I promised Vanessa I'd look after her place while she was away.'

Lance parked the car outside Vanessa's and killed the engine. He draped his arm along the back of Danny's seat. His eyelids slid to half-mast and he smiled. Danny wondered if he practised in the mirror. 'Let me come inside and look after you.'

Danny smothered a yawn and patted his cheek. 'No, thanks. All I want to do is sleep.' She gathered up her purse. 'Thank you for the meal.'

He searched her face in disbelief. 'Don't I even get a kiss?'

'OK, but make it quick.'

It was like throwing him a challenge. Lance bent Danny back across his arm and devoted long moments to soul-kissing her. He gave it everything he had.

'Are you finished?' she gasped when he let her up for air.

Lance mistook her gasps for excitement. 'Can I come in now?'

Danny shook her head. 'No.'

He was bewildered. 'No?'

'*No*.' She opened the door and stepped out onto the pavement. 'Thanks again, Lance, but let's not repeat this, OK?' She said goodnight and let herself into the house.

Inside her bag, Danny had her toothbrush and a change of underwear. She deliberately hadn't brought a change of clothes, because she didn't want to give Lance ideas and she wanted to arrive home in the morning wearing the same clothes she'd gone out in. She'd make sure she looked rumpled and just a little slutty, as if she had climbed back into her dress after a night spent in Lance's bed. Ross wouldn't know she'd spent the night at Vanessa's watching *Lord of the Rings* and eating chocolate.

Viggo Mortenson and a bar of Cadbury's did a whole lot more for her than Lance Ashburn.

Danny sloped home around ten-thirty the following morning, looking like a woman who'd spent the night having sex. She oozed into the house, a feline smile on her lips, and her shoes dangling from her fingertips. Her pink dress was creased, her hair mussed, and there were half-moons of mascara beneath her eyes.

Ross wanted to explode — or shake her until her teeth rattled.

'Where have you been?' Matt asked disapprovingly.

Ross's ears rotated like satellite dishes.

'You know I went out last night.'

Mia pursed her lips. 'You didn't come home. I looked in your bed and you weren't there. Where did you sleep?'

Yeah, Ross thought, *where did you sleep?*

'I'm a grown-up, Mia. I can stay out if I want to.' Danny slanted a look at Ross. 'Just ask Uncle Ross.'

'Those racoon eyes remind me of how you looked when I met you.' He took Mia's hand. 'Come and eat your French toast, Mia.'

Danny flounced into the bathroom and spent the rest of the morning sulking in the bath because Matt and Mia had sided with Ross.

Around midday, three dozen long-stemmed roses were delivered. *Yeuch!* Danny thought. 'How lovely!' She hoped Lance really *had* got the message that she wasn't interested.

'Sorry to tear you away from your reward,' Ross said coldly, 'but I need to talk to you about something.'

'What do you mean *my reward?*' Danny demanded hotly.

He spoke through clenched teeth. 'I apologize. Your personal life is none of my business.'

She gasped theatrically. 'Can you say that again? And can I video you while you do it?'

'I'm going back to the States in November.'

Had he just said he was going back to America? That he was going *home?*

'I'm going back for—'

She heard nothing beyond *I'm going*. Ross was *leaving*; he was going home. Why wasn't she turning cartwheels around the kitchen? It was what she wanted.

Wasn't it?

'Danny, are you listening to me?'

'You're going home,' she repeated tonelessly. 'You're leaving.'

Ross frowned. 'Only for a couple of weeks. I'll be back early December.'

Relief made Danny feel light-headed. He was coming back.

He peered at her. 'Are you OK?'

Her smile was radiant. 'Yes, I'm fine, just a little tired.'

'Perhaps you'd better go and get some sleep,' Ross suggested icily. 'To recharge your batteries. I'll take the kids down to the beach.'

'Ross, I didn't mean—'

After he'd driven away with Matt and Mia, Danny went to the calendar hanging by the refrigerator and lifted the page to November. She wanted to forget all about November. She wanted to jump right from October to December. She wanted to scrub November the seventeenth from all the calendars of all the years to come.

Her first birthday without Nella.

As October came to an end and November arrived, Danny became more and more subdued. She seemed not to notice Ross's verbal digs, and the things about him that usually drove her mad barely registered. She didn't care about the paparazzi parked outside the house, and she didn't care that his family continued to get the time difference between New Zealand and San Diego wrong and called at all hours of the day and night. When Ross asked what her colour preference was for the new steel roof, she shrugged and said he could choose. The sass and snap that drove him nuts seemed to have drained right out of Danny. She put on a good face for the kids, but Ross wasn't fooled: something was bothering her, something that made her sad and depressed. And for once, he wasn't the culprit.

Ross thought Lance Ashburn might be to blame. Danny hadn't gone out with him again, and Jeff told him that Lance was seeing one of the nurses from the Emergency Department. Instead of being pleased, Ross wanted to rearrange Ashburn's cheating face. 'I thought he was seeing Danny.'

Jeff shook his head. 'That's not what I heard. John Miller told me Lance was keen, but Danny wasn't. He said she's been trying to get Lance interested in this nurse Gabby ever since they started working together.'

Ross was confused. But then, what man understood how women thought?

He forgot all about his birthday until cards began arriving from his family. Ross had mentioned that Danny's birthday was the same day as his, and his mother and sisters sent cards for her, too. Danny continued to keep Ross's family at a distance, so he was wary of her reaction when he mentioned there was some mail for her.

Danny looked at the red, yellow and pink envelopes propped on the mantelpiece. His cards were all around the room, on top of tables, the mantelpiece and hooked over the curtain rod. She made no move to pick up her mail.

'Aren't you going to open them?' Ross asked.

'Later . . . I've got a few things to do first,' she said and walked out.

Ross was hurt by her rejection of his family's kindness; why was she being such a bitch? He noticed Matt watching him anxiously. 'What's the matter?'

Matt shrugged. 'Nothing.'

Mia buried her face against her doll and burrowed into his side. Ross had the feeling he was missing something important. 'Is something bothering Auntie Danny?'

Mia chewed her thumbnail.

Matt changed the channel.

When the envelopes were still unopened the following morning, Ross found Vanessa's phone number and called her.

'Hi, it's Ross Fabello. You know — the Serial Killer?'

'What do you want?'

'I want to know what's wrong with Danny.'

'What do you mean what's wrong with Danny?'

'She's miserable, and for once I don't think I'm to blame,' Ross replied. 'Now can we cut the crap and have a serious conversation about this? Is she upset because Lance Ashburn dumped her?'

Vanessa snorted. 'Lance Ashburn didn't dump Danny, you idiot! She dumped him! She only went out with him to . . .' Her voice trailed away.

'To what?'

'To . . . make him realize they didn't have anything in common.'

It was the dumbest thing he'd ever heard. Ross wanted to ask if sleeping with Ashburn had been part of Danny's plan to prove they had nothing in common.

'Lance Ashburn drives Danny mad!' Vanessa said. 'She's been trying to get him to go out with Gabby for weeks.'

Ross didn't believe a word, but was unprepared for what Vanessa said next.

'Danny's upset about her birthday. It's her first one without Daniella.'

It was as if somebody had dropped a rock on his head. *Of course* Danny was dreading her birthday. She was a twin. Her birthdays had always been shared with her sister. That was why Danny didn't want to open her cards, and why Matt and Mia had been so subdued.

'Ross? Are you still there?'

'Yes, I'm still here. I'm an idiot, but I'm still here.'

Vanessa sounded almost friendly. 'I've been worrying myself sick trying to think of a way to help her, but I don't know what to do. November seventeenth is your birthday, too, isn't it?'

'Yes — yes, it is. Vanessa?' Ross murmured thoughtfully.

'Yes?'

'Can you take the kids for the night of the seventeenth?'

'Why? What have you got planned?'

'It's a Saturday and Danny isn't working the next day.'

'You're going to take her out for the night?'

'Even if I have to dress her myself and handcuff her to the seat of my car.'

'I'm beginning to like you, Ross.'

'Let's hope Danny feels the same way on Saturday night,' Ross replied grimly. 'Oh, and Vanessa?'

'Yes?'

'Let's keep this between us. Come and pick the kids up around midday, OK? I'll tell them it's a surprise and they mustn't tell Danny.'

'You know Mia's not great at keeping secrets.'

'That's true, but she has a redeeming quality — she can be bribed.'

'We mustn't tell Auntie Danny anything about next Saturday,' Matt repeated solemnly.

He and Mia sat cross-legged on the trampoline listening to Ross, who was grabbing the chance to speak to them both while Danny was out. Ross looked at Mia and repeated slowly, 'You mustn't tell *anybody* about what we've just discussed. *Nobody*.'

Matt shook his head. 'Won't work: Mia can't keep a secret.'

'Yes, I can!' she cried indignantly.

'No, you can't. Remember when Mum hid Dad's birthday present under your bed and you showed it to him and told him what it was before he even opened it?'

'I was only little then! I'm *eight* now!'

'You're still a blabbermouth.'

'I haven't told *anybody* about our performance reviews!' Mia exclaimed. The lure of extra pocket money had kept her mouth shut tighter than a clam.

'Just to help you remember, Mia: I'm going to give you both an incentive,' Ross said.

Mia's blue eyes narrowed. 'Is an incentive the same as a performance review?'

'It's a bribe,' Matt said.

She smiled and bounced up and down a little on the trampoline.

'*If* you can keep your lips zipped, I'll buy you that Black Eyed Peas CD you've been wanting.' And, God help him, he'd then have to listen to her sing him every song.

'Cool!'

Matt opened negotiations. 'What about me?'

'I'll get you the new Captain Underpants book or the *Stadium Arcadium* CD.'

He considered. 'The CD costs more than the book.'

Ross raised a brow. 'So?'

'So if I get the book and Mia gets a CD, there'll be some dollars left over.'

Ross considered. 'I'll make up the difference by buying you

some of those Draco magnets.'

Matt considered. 'Four packs?'

'Two.'

'Three?'

'Deal.'

Matt punched the air. '*Yesss!*'

Ross stared hard at them. 'If one of you spills the beans, the deal's off.' He put out his hand. 'Now, shake on it.'

Danny didn't notice the meaningful looks that Ross shared with the children or the conversations that suddenly ended when she walked into a room; she was too sunk in despair. Because it was Ross's birthday, too, she tried to put on a brave face. On Saturday morning, Danny managed to get through opening her present from the children. Matt and Mia had bought CDs for her and Ross — Split Enz for Danny and Nickelback for Ross.

'Deryl took us to buy them,' Mia said. 'She asked the girl in the shop if they had any Perry Como elle pees, but she didn't know who Perry Como was or what an elle pee was.'

Ross picked up Danny's Split Enz CD. 'Who's this?'

'One of the best New Zealand bands ever.'

'They're really old,' Matt said.

Ross didn't ask Danny to speak to his family when they called to wish them both happy birthday; he said she was out. Danny was grateful . . . until Vanessa arrived to collect Matt and Mia.

'I never asked you to babysit.'

'No, Ross did.'

Danny's voice rose along with her eyebrows. '*Ross did?*'

'Yes,' Vanessa said. 'You can pick them up tomorrow around lunchtime.'

And they were gone.

Ross was sitting outside enjoying the sunshine and reading *The Horror at Camp Jelly Jam* when Danny found him.

'What are you up to, Fabello?' she demanded.

He checked the book. 'Page fifty-three.'

'Don't get smart with me,' she snapped. 'Why have you sent the kids to Van's for the night?'

'Because we're going out.'

'*We are not!*'

'Yes, we are,' Ross nodded. 'It's my birthday.'

What about me? Danny thought. *It's my birthday, too.* She bridled. 'What if I don't want to go out with you?'

He was unmoved. 'Has that ever stopped me before?'

She glared at him in frustration. 'Where are we going?'

He went back to his book. 'It's a surprise.'

'Don't expect me to dress up.'

Ross looked at her T-shirt and grimaced: it was the *I Started Out With Nothing And I Still Have Most Of It Left* one he hated so much. 'The jeans are fine, but the T-shirt has to go.'

'I like it,' she said obstinately.

'I don't. Because it's not true.' Ross made himself more comfortable on the sun lounger and turned the page. 'We both know you're something.'

Danny didn't know what to make of that.

It's been too easy, Ross thought as he drove across town to his apartment. She would eventually crack and start yelling and swinging at him.

'What are we doing here?' Danny asked as he parked under the building.

'I told you: it's a surprise.'

She followed Ross into the elevator. 'Don't tell me, you're going to initiate me into the coven.'

He pushed a button on the panel. 'Not today. It's my day off.' They rode the elevator to the top floor.

When they stepped into the living room of his apartment, two tiny Asian women wearing white tunics were waiting for them. They looked like beauty therapists, and beside them Danny felt like a cart horse that had just been led in from the field covered in mud after a long winter. Her hair needed a wash, her nails were a mess, and she couldn't recall the last time she'd had a pedicure. She glared at Ross. He looked great in a long-sleeved white shirt over jeans, black loafers and a pair of mirrored aviator sunglasses.

Ross correctly interpreted her look. He slipped off his sunglasses and looked pointedly at her clothes. Danny got the message: it wasn't *his* fault she looked a mess.

'Good afternoon, sir. Good afternoon, madam,' one of the women said. She gestured towards the bedroom. 'Would you like to come with us?'

Had Ross arranged a foursome?

Ross read her mind and rolled his eyes. 'She means you.'

Danny allowed the women to lead her away towards the bedroom.

'Although,' Ross called after her, 'if you twist my arm I'll join you.' He grinned when Danny shouted back, 'That's not the only part of you that's twisted, Fabello!'

It was heaven.

Ross had bought her heaven — even if it was just for one day. The women were called Hisayo and Noriko. They handed Danny a flute of champagne — 'From *sir*' — and showed her into the bathroom where the Jacuzzi was bubbling gently. The bottle of champagne was chilling in a bucket alongside.

'You soak in the Jacuzzi,' Hisayo/Noriko said. Who was she to argue? Danny couldn't get out of her clothes and into the water fast enough. She drank two flutes of champagne and was nearly asleep when she felt a gentle touch on her shoulder.

'You have massage.'

Danny smiled at Hisayo/Noriko through a warm haze. The only sticky moment came when they saw the state of Danny's neglected armpits, legs and bikini area. 'You have leg, underarm and bikini wax?'

Danny nodded and hung her head in shame. Hisayo and Noriko were superb at their job, but Danny still yelled as the wax was ripped off. Noriko gave her a facial, an eyebrow shape and lash tint, while Hisayo soaked Danny's hands and feet and started on a manicure and pedicure.

They rewarded her with a scalp, shoulder and neck massage that left Danny feeling as if she could levitate to the ceiling. Her muscles sang like a dawn chorus.

When Hisayo and Noriko had gone, Danny floated into the living room clutching the bottle of Brut and her glass. Ross was sitting on one of the sofas with his laptop in front of him on a glass coffee table. She was wearing his white bathrobe; it hung to her ankles, and the sleeves were rolled back.

'I'm going to marry Hisayo and Noriko and have their babies,' Danny said dreamily. She upended the champagne bottle above the champagne flute and was perplexed when only a trickle of golden liquid came out.

Ross watched with amusement. 'Are you drunk?'

She squinted down the neck of the bottle. 'Not yet, but I'm getting there.'

He rose from the sofa and took the bottle from her. 'Slow down a little. Dinner's arriving soon and you can have some more then.'

For once she didn't argue.

He led her to the sofa. Danny sat down and tucked her feet beneath her. Ross resumed his seat and began to shut down his laptop.

'Why are you being so nice to me?' she asked. 'I'm horrible to you.'

'You're not always horrible.' He closed the lid of the laptop. 'And sometimes I *am* nice.'

She watched him. 'Yes. You are.'

When Ross wasn't doing PR for his books, a person had to dig deep to get to the nice. Ross kept it well-hidden. He had no tolerance for bullshit or idiots, and he could spot a fake a mile off. He wasn't pretty or charming like Lance Ashburn. His black scowls and sarcastic tongue made most people run a mile. But he'd known how Danny was feeling today. He'd known not to wish her a happy birthday; he hadn't said anything — but he'd done a lot.

Ross looked embarrassed by her praise.

Danny giggled. 'You're blushing!' She leaned back against the arm of the sofa, and poked him in the thigh with her toes.

He trapped her foot against his leg, and Danny kneaded him with her toes like a cat. Ross watched the white bathrobe slip down and bunch between her thighs. Suddenly, his jeans felt too tight and his skin too hot. Was she naked beneath it? He let go of Danny's ankle and slid his hand slowly up her calf to the back of her knee. His conscience reawakened. He shouldn't be touching her like this — she was drunk. Reluctantly, he dropped his hand.

Danny planted her foot against his chest. 'Why did you stop?'

The front of the robe had parted and he could see the inner curves of her breasts and the silky skin between. He looked away. 'You're drunk.'

She levered herself up on her elbows and exclaimed indignantly, 'I am not!'

Ross turned to argue, but instantly forgot what he was about to say. The lapels of the robe were wide apart. His gaze snagged on a rose-brown nipple, puckered like a rosebud. Danny might not be drunk, but she was aroused. The temptation was too much. He raised his hand and reached towards her.

The doorbell rang.

They both started. Danny looked down to see what Ross was reaching for, snatched the robe together and scooted backwards on the sofa. 'Who's that?'

Ross stood up and adjusted his pants. 'Dinner,' he said gruffly and went to answer the door.

Ross had emphasized he wanted a small, quiet dinner party for two. He supposed the caterer thought he meant a romantic evening. Ross watched one of the catering staff set two places at the end of the dining room table and fat white candles in a wreath of waxy white flowers and green leaves. He was shaken by what had happened on the sofa. Danny was like smoke, seeping inside him, making him want to touch and taste her properly. It was just as well the caterer had arrived when he did.

'Grab a seat,' he told Danny brusquely. 'Chow time.'

She took her seat in silence.

The waitress brought the first course, pan-seared scallops in a lemon sauce. For the first time in days, Danny had an appetite. She closed her eyes and chewed slowly. 'Ohhh!' she moaned. 'This is wonderful.'

Ross watched her, the wine bottle in his hand poised above her wineglass. Did she have to moan like that? 'Wine?' he asked.

Her lids fluttered open. 'Mmmm?'

'Do you want some wine?'

'No, thank you.'

He filled his glass and took a hefty swig.

The waitress cleared the first course and returned with the second: seared hapuka steak with tiny vegetables.

They ate in silence. The shadows lengthened on the tiled patio area beyond the glass doors, and the cars trailing across the harbour bridge became dancing points of light as drivers turned on headlights. Boats returned to Westhaven Marina after a day spent out on the Hauraki Gulf fishing or sailing. Danny watched them. 'It looks like a movie — too perfect to be real.'

Ross watched her over the edge of his wineglass and silently agreed.

When the waitress brought the third course, he noticed Danny staring at her. 'What's wrong?'

She looked away. 'Nothing.' But she didn't attack her lemon-and-lime sorbet with nearly as much gusto as she had the scallop and fish courses.

'Don't you like it?' Ross asked.

Danny toyed with the dessert with her spoon. 'I love it. It's perfect. I've just run out of room.'

The waitress reappeared to ask if they wanted coffee. Danny stared at her again and silently shook her head. The waitress left. Ross was puzzled. 'You keep looking at her as if she's grown two heads or something.' She sat back in her chair and looked at the table. 'What's wrong, Danny?'

The caterer and his two helpers were leaving. When Ross went to say thank you and see them out, he got a good look at the two women. He'd thought it was the same waitress who'd served them. But he'd been wrong. There were two waitresses.

They were identical twins.

Chapter 17

Danny pleated and unpleated the belt of Ross's robe. She would not lose it and bawl like a baby. So the waitresses were twins. There were lots of twins in the world; Ross had twin sisters, for goodness sake. She'd guessed somewhere between the second and third course that they were being served by two different women who looked almost exactly alike, and had tried to ignore it. But as the meal progressed, the pain in her chest forced its way into her throat, making it impossible to swallow. The fact that Ross seemed to be getting annoyed with her hadn't helped. How could she explain she was a nutcase?

She heard Ross see the caterer and women out. He reappeared beside her. 'They've gone.'

Danny looked up and pinned a smile on her lips. 'Thanks a lot for a wonderful day and an awesome meal, Ross. I owe you.' She put her hands on the tabletop and pushed herself to her feet; she couldn't trust her legs to do it alone. Ross had already told her they were staying the night at the apartment and she was sleeping in the guest bedroom. 'I think I'll go to bed now.'

He didn't move. 'You can't keep running away from this, Danny.'

'I don't know what you're talking about.' She tried to step around him.

Ross moved, blocking the way. 'There's always going to be twins in the world.'

Danny sidled the other way, but he barred her way again.

'You have to get used to seeing twins together,' he said. 'The way you used to be with Daniella.'

His lack of sensitivity stunned her. 'Shut up!'

Danny tried to force her way past him. Ross caught her arms and gave her a little shake. 'You can't climb in that hole with her.'

'She's not in a hole! We burnt her!' She grabbed her mouth.

Ross caught her wrists. 'But you aren't dead, and you can't carry on acting as if you are.'

Her bottom lip wobbled and her eyes brimmed. 'But I *feel* dead! I *feel* like part of me has died! And — I can't *bear* it!' Danny buried her face in his chest and wailed like a child. *'I miss her . . . I miss her!'*

Ross wrapped his arms tightly around her. 'You're alive!' He said fiercely and kissed the top of Danny's head. *'You're alive!'* He pressed his lips to her neck and caught her skin between his teeth.

Danny yelped.

'Feel that?' He raised his head and bit her none too gently on her bottom lip.

She gasped against his mouth.

'Feel that?' he said harshly. His heart was beating so fast he could feel it throbbing in his ears.

Danny's eyes were huge. She couldn't seem to get enough air into her lungs. Her breasts rose and fell quickly. She nodded.

Ross cupped her bottom and pulled her against him. *'Do you feel that?'*

He was rock-hard. *'Yes,'* she whispered and leaned into him.

He took her hand and walked into the bedroom. He stopped at the end of the bed and opened the robe. Ross studied her body intently and said in a low voice, 'I've wondered what you looked like ever since the night of that damned party.' He pushed the robe from her shoulders and tossed it on the floor.

Danny's breath hitched. 'Now you know.'

'Yes.' Ross stroked the underside of one of her breasts with the tip of one finger. 'And now I know.' He dipped his head and touched her nipple with his tongue. 'Do you feel that?' he asked huskily.

Tears slipped down her cheeks. She nodded.

Ross pressed her down onto the cool, white bed linen and traced a pathway across her breasts with his lips and tongue. He moved downwards, stopping every so often to murmur 'Do you feel that?'

Her sobs quietened. She caught his head and buried her fingers in his silky, black curls and moaned. Ross dipped his tongue into her navel. Danny dragged his shirt up his back and smoothed her hands across his warm skin. *'Take it off...'*

Ross rose from the bed and stripped off his clothes.

Danny raised up on her elbows and looked at him. She bent her knees and reached for him. He caught her ankles, knelt on the edge of the bed and pulled her down the bedcovers towards him.

'What're you doing?'

'I bet you've always called the shots in bed, haven't you, Danny?' Ross lifted her legs and placed them over his shoulders.

'What does that mean?' She was struggling to breathe, let alone talk. Why was he talking so much?

'I bet guys couldn't believe their luck. I bet you turned them inside out — and then you walked. Didn't you, Danny?'

She punched him on the arm. 'Just *do it.*'

'You're not going to use me for a quick poke, Daneka. You're not going to use my dick to run away and hide.' He pressed his hands against the insides of her thighs. Danny pressed back. 'Open for me,' Ross said softly. '*Please.*'

She hesitated and slowly parted her thighs. Ross looked down. He dipped his head and laid his tongue against her.

Danny fell back on the bed. She closed her eyes and clutched his shoulders. He was her anchor as her world flew apart. She sprawled on the bed like a rag doll; beneath her palms Ross's shoulders were slick with sweat. Danny could hear the ragged sound of his breathing as he moved away and the bedside drawer opened and closed. Ross stretched out beside her. Danny felt him pressed against her thigh and whimpered, *'I can't!'*

'We've got all night, Danny.' His words were in stark contrast to the tension she could feel in him.

Danny turned her head. Ross was watching her. The look in his intense, dark eyes scorched her; she stroked her thigh against him. Ross closed his eyes and inhaled deeply. She rolled on her side and hooked a leg over his hip. His eyes flared. He caught her thigh and eased it higher. Danny traced the tip of her tongue along the seam of his lips, and when he opened them for her she slipped her tongue between them.

Ross pushed himself inside her, and Danny arched her back greedily. Ross cupped her bottom and changed the angle. *Even better.* Danny didn't miss a beat. They climaxed together, shuddering.

'You OK?' Ross asked when he was able to speak again.

'I'm good,' Danny said. 'I'm *very, very good.*'

Ross caught her chin and smiled. 'But you do bad better.'

He went to the bathroom to deal with the condom, and stared at himself in the mirror as he tried to come to grips with what had just happened. He'd just had sex with Danny. And he wanted to go right back out there and start all over again.

Danny was so vulnerable. And his track record with women was abysmal. He braced his arms on the vanity, hung his head and murmured 'Shit.' Danny wasn't the only person who used sex as an escape. Ross was guilty of the same thing. He'd slept with a lot of women, but he'd never connected with one the way he had with her tonight. It was . . . *disturbing*.

Danny rolled onto her stomach and tried to decide what to do. How had Ross known what she'd been trying to hide, even from herself? How had he known that Daniella's death made her feel like an amputee — she hadn't lost an arm or a leg, she'd lost part of her soul. What began as sex and comfort had turned into something else. And Danny wanted more. When it came to Ross she had a feeling that she'd always want more, and that would be a fast track to disaster. She was considering getting dressed when Ross reappeared, and her heart began to hammer at the sight of him walking towards her naked. He looked as wary and uncertain as she felt, and some of Danny's tension dissolved.

Ross looked at Danny stretched out on his bed on her stomach. She had her cheek propped on one hand and a guarded expression in her eyes. He followed the smooth, supple curve of her spine as it rose up to her pert little ass. His gaze halted at the cleft of her bottom and his eyes widened.

'I knew it!' he exclaimed triumphantly and came closer. 'I knew you'd have a tattoo!' Danny tried to roll onto her back, but Ross caught her shoulders and turned her over. She tried to cover the tattoo, but he pushed her hand away.

'I had it done years ago when I was young and stupid! It was a dare!'

Ross sat on the bed and traced the tattoo with his finger. Danny had three tiny black moles at the top of one buttock. A dice had been drawn around the moles, and looked as if it were tumbling into the cleft of her bottom.

'I might have known you wouldn't have a rose or a bluebird.'

She looked at him over her shoulder. 'What did you expect me to have?'

'A skull and crossbones.'

She took a half-hearted swing at him, and Ross used it to flip her onto her back. He caught her hands, raised them above her head and covered her body with his.

'You said I could stay in your guest room.'

'You're not staying in the guest room.'

Danny stroked the sole of her foot along the back of his calf. 'No? Why not?'

'Because,' Ross smiled down at her, 'I think I'm going to get lucky.'

When it came to sex, they were a perfect match. They left the curtains open to let the moonlight into the room, and made love twice more before falling asleep.

Ross woke around three o'clock to find Danny crying in her sleep. She wasn't making a big noise about it or thrashing about the bed, just sobbing softly, tears making wet, silvery tracks down her cheeks. Watching her made his insides feel as if somebody had scraped them raw and left them oozing. Ross touched her shoulder. '*Danny.*'

Her eyelids flickered and opened. She lifted her head and looked up at him bemusedly. 'What . . .' Danny touched her wet cheek and her face crumpled. 'I was dreaming about getting the tattoo. You know who dared me?'

'Nella?'

She nodded.

Ross caught her sob in his mouth and made love to her slowly and gently, rocking his big body against her much smaller one, trying to wipe away her loneliness and grief for just a little while and replace it with the tangle of tongues and legs and arms and his hardness buried deep inside her warmth and softness.

When it was over, he looked down at Danny and said quietly, 'Happy birthday.'

'Happy birthday,' her bottom lip wobbled. 'I didn't get you

anything.' She hoped he wouldn't say something crass about how she'd been his present.

'There is something you could do for me that I would really like,' Ross said gently.

Danny stared at him. What was he? The Energizer Bunny?

'Tell me where you're hiding my socks.'

Ross expected Danny to want to talk about *things* in the morning. Women always wanted to talk about *things* after they'd slept with a guy for the first time. Talking about whatever the thing might be didn't mean a casual conversation based on sound logic. It meant dissecting the hell out of something, looking at it from every conceivable angle, postulating on the possible outcome from both a positive and a negative perspective, and basically making something that was straightforward and fun a pain in the ass and awkward. While Ross knew he wasn't exactly a sensitive New Age guy, he also knew he didn't qualify for Neanderthal of the year. Danny had been through the emotional wringer on her birthday, and even he thought that what had happened between them qualified as a big *thing*.

On the drive back across the harbour bridge, Danny talked about everything but things. She'd borrowed a pair of his too-big boxer shorts, and the sight of them hanging over the waistband of her jeans made him horny. In desperation, and to his eternal regret, Ross raised the subject of *things* himself.

'What's the deal with us once we get back to the house?' he asked.

Danny looked at him blankly. 'Us?'

'Yeah — *us*. As in: was last night a one-off or are we planning to continue?'

'You mean . . . have sex again?'

Ross was exasperated. 'Yes!' When Danny didn't answer, he began to get a bad feeling about *things*. 'A straight yes or no will suffice,' he said curtly.

'No.'

Ross prayed he'd misheard. *'No?'*

Danny stared out the passenger window. 'No.'

He was stunned. 'Are you trying to tell me you didn't enjoy last night?'

'No, I'm telling you I don't think it'd be a good idea to do it again.'

'Why the hell not?'

'Because this isn't just about us — there are Matt and Mia to consider.'

'What does us sleeping together have to do with Matt and Mia?'

'Plenty,' Danny said. 'I don't want them to think of us that way. It'll be enough of a wrench for them when you eventually leave. Besides,' she pursed her lips, 'it's not as if you'll have to go without.'

'You think I've got somebody *else?*'

'No, I think you've got lots of somebody elses.' Danny shrugged with a nonchalance she didn't feel. 'That's the way you are. The way we *both* are. We don't get attached.'

What was left of his ego deflated and fizzled like a flattened whoopee cushion. Danny's indifferent attitude was totally at odds with the passionate woman he'd made love to the night before — and they *had* made love, certainly the last time, when she'd been crying in her sleep, no matter how determined she might be to label it otherwise.

'Don't feel under any pressure,' he said flatly. 'If you don't want to sleep with me, I'll cope with the disappointment.'

'I'm sure you will,' Danny retorted. 'There's always Selena.'

For a moment Ross didn't have a clue who she meant.

'Not to mention the nutter in the supermarket. You could

always hang out there if Selena has to work late.'

'And of course there's always Lance if you've got an itch that needs scratching,' Ross snapped.

'I never slept with—' Danny closed her mouth abruptly.

'Is that so?' Ross almost smiled until he recalled the night he'd spent wondering where she was and what she was doing with Ashburn. 'Where were you that night? You never came home!'

'None of your bloody business!'

'What's the matter?' Ross taunted. 'Did he turn you down?'

'No! I realized when he had his tongue down my throat that I didn't want him!'

Ross strangled the steering wheel between his fists at the picture her words painted in his head. 'Damn fairy!'

Danny rounded on him. 'Oh? Oh, *really?* So it's not OK for *me* to sleep with Lance Ashburn, but it's perfectly fine for you to shag Selena what's-her-face. Talk about bloody double standards!'

Ross bought himself time by checking the wing mirror to make a lane change as they descended onto the northern motorway. 'What was I supposed to do? She's Christine's cousin.'

Danny's brows rose and her lip curled. 'You *shagged* her because she was Christine's cousin?'

'Will you stop saying that?' Ross shifted uncomfortably. 'She's a nice woman. It seemed . . . rude not to.'

She flung up her hands. 'Am I really hearing this? Did you just say you had sex with a woman because she's your best friend's wife's cousin and because *it seemed rude not to?* Just when is the Mother Ship coming back to collect you, Ross?'

'It happens more often than you think,' he said defensively.

'What? *Pity fucks?*'

Ross winced.

Danny pointed a finger at him. 'Don't you dare correct my language! That *poor* woman! How would she feel if she knew?'

'I made sure she didn't know! I made sure she . . .' Ross trailed off. He'd already dug a big enough hole.

'Had a good time?' Danny cooed. 'Multiple orgasms?'

She was *jealous*. Ross had shared with Selena what he'd shared with her last night. It was better that she thought about it now, better to feel the anger and jealousy than imagine something that wasn't there.

'Tell me, Ross, was I another one of your pity fucks?'

The Explorer swerved and the driver in the next lane honked his horn. *'No!'*

Ross took a deep breath and slowly let it out again. 'Last night was different, Danny. It was *completely* different.'

She looked out the window, thinking wearily that it really didn't matter, because she wasn't doing it again. '*Whatever.*'

They collected the kids from Vanessa's and drove home listening to Matt and Mia's excited chatter about their trip to McDonald's and the movie they'd seen. Their noise filled the silence that stretched between Danny and Ross.

'Did you have a nice birthday?' Mia asked.

'Yes,' Danny said.

'Did you do anything special?' Matt wanted to know.

Danny didn't answer.

'Auntie Danny had a massage and manicure and all that girl stuff,' Ross said to fill the silence.

Matt rolled his eyes. 'Bo-*ring*.'

'No, it's not! It's nice!' Mia insisted. 'Bet it was *really* nice, wasn't it, Auntie Danny?'

'Yes, it was . . . very nice.'

It was way better than nice, Ross thought bleakly, *and unlikely to ever be repeated*.

He thought Danny had changed her mind when she knocked on his bedroom door later that night after the children were in bed. She was dressed in a pair of green cotton pyjama pants and a matching camisole top. Danny handed Ross a small package wrapped in bright blue paper printed with yellow and red party streamers. 'Your birthday present.'

He looked at her breasts beneath her thin cotton top and remembered how they had felt in his hands and against his tongue the previous night. 'You got me a birthday present?'

'It's not just for you; it's for your family.' She turned away and headed back to her bedroom. 'Goodnight.'

Ross watched her go and wondered why they always hurt one another.

He sat on the bed to open the gift, thinking that it wouldn't surprise him if it exploded. But when he peeled away the wrapping paper, Ross discovered a small yellow photo album filled with pictures of Pat, Daniella and their children. There were photos of when Pat and Nella first met, taken on the beach sunbathing and with their arms wrapped around one another beside a roaring bonfire.

Ross flipped a page. A heavily pregnant Nella posed in front of Pat and smiled at the camera. Pat was holding her belly in his hands. The next shot was taken in the delivery room at what Ross presumed must have been Matt's birth. Pat was staring down at a waxy, wet looking baby with black hair stuck to its pointy head, while a tired, dishevelled-looking Nella leaned over his shoulder to look at the baby.

Ross slowly turned the pages and watched his brother's secret life with Danny's sister unfold. The last photographs showed Matt and Mia a couple of years younger than they were now, riding boogie boards in the waves at the beach with their parents.

'Pat, you damned fool . . . Why did you have to shut us out?'

He took the book and tapped on Danny's door.

She didn't seem surprised to see him.

He held up the photo album. 'Thank you,' he said huskily. *'Thankyou.'*

His eyes were damp. Tonight, he was the vulnerable one, mourning the loss of something he'd never had, an opportunity missed and gone forever.

Danny sighed and pulled him into her room. There was always one guy a girl was a sucker for, and it seemed Danny wasn't immune after all; she was a sucker for Ross Fabello.

'I didn't come down here to—'

'You better not have.'

She closed the door and propped her hands on her hips. Sleeping with him last night had messed everything up, but it had been precious, and Danny couldn't regret it. Taking the album from him, she placed it on the chest of drawers. Tonight he needed her. Danny gently tugged Ross towards her. 'Come here, Darth.'

Ross's hands hung in midair while he wondered if he was imagining this because he wanted it so much. He sighed deeply, wrapped his arms around Danny and buried his face against the side of her neck. She stroked his back and turned her face to find his lips with hers.

'Was that a pity kiss?' Ross asked when they finally broke apart.

'It might be. How bad are you feeling?'

'Real bad,' he said quickly, and she laughed, but stopped when she saw the look in his eyes.

'I guess there's nothing for it but a trip to the Death Star.'

'What?'

'Nothing. Come to bed, Darth.'

Vanessa cornered Danny at work the next day and said, 'You've slept with him, haven't you? I couldn't say anything in front of the kids yesterday.'

Danny considered lying, but decided there really wasn't much point.

'D'you think everybody else will be able to tell?' she asked anxiously.

'From your face?' Vanessa asked dryly. 'No. But I'd try to kill the John Wayne walk if I were you — bandy legs are a dead giveaway.'

'Shut up!'

'So, was he any good?'

Danny pursed her lips.

'Don't be cruel!' Vanessa pleaded. 'How else will I have a sex life if I can't live it vicariously through my friends?'

Danny glanced around to make sure they couldn't be overheard. 'He was good,' she muttered.

'How good?' Vanessa demanded.

She checked again for eavesdroppers. '*Very good.*'

'On a scale of one to ten?'

'Oh for chrissakes, Van! What are you? Sixteen?'

'No, thirty-three and very horny.'

Danny took pity on her. 'You know how Cosmo always has those articles about the G spot?'

'Yes?'

'Well, Ross Fabello knows *exactly* where it is. He also knows where to find H, I, J and K.'

'You . . . lucky . . . cow.'

'Yeah, I know.' Danny paused. 'But it won't be happening again.'

'Why on earth not?'

'Because my life is here and his is in America,' she said firmly. 'And I'm never going to be like Nella, waiting for crumbs to be thrown my way when Ross finds the time to fly in for a quick visit to see Matt and Mia.'

Vanessa frowned. 'Danny, Ross isn't anything like Patrick. And you're nothing like Daniella. You'd never in a million years become some guy's doormat.'

Danny studied her pensively. 'Problem is, somewhere along the way he stopped being just some guy.'

Ross soon realized that Danny's lapse the night he opened his birthday present was definitely not going to be repeated, which infuriated him, because if anything their second night together had been even better than the first — which he would have insisted was impossible.

Danny tried to morph herself into his *friend*. If Ross hadn't been so sexually frustrated, it might have been amusing watching her bite her tongue when he went out of his way to bait her, which was the only way he could let off steam. He didn't want her friendship — well, not the lukewarm, polite variety she was offering. Ross wanted her wild and naked beneath him, and when she wasn't there he wanted her smart mouth and sharp brain. It was like taking a mouthful of your favourite coffee and finding non-fat milk instead of rich, velvety cream. Ross wanted full cream. He wanted Danny back. But the more he pushed for her to reappear, the more Danny withdrew.

It was a relief when the time finally came to pack his bags for the trip back to the States.

On the morning Ross left, Mia cried and clung to him, and even Matt looked upset. 'I'll only be gone a couple of weeks.' He rubbed Mia's back soothingly. 'I'll be back before you know it.'

He looked at Danny's composed expression and felt the helpless, angry frustration that was becoming his constant companion. 'I'll be back by early December. You've got the numbers I gave you if you need to contact me for anything?'

She nodded. 'Yes. We'll be fine. Robyn's found somebody to cover the Walking School Bus while you're away.'

Ross stared hard at her.

Danny concentrated on picking a speck of paint off the handle of the front door.

He grabbed his suitcase, flung a leather holdall over his shoulder and said curtly, 'See you, then.'

'Yeah,' she pushed the door wide open. 'See you.'

Chapter 18

It hurt. It really hurt. The very thing she'd tried to prevent had happened. Danny felt the loss of his presence as keenly as if the air had suddenly been depleted of oxygen.

She changed the sheets on his bed and had to sit down when the smell of his aftershave wafted up and hit her in the nostrils. Danny didn't know the name. The next time she was in a chemist, she began sniffing the tester bottles of men's cologne like a bloodhound. The instant she inhaled from the bottle of Dolce & Gabbana, Danny gave a deep sigh of pleasure and began snorting it like a junkie.

'Can I help you?' the startled shop assistant asked.

'No. You can't. Sorry.' Danny fled the shop.

One moment she longed for Ross's return, and the next she prayed he'd stay in America so she wouldn't have to go through the pain of saying goodbye again. How had Nella stood it? How had she managed to wave Patrick off with a smile each time he left? Danny pictured herself clinging to Ross's ankles as he walked away. Maybe that was why Nella and their mother had been so accommodating: letting them go meant they'd come back.

Maybe.

Joe continued working on the house doing the smaller jobs he could manage on his own. Ross had told Danny not to let Joe tackle the roof again until he returned. 'His back is still giving him problems, and I don't want him up there alone.'

They all liked Joe. He was kind and funny and had no hidden agendas. Provided he got his money on time and a steady supply of mugs of tea and a piece of cake for his morning break, he was happy. Danny started helping him when she wasn't at the hospital. She liked fixing things, and if she was busy she had less time to think about Ross and the future.

'Where are your people?' Joe asked one day when they took a break from replacing the deck.

'My people?' Danny held out a mug of tea and the last slice of a cake that Deryl had made.

'Your whanau — *your family.*' He took the tea and cake and sat down on a pile of decking.

She suddenly understood; Joe was Maori. 'I know what whanau means, Joe,' Danny said. 'I don't know where my whanau are. I've never met them.'

He took a bite of cake. 'How come?'

Danny was silent. Sometimes she wondered if Rose had been ashamed to be an unmarried mother because her family were strict and wouldn't accept her illegitimate children.

Joe swallowed the cake and looked at Danny expectantly. Reluctantly, she began to tell him about her mother.

'She was from Rotorua?' he asked when she'd finished.

'Yes, but that's all I know; and her surname was Smith, which doesn't help. Why couldn't she have been something unusual? Like Foghorn or Possumbreath?' Danny joked weakly.

Joe grinned. 'Never heard of any Foghorns, but I've got a cousin who would suit Possumbreath.'

Danny smiled.

'Your mum's people are Te Arawa?'

She sat down beside him. 'Yes, so far as I know.'

Joe polished off the last of the cake. 'You got a photo of your mum I can have?'

'Yes.' Danny was puzzled. 'Why?'

'My mum is Te Arawa. She knows everybody, and if she doesn't know them then she'll know somebody who does. If you give me a photo, I'll show it to my mother.'

'You'd do that?' Danny asked, incredulously.

Joe looked bashful. 'Sure. No skin off my nose.'

'Thank you, Joe.' Danny wanted to hug him, but knew she'd only embarrass him. She tried to think of a way to thank him. Inspiration struck. 'Tell you what: I'll make you a cake.'

Joe's smile slipped: Matt and Mia had warned him about Danny's cooking. 'Thanks . . . Choice.'

Ross phoned most nights. After the episode in the chemist shop, Danny was scared that the sound of his voice might make her do something equally irrational, such as start howling like a wolf, so she kept their conversations brief and handed the phone to one of the kids.

'Everything OK?' Ross would ask politely.

'Just fine,' Danny would answer politely. 'I'll get the kids.'

And everything *was* fine until Danny got a phone call from the school to say that Matt had been involved in a fight. When she arrived to pick him up, she was shocked to see he had a bloodied nose and that his clothes were torn. Matt refused to answer either Danny's or the principal's questions, and when he got home he shut himself away in his room.

Danny wasn't sure who was more upset: Matt, Mia or her. She couldn't believe Matt had been in a fight, it just wasn't in his nature to be confrontational. Mia had seen it happen and run to get help.

'Two boys were picking on Matt,' she told Danny. 'They always pick on him.'

'What do you mean they always pick on him? What about?'

'His hair. They say he looks like a girl.' Mia began to cry again.

Danny pulled Mia onto her lap to comfort her, wishing it was as easy to comfort Matt. It was her job to keep him safe, to shield him from the nastiness in the world, but she'd failed and didn't know what to do. How could she help Matt if he wouldn't even talk to her? It was the lowest Danny had felt since Nella had died.

Ross called that night.

'Are you OK?' he asked when Danny answered the phone.

'Yes, fine,' she replied.

'You don't sound it. What's wrong?'

There was a click as the extension in the living room was lifted, and Mia sniffed, 'Uncle Ross! Mattie got in a fight at school and got a bloody nose and torn clothes. He got sent to the principal's office and Auntie Danny had to come and get him.'

Danny's heart sank. Now he would know how useless she was. 'Hang up the phone, Mia.'

'Is he OK?' Ross asked sharply.

'No! I told you he's got a bloody nose and ripped his favourite T-shirt—'

'Hang up, Mia!' he exclaimed.

'But—'

'Hang up the phone!' Danny and Ross cried together.

There was a click as Mia finally did as she was told.

'Tell me what happened,' Ross demanded.

'I don't know exactly. I got a call from the principal to say that Matt had been involved in a fight at school and he was refusing to answer any questions.' Danny's nose stung, and tears welled in her eyes as she recalled the vulnerable, wounded expression on Matt's face when she saw first him.

Ross heard a telltale sniff and wished he was there. His voice softened. 'Where is he now?'

'In his bedroom, he won't come out.'

'Take the phone and go and knock on the door. Tell him I want to talk to him *now*. Don't ask him — *tell* him.'

Danny doubted it would work, but she did as Ross asked. She was astonished when Matt opened the door, took the phone from her and shut the door again. Minutes ticked by before Matt finally opened the door and held out the phone to her.

'Uncle Ross wants to talk to you.'

'Oh.' She took the phone into the kitchen. 'Hello?'

'Take him to a barbershop and get his hair cut first thing tomorrow morning.'

'Tomorrow morning? But he's got school.'

'Forget about school. He can be a couple of hours late for once. Just get his hair cut.'

'But he'll say no,' Danny insisted. 'I've tried to get him to have it cut before, but he always refuses.'

'We've discussed it, and he's agreed to have it cut. Make sure the barber does a really good job, it needs to be *short* or he'll end up looking like he's wearing an afro wig.'

Danny laughed weakly.

'Can you give my father a call and tell him what's happened? Ask him to speak to Matt, OK?'

'OK.'

'Do *not* let my mother speak to him. It'll only get her started about the first time that Dad took me and Pat to get our hair cut because we were getting into fights at school.'

'It happened to you, too?'

'Yes. I got my butt kicked more times than I can count, until Dad realized what was happening and took me to the barbershop. Ma hit the roof when he brought me home, but I didn't get into any more fights; well, at least — not about my hair.'

Danny gripped the phone. 'Thanks, Ross.'

'If Mia hadn't spilled the beans, would you have told me about

Matt?' He didn't sound very friendly.

'I don't know. I suppose so . . . eventually,' she hedged.

'You mean *no*,' Ross replied cuttingly.

'I — well — I mean —' Danny muttered. 'You're busy.'

'Not too busy for something like this,' he said coldly.

What was his problem? Why was he so angry with her? She *had* told him.

'When are you going to get it through your head, Danny, that this deal is fifty-fifty? Matt and Mia are half-Lawton *and* half-Fabello. We *share* responsibility for them.'

'OK,' Danny said.

Ross disconnected the call and ground his teeth. She didn't mean it: if Mia hadn't opened her mouth, he would have been none the wiser. He tried not to get angry. Danny suffered from an almost pathological fear of being dependent, a direct result of her childhood. When it came to relying on other people — particularly men — the only blueprint Danny had to work with was the one she'd cobbled together from watching her mother's relationship with her father and Nella's with Patrick. The lack of an extended family had compounded the problem. If she'd had grandparents or aunts or uncles, she would presumably have been exposed to normal family life. She would have grown up with what Ross had taken for granted — his family. They might be interfering and drive him to distraction at times, but nonetheless he loved them and knew they loved him — as he loved Matt and Mia.

Ross was unprepared for how much he missed them. He'd fallen for the dubious charms of an eight-year-old chatterbox with a singing voice that could strip paint from a wall, and a prematurely old eleven-year-old with a complete disregard for his famous uncle's writing or cooking skills.

And their aunt.

Joe carried his empty mug into the kitchen and rinsed it at the sink.

'I'm making a banana cake, Joe.' Danny stared at a pan of cake batter in the oven, willing it to rise. 'It should be ready soon. Do you want some?'

Her cooking had suffered since the confusing conversation with Ross. The night before, she'd managed to ruin one of the few edible things she could produce — chicken nuggets and chips. If Ross didn't return home soon, they'd all starve or have to live on porridge.

The children shared Danny's feelings. Matt stared at the burnt offerings on his plate and said, 'I *really* miss Uncle Ross.'

Mia tapped a blackened chip with her fork. 'Me, too.'

Me three, Danny thought dismally, and not just for his cooking.

Joe eyed the cake in the oven and snuck a look at Matt, who was doing his homework at the kitchen table. Matt shook his head vigorously. 'Ah, maybe some other time, Danny. My missus is doing roast pork tonight, and she'll kill me if I'm not hungry.'

Danny eyed Joe beadily.

'Not that I wouldn't be hungry because I ate your cake, or anything. It's just that if I ate it I might not have room for the roast pork, you know?'

Joe set his mug upside-down on the draining board, and pulled a slip of paper from the pocket of his shorts. 'By the way, I heard from my mum: this is your nan's telephone number in Rotorua.' He held it out as a peace offering.

Danny stared at the piece of creased white paper in disbelief. Had he just said that he had *her grandmother's telephone number?*

'Turns out we're cousins,' Joe said.

'We're cousins?' she repeated faintly.

'Yeah.'

Danny stared. He *was her cousin?* She *had a cousin?* She hadn't expected anything to come of Joe's offer to find her family, and certainly not this quickly. Danny looked at him sceptically. 'First or second?'

'First or second what?' Joe repeated blankly.

'Cousin — first or second?'

It made no sense to Joe. Pakeha — European New Zealanders — kept track of first, second or third cousins. In the Maori world you were just cousins.

'I dunno. Who cares? Here, take it.' He thrust the paper into Danny's hand. 'Funny thing is, Mum said some fella had already been asking around about your mother's relatives.'

Danny preferred her bombshells one at a time. 'She did? Who was he?'

'A stranger. He got given the run-around, nobody told him anything useful.'

Ross was the only person she could think of who would send a stranger to ask questions about her family. Why? Because he cared that she was alone? Or because knowing Danny had relatives to call on would make it easier to leave? She believed Ross when he said he felt jointly responsible for the children, but she didn't think that included her. He was only in New Zealand by default. If somebody else in his family could have made the trip, they would have. When he eventually went back home to the States, Danny knew the children would keep in touch with their American relatives by phone and email, and *maybe*, when Matt and Mia were older, Danny would let them visit in the school holidays. Once Ross left, she only expected to hear from him if there was a problem, in his role as the family troubleshooter.

Danny looked at the note in her hand and wished it was Ross who had given it to her, because then she could be sure the information it contained was accurate. Ross would check and double-check before he would say anything to get Danny's hopes up. Her fingers tightened around the paper. She hoped Joe hadn't made a mistake. 'Are you sure you've got the right person? I mean, what if it's not her?'

Joe wondered why women always found problems where there weren't any. 'My mum recognized your mum from the photo. She knows your nan. If you don't believe me, give her a call and find out for yourself.'

'Oh, Joe.' Danny clutched the paper against her chest. 'How can I thank you?'

He glanced at the oven. 'Buy me a Lotto ticket.'

Chapter 19

Danny's grandmother was called Pania.

Her grandfather's name was Ted.

She had three uncles — Henare, Hemi and Tipene (or Henry, James and Stephen if you preferred English). *The boys,* as their mother called them, didn't care what they were called. They answered to their Maori and English names, and several others which Pania didn't share. Rose had been Ted and Pania's only daughter.

Danny's phone call to her grandmother had been eerie: Pania sounded like an older version of her mother. Hearing her voice put a lump in Danny's throat. Pania took pity on Danny's tongue-tied silences and said, 'We'll talk properly when you get here. You're staying for the week, aren't you?'

Danny cleared her throat. 'I can't. I have to go to work on Monday, and the children have to go to school.'

'Oh.' Pania sounded disappointed. 'Alright, but next time you have to come for a month.'

'OK, if you want us to.'

'We want you to,' Pania said firmly.

They made arrangements to visit the following weekend. Danny wrote down the address and directions. 'I'll see you on Saturday.'

'Yes.'

'I'll go now.' Danny didn't want to hang up.

'Yes.'

'Goodbye.'

'Goodbye.'

Danny waited for Pania to hang up.

'What do you look like?'

Her shoulders slumped. Pania probably hoped she looked like Rose. 'I'm more like my father than my mother, but my eyes are brown . . . kind of.' She hated the desperate note in her voice. 'You might be disappointed. Joe's mother might be wrong.'

'Kiri's not wrong.'

'How do you know?'

'Have you ever noticed how the women or the men in a family sound alike on the phone?'

'Yes.'

'You sound just like Rose.'

Danny left a message on Ross's voicemail, saying she was taking the children to Rotorua for the weekend. She was a bundle of nerves and excitement, so when her cellphone started crowing as she was loading the car for the trip on Saturday morning Danny promptly dropped it and had to dive under her car to retrieve it.

'Hello?' she panted into the phone.

Ross was still upset Danny hadn't asked him for help over Matt, and didn't waste time saying hello. 'Why are you going to Rotorua?'

Danny went on full alert. What was it to him? 'Did I give you the third degree when you said you were flitting off to America?'

'I did not flit off,' he retorted. 'This is work.'

'Oh yeah, it must be hell spending all day bent over while strangers kiss your arse.'

'It's hard work. You wouldn't last a day: I have to repeat the same thing over and over to strangers and be nice.'

'I'd be great at it.'

'You'd stink. By the way, I'm not in America.'

'What do you mean you're not in America?' How dare he move countries without telling her? 'Where are you?'

'Oh I get it, it's OK for *you* to flit off to Rotorua but it's not OK for *me* to flit off to London.' Ross paused. 'You still haven't said why you're going to Rotorua.'

'You're right, I haven't. What are you doing in London? Does the queen know you've been let in the country?'

Once they got started, they could keep up this verbal barrage forever. Ross decided it was better not to make a big deal about her trip to Rotorua, although he badly wanted to know why she was going. Allan Nicolls had emailed him the private investigator's report with the names and addresses of Danny's grandparents and three uncles and the background checks he'd completed. The Smiths seemed solid enough; Edward and Pania Smith had retired four years ago and moved into town, leaving one of their sons to manage the farm. The other two brothers owned and ran an auto-repair business in Rotorua. The family farm had been split equally between the sons. If Danny's mother had lived, her inheritance would have solved all their financial problems. Danny was Rose's heir, and so by rights she was entitled to her mother's share in the farm, but Ross knew money was the furthest thing from Danny's mind — it was family she was looking for, not dollars. Ross hoped her grandparents and uncles would rectify matters without him having to step in and make Danny hate him even more than she already did. He'd planned to give her the report once he'd asked Allan and the investigator some questions. But, as usual, Danny had upset his plans.

'Ross? Are you still there?'

'Yes.'

'Tell me what you've been doing. You don't really hate it do you?'

'I was getting bored, so I broke into the Tower of London to steal the Crown Jewels. It was a bad idea. I'm tunnelling my way out as we speak. I want you to meet me under Tower Bridge in a year's time. Bring a small inflatable boat.'

'Only if you send me the money for the flight and the boat.'

'I'm in a crisis, and you're trying to squeeze money out of me?'

'You'd better include childcare expenses: I'm a solo mother.'

'You're a tightass.'

'That too,' Danny agreed. 'Is the boat for when I fish your sorry carcass out of the Thames?'

'Has anyone ever told you you're heartless?'

'Yes, but he was puking into a bucket at the time so I didn't pay attention. Tell me why you're in London.'

'It's the English premier of *John Doe* tonight. I flew over with Kevin.'

'Kevin? Kevin who?'

'Kevin Spacey.'

She gasped. 'Omigod! Can you get me his autograph?'

'Why do you want his autograph?' Ross asked irritably. 'You've never asked for mine.'

'Why would I want your autograph?' Danny threw Matt's soccer ball and Mia's skateboard beside the bags in the boot of the car. 'Hang on a moment: is it worth anything? Come to think of it, do you think I'd have any takers for your dirty laundry? You certainly left a big enough pile of it in the hamper.'

'You keep your hands off my laundry. I know exactly how many pairs of socks I left behind.'

Danny closed the boot and rested her hip against it. She was wearing the blue skirt and top Ross liked and her blue ballet pumps; and out of respect for the Smiths, her hair was *au naturel*.

She didn't want to frighten them on her first visit.

'This obsession with socks is unhealthy, Fabello. You need help.'

'Danny, I'm warning you—'

Danny sighed with pleasure. It was like old times. 'What are you going to do? Set your private investigator on me?' She waited with bated breath, but Ross remained silent. *Interesting.* 'How's everything going?'

'What? You mean the film?'

'Did you take an extra dumb pill this morning, Fabello? Of course I mean the film.'

Surrounded by sycophants and people dedicated to making sure his world was perfect, Ross smiled as he realized how much he had missed Danny's smart mouth and attitude. He thawed some more. 'The box-office takings are great, so everybody seems to be happy.'

'Excellent,' she replied with satisfaction. 'That means I can ask double for your socks when I post them on TradeMe. I hope you're not overdosing on popcorn and coke — I'll have to lower my asking price if you're fat and covered with zits.'

'I've been pacing myself,' he said reassuringly. 'Or it goes straight to my hips.'

Danny smiled. Oh, but she missed this.

'Besides, I share with Kevin.' He paused significantly. 'Or Marisa.'

Danny's smile slipped. 'Marisa? Who's Marisa?'

'Marisa Tomei. She plays Maria, the wife.' Ross smirked. Just throw out the right lures and Danny could be relied upon to bite. 'Dark-haired, *very* pretty, *great* actress.'

'How nice for you,' she sneered. 'If you'd taken me, Kevin and I could have made up a foursome.'

'I don't think he's attracted to women wearing boiler suits and clown pants.'

'I *do not* wear boiler suits, and my yellow pants *are not* clown pants.' Danny straightened from the car and shook down her skirt. 'I haven't got time to stand around talking to you. I've got to get on the road.'

'Don't pick up any hitchhikers: you'll only frighten them.'

'If I don't get going, I'll be late.'

Ross pounced. 'For what?'

Danny wasn't biting. 'Have fun with Kevin and *Marisah*, and good luck with digging the tunnel. We'll be back on Sunday night if you want to talk to the kids.'

But only after she'd discovered a way to bribe Mia not to blab; Danny still hadn't found out how Ross had managed to keep her quiet about the arrangements for their birthday. She was certain it had taken more than the promise of a CD and a few magnets.

From the bedroom of his hotel suite, Ross watched the lights from Tower Bridge spangle the black surface of the Thames like sequins, and chided himself for being such a fool. He knew Rotorua was a popular holiday destination with geysers, hot bubbling mud and Maori cultural attractions, but he was certain this was no weekend jaunt for the kids. Danny didn't do weekend jaunts.

He'd toyed with asking Allan Nicolls to find Danny's family for weeks, only to make his mind up too late. In her usual independent fashion, Danny had taken matters into her own hands and found them herself, proving yet again that she didn't need Ross for anything. Well, apart from a new roof, bathroom, and to replace the rotten decking. And in bed, Danny definitely liked having him there, so much so that she'd panicked and tried to back-pedal their relationship to being friends. The only time Danny let down her barriers was when they were naked, and each time they made love he felt another layer of his tough, cynical outer shell slough off and light creep into corners of his soul that had lain dark for too long.

Ross told himself the reason that he wanted to find Danny's relatives was so he could leave New Zealand with a clear conscience, safe in the knowledge that she wouldn't be alone. But if he were honest, the real reasons he'd contacted Allan was because Danny needed her family and Ross wanted to find a way to convince her that he wasn't like her father or Patrick; he could be relied on to be there for her; he wouldn't disappear when bad times came or tough decisions had to be made.

Aoife had said he needed a woman who'd kick his ass, and Danny ticked all the boxes. She'd not only kick his ass, she'd pull the rug from under his feet and give him a right hook while she was at it. She'd held up a mirror and shown Ross how he'd become an arrogant, petulant, self-centred pain.

Thousands of miles separated them, but the essence of her had travelled with Ross. In the middle of an interview he'd think about something she'd said or done and have to ask for the question to be repeated. Matt had downloaded some extra songs onto Ross's iPod to listen to on flights and during car rides between publicity appearances, including Danny's Split Enz CD. As soon as he heard 'I See Red' he recognized it as the tune Danny had hummed a lot when they'd first met. When he heard the lyrics he laughed. Now he understood — and also realized that she seldom hummed it anymore. When he listened to the plaintive 'Message to My Girl' and Neil Finn sang about being scared to admit what he felt because it might give away too much, Ross knew exactly what he meant. He had to figure out a way to coax Danny out of the emotional trenches she'd dug around herself without spooking her.

What had happened on their birthday hadn't been about seduction, it had been about need. It had been so long since Ross had to bother seducing any woman that he wasn't sure he even knew how to anymore. Seducing Danny would be like trying to get up close and personal with a porcupine. If she even suspected he wanted more than her body, Lloyd might have to make good on his promise to exhume Ross's remains from the back garden and ship him home to the States. Ross didn't want to be Danny's friend; he wanted the total package. Since he'd begun doing the publicity for John Doe, Ross had been surrounded by beautiful women who'd made it clear they found him attractive. But he wasn't even tempted. None of them had blue hair or dressed like bag ladies. He returned to his solitary bed each night to stare at a strange ceiling, stubbornly refusing to take his hands from behind his head and do something to ease the throbbing in his groin.

The phone rang. It was the concierge. 'The limousine is waiting to collect you from the lobby, Mr O'Rourke.'

'Thank you. I'll be right down.'

Ross shrugged into his suit jacket, shot the cuffs, and picked up his iPod for the journey to the London theatre, where the premiere was being held. As he walked to the door of the hotel suite he knew he wouldn't take in any of what he saw or heard on the screen; he'd be too busy worrying about what might go wrong if Danny was meeting her family. What if they let her down the way her mother and father had? Even Danny had her breaking point, and when it came to her family she was defenceless. Ross wished he wasn't so far away. He wanted to be there if things went wrong.

He wasn't a man who spent a lot of time praying, but Ross sent a silent prayer winging to New Zealand, to Edward and Pania Smith and their sons.

Don't let her down. Don't hurt her. She's waited so long. She needs you.

And I need her to be happy.

Several hours later in Rotorua, Danny gasped as a red tractor barrelled up the driveway to her grandparents' house, narrowly missing the rear bumper of her car.

'Hemi!' Ted, her grandfather, got up from the table to bang on the window. 'Watch Danny's car and my bloody roses, d'you hear?' He was a big, tall man who stood straight as a rugby goalpost. His eyes were bright blue and he had a head of white hair.

Danny held her breath as the tractor veered to the left and stopped just short of Henare's black SUV and Tipene's ute. The black-singleted driver cut the engine and climbed down.

'Hemi drives . . . a tractor?' She'd always thought farmers driving around town on farm bikes and tractors were just a myth created by townies.

'Not usually.' Pania Smith made her way slowly towards the table with a plate of pikelets, adding them to the fruit cake, sandwiches and sausage rolls spread across the yellow-flowered tablecloth. 'But he was working on the farm when we called to say you were here, so he probably thought it was quickest to drive straight over.'

Pania was stooped and tiny and walked with the aid of a stick. When Danny looked into her face, she saw what her mother would have looked like if she'd lived to old age.

Hemi Smith stepped into the room and immediately filled it with his smile and size. 'Morning.' He winked at his father. 'Those roses of yours are looking good, Dad.'

Ted growled and sat down at the table.

Hemi looked at Danny sitting at the other end of the table. 'So, you're Rose's girl.'

Like Tipene and Henare had before him, Hemi inspected Danny thoroughly before coming forward to take her hand, kiss her cheek, and smother her against his chest. The brothers were so much alike that Danny had trouble telling them apart. Fortunately, Henare had the beginnings of a paunch, Tipene's ears stuck out, and Hemi was missing a front tooth.

Hemi looked out the window at Matt and Mia, who were

inspecting the tractor. 'Are those your kids?'

'No,' Danny replied. 'My niece and nephew.'

He scratched his head and pulled out a chair. 'Hard to imagine Rosie as a grandmother.'

Pania beckoned Henare and Tipene to the table and eased herself carefully into the chair that Ted pulled out for her. 'Now we're all here, we can talk. I'm sure Danny has got lots of questions.' She picked up the plate of pikelets and held it out to Danny. 'You'd better get in quick before those three clean us out.'

Danny obediently took a pikelet, but was too nervous to eat it so she put it on her plate.

Ted pointed to a big stainless-steel teapot and a coffee plunger. 'Tea? Or coffee?'

'Tea, please. I don't like coffee.'

'Me, neither.' Pania handed her walking stick to Henare, who hooked it on the back of her chair. She looked at Danny. 'You've been waiting longest, so you should go first. What do you want to know?'

Danny replied, 'Everything.'

Rose Smith had left home when she was nineteen, after her father found out she was having an affair with a married man.

'I told her I didn't want her under my roof if she was going to carry on with a scoundrel like Dave Blackstaff.' Ted shook his head. 'I never expected she'd actually go. She packed her bags and asked Blackstaff to leave his wife and set up with her, but he never meant any of the things he'd promised her, and next thing we knew she'd disappeared to Auckland.'

'We tried to find her,' Pania said. 'The boys went back and forth to Auckland for months.'

Henare took up the story. 'We never got so much as a whiff of her; it was as if she'd disappeared into thin air. Rosie was always her own worst enemy. She lived in a dream world and she wouldn't have it when you tried to put her straight about anything.'

Tipene nodded agreement. 'If bullshit was music, Rosie would have had her own orchestra.'

Danny slanted a look at her grandparents, who were nodding.

'Too pretty, that was Rosie's problem,' Hemi pronounced. 'All the boys were after her.'

'Which was why seeing her with a mongrel like Dave Blackstaff was so hard to swallow,' Ted added bitterly. 'She could have taken her pick.'

'We're just going round and round in circles,' Pania said wearily. 'It won't change anything. Rose made her choices and we just have to live with that.' She watched Matt and Mia come into the room and stop when they saw all the food on the table. 'How about you kids take some of this food and go and watch the television while the grown-ups talk their boring old talk?'

Mia and Matt looked questioningly at Danny, who nodded. They heaped pikelets and sausage rolls onto two plates and went into the living room.

'So what happened to her?' Hemi asked when they were out of earshot. 'What happened to Rosie?'

Danny told them, leaving nothing out. When she said Rose had died of breast cancer, they all looked shaken.

'And your sister?' Pania murmured.

'Breast cancer — earlier this year.'

Tipene shoved his chair back from the table. 'That bloody disease! It's a curse on this family.'

'What do you mean?' Danny searched their faces. 'What does he mean?'

Hemi muttered, 'Two of Mum's nieces and one of her sisters died of breast cancer.'

Danny's hands trembled. She pressed them against the table. A pair of small, wrinkled brown hands covered them. Danny looked up into Pania's warm, brown eyes and saw understanding. 'I'm still here, Danny.' Her grandmother's grip was surprisingly strong. 'It got my twin sister, but it didn't get me.'

Danny clutched her hands. 'You're a twin?'

Pania nodded. 'We're the strong ones, you and I; we're spared for a reason. Ted and your mother and my boys were my reason.' She nodded towards the living room where Mia and Matt were sprawled on the floor in front of the television. 'Those are yours.'

'Auntie Danny!' Mia yelled.

'That girl's got an awesome set of lungs,' Tipene observed dryly.

'Auntie Danny! Uncle Ross is on the TV!'

'Hurry up!' Matt yelled. 'You're missing it!'

Danny rushed into the living room.

Ross's stay in New Zealand had generated enough local interest to warrant the premiere of *John Doe* making the national news. The interview had been filmed a few hours earlier. Ross stood on the red carpet outside a London theatre flanked by Kevin Spacey and Marisa Tomei while crowds braved the chilly night to shout and scream their excitement at seeing their idols.

Danny studied Marisa critically. She wasn't *that* pretty. She stared hungrily at Ross. He'd had his hair cut since she'd last seen him, his black curls were tamed and his jaw was stubble-free. He wore a dark suit and white shirt and looked relaxed and very at home in front of the camera. The top button of the shirt was open and showed his beautiful olive skin and the crisp dark hair at the base of his throat.

Sarah, the interviewer, was the European correspondent for one of the New Zealand television channels. 'So when will you be back in New Zealand, Ross?' she asked and tilted the microphone towards him.

'Early next month. I've got to finish fixing the roof on the house.'

'He's got sheep problems, too,' Kevin said, and Marisa laughed.

'Oh yes, the sheep!' Sarah exclaimed. 'There's been some very interesting photographs of you making the rounds in recent months.' She smiled coyly at the camera before turning back to Ross. 'Do you make a habit of driving around with two sheep in the back of your car?'

Ross arched a brow. 'I have to explain that to a Kiwi girl? The sheep got out. How else was I supposed to get them home?'

Sarah giggled up at him, and Danny longed to slap her. Ross's temporary residence in New Zealand seemed to have turned him into an honorary Kiwi. Sarah asked Ross, Kevin and Marisa some questions about the film. It was obvious from their easy banter and the jokes made at each other's expense that they enjoyed one another's company. Ross smiled and hugged Marisa when she complained about how he and Kevin constantly ganged up on her, and Danny ground her teeth. She wanted to slap them all.

There was a call for Ross and the actors further along the red carpet, so Sarah thanked them all for talking to her and turned back towards the camera.

Ross lingered. 'Is it OK if I say hi to my family in New Zealand before I go?'

Sarah beamed. 'Of course.' She handed him the microphone.

He smiled into the camera. 'Hi Matt, hi Mia. I hope you're getting something to eat besides oatmeal.'

Mia bounced up and down on the floor. 'That's us! He's talking to us!'

Matt shushed her.

Ross stared into the camera lens. His smile grew more intimate and his voice dipped: '*Hi Danny.*'

Danny's stomach somersaulted. She felt as if she was being sucked through the camera and into Ross's warm, dark eyes. He handed the microphone back to Sarah, who asked, 'Who's Danny?'

Ross smiled. 'Ah, now *that* would be telling.'

Sarah turned to the camera and began to speculate about who the mysterious Danny might be.

Danny, meanwhile, had the undivided attention of everybody in the living room.

'Who,' Ted demanded, 'is *that?*'

Chapter 20

When his plane touched down in Auckland, Ross was weighed down by enough Christmas presents to make the elves redundant for the next five years. He'd caught up briefly with Wanda in New York, and then made a quick visit to see his parents in San Diego. Predictably, his mother and sisters had taken the opportunity to give him the job of mail boy for Matt, Mia and Danny's Christmas presents.

It wasn't until Ross was settled on the plane with a glass of single-malt Scotch in his hand that he realized he'd been set up. One of Mia's presents turned out to be a battery-driven puppy, which according to the box was so much like the real thing it did everything but poop. The instant the plane was airborne it started barking nonstop, upsetting all the other passengers in First Class. Ross and one of the cabin attendants had to empty his cabin bag onto the floor before they located the puppy and popped the batteries on the little bastard. He wasn't too surprised to see Deirdre's handwriting on the gift tag attached to the torn wrapping paper.

'How many children do you have, sir?' the flight attendant asked.

He opened his mouth to say none, and stopped. 'Two,' Ross said slowly. 'I've got two.'

A fellow passenger who was already halfway through her first bottle of champagne spoke up from the other side of the cabin.

She had the lifted, suctioned, immobilized face of a sixty-year-old trying to pretend she was still thirty.

'Tell me, O'Rourke,' she slurred, 'are any of those for Danny?'

Her remark alerted Ross to what he'd find when his cab finally pulled up in front of Danny's house. When he'd left there'd been only two or three photographers outside, but when he stepped from the car at least ten of them leapt from their vehicles and began frenziedly snapping his photo.

Months earlier, when Ross had flown into New Zealand Danny had been fast asleep and oblivious. The second time around, she was watching the digital clock on her bedside table when it flicked over to 5.30 a.m. and knew his flight had just touched down at Auckland airport. Just as Nella and her mother had done before her, Danny was watching the clock and counting the minutes until a man came through the front door, and just like them she'd made an effort with her appearance and dressed in the blue skirt and top and matching shoes that Ross liked so much. She'd washed the mascara from her hair, but at the last moment panicked, thinking she looked too obvious, and painted it silver and blue and added her safety-pin earrings.

She needed her head read. Lawton women were hopeless when it came to choosing men. They were genetically predisposed to two things: falling in love with the wrong man, and dying young. Danny shied away from labelling what she felt for Ross as love — lust was better. Long-term commitment was no more Ross's thing than it was hers. He was thirty-seven years old and didn't have so much as an ex-wife or illegitimate child to show for it. He lived alone, in a house with a turret, only emerging to do publicity for his books, or when something like Patrick's death conspired to put him on a plane to the other side of the world.

But when Ross came through the front door trailing glamour

in his wake like some kind of high-octane aphrodisiac, Danny knew she was sunk. He was clean-shaven, clear-eyed and dressed in a smooth dark suit, loosely buttoned white shirt, and aviator sunglasses. He was smiling and rakish and dangerous-looking. The Serial Killer was nowhere in sight. Right there on the floor, in front of the children, Danny wanted to jump his bones.

Instead she watched Ross spill his luggage and duty-free bags across the wooden boards, and scoop Mia into his arms.

'Ouch!' She giggled. 'Uncle Ross! You're squeezing me too hard!'

Ross grabbed Matt and hauled him in for a hug. He scrubbed a hand across Matt's short curls and told him, 'Like the hair, Matt. It looks mean.' Matt ducked away, grinning.

Across their heads, Ross and Danny's eyes met.

I missed you.

I'm so glad you're back.

Ross wanted to haul her against his chest and kiss her until she was dizzy. She was wearing the short blue skirt and blouse he liked. Ross tried not to read too much into that; he'd watched Danny dress the morning after he'd spent the night in her bed and seen the way she plucked clothes from her closet without bothering to see if they matched. Still, it was unusual that she was wearing her blue ballet flats and that her hair didn't clash with her clothes.

'Well,' Ross drawled, 'if it isn't Auntie Danny.'

It was as if a plug had been pulled and all the moisture suddenly drained away from her mouth. Danny licked her lips. 'Auntie Danny, my bum. Do you realize the aggravation I've had since your little television performance?'

He watched her across Mia's head, his eyes glinting. 'What did I do?'

Danny's brows lowered. 'You know what you did.'

Mia grabbed Ross by the jaw and turned his face towards her.

'You've made Auntie Danny famous, Uncle Ross.'

He gasped mockingly. 'I have?'

Danny scowled. 'Ever since you said "Hi, Danny", journalists having been ringing at all hours asking me for interviews, and photographers have been *breeding* on the front lawn. Every time I look out the window there's another one.'

His time spent in the publicity circus meant that Ross had become immune to it, but he'd had the services of a well-oiled security contingent to keep the weirdos and the over-zealous at bay. Danny and the children hadn't had that luxury. 'I'll do something about it.'

Danny hadn't finished. 'Yesterday, a patient asked me if I was "that rich Yank writer's Danny", and if I was could she have my autograph?' She omitted to mention that the woman had actually said 'that spunky, rich Yank writer'. 'It's like I'm being stalked.'

Ross put Mia down and peered through the glass panes in the front door at the photographers prowling up and down the roadside like lions waiting for feeding time. 'I promise I'll do something about it. In the meantime, you and the children keep away from the front garden.'

He picked up his bags and headed towards the kitchen.

Danny stepped in front of him. 'When will you do something about it?'

He tried to step around her, but she blocked him. Ross looked more amused than annoyed. 'I don't know; I left my crystal ball in the States.'

'What are we supposed to do while you decide?'

'Be patient.' He craftily waved the duty-free bags in the air at Matt and Mia. 'Look! I bring gifts. Shall we open them in the kitchen?'

The children raced for the kitchen.

Danny recalled him pulling a stunt like this before; only last time he'd come bearing Starbucks instead of duty-free, and she'd been sporting black eyes. 'Don't try fobbing me off with bottles of cheap booze, and eye shades and slippers from Business Class,' she warned.

His lids dipped and his voice lowered just the way it had on television, and Danny's vertebrae did a little shimmy. 'It isn't cheap booze, and I fly First Class.'

Danny lowered her eyes to his mouth and remembered how it felt to be kissed by him. 'That's . . . that's not the point.'

'I have got a present for you.' Ross dipped his head and leaned closer. 'Do you want to see it?'

Just a few centimetres separated their mouths. It was too much temptation for Ross. He tilted his head and brushed his lips against hers.

'Uncle Ross! Auntie Danny! Are you coming?' Matt shouted from the kitchen.

They sprang apart, Ross grunting as his nose collided with hers. Danny turned one way and then the other in the narrow hall, like a dodgem car without a driver. Ross gave her a nudge in the direction of the kitchen.

He'd brought CDs and books for the children, and a bottle of perfume for Danny. When Ross mixed up Matt and Mia's presents, Danny's lips curved in a small, satisfied smile. He was just as rattled as she was.

He handed her a bag, and she looked inside. 'Perfume? For me? But you don't know what I like.'

'Trust me,' Ross said and she snorted. 'It's perfect for you.'

Danny pulled the cellophane-wrapped box from the yellow bag. It was a bottle of Poison.

'See?' he said. 'It even has your name on it.'

Mia and Matt asked Ross to make dinner.

'Why?' he asked. 'What have you been eating?'

'Burnt chicken nuggets and chips,' Mia replied.

'They weren't always burnt!' Danny protested. 'And I made a cake.'

'You forgot to put the eggs in,' Matt said. 'Even Deryl's pigs wouldn't eat it.'

Ross laughed so hard that Danny hoped he'd have a cardiac arrest. He stopped laughing when the children mentioned their new relatives in Rotorua.

'You've made contact with your family?'

She watched his face closely for some sign that he was responsible for the man who'd been asking around about her family. 'Yes. It turns out that Joe's mother knows my grandmother.'

'That's great, Danny, I'm pleased for you.'

Did she imagine it or was there an edge to his smile? It only added to Danny's confusion. *Why* was he being so nice?

'We've got photos of Nana Pania and Grandad Ted and our uncles.' Matt went to get the digital camera.

When he returned, Ross stared at a photo of Pania for a long time. 'You look like her.'

Danny's cheeks turned pink. 'Do I?'

He scrolled through more photos. 'Do your uncles come in any size besides extra-large?'

Later that night, Danny helped Ross hide the Christmas presents his family had sent for Matt and Mia, and listened to him describe the good, the bad and the downright insane things that had happened during his publicity trip. She laughed when he told her how Deirdre had set him up on the plane with the yapping puppy. The longer Danny listened, the more confused and bewildered she felt. He was handsome, charming and agreeable. He was a certifiable genius in bed, and she only had to look into his eyes to know Ross was intent on getting her back there again. Danny was sorely tempted.

Ross was careful not to overplay his hand. If he pushed too hard, Danny would either bolt or murder him in his sleep, so he made a point of insulting her from time to time to keep her guessing.

For the first few days he didn't do any writing, but gave Danny and the kids his undivided attention. Summer had arrived, and the heat and humidity climbed. Ross rose mornings to run on the beach and take a swim before returning to shower and dress for the Walking Bus. He wore a shirt, shorts, his Chargers cap, and aviators to thwart the photographers' attempts to get a good shot of him, but on his return he stripped down to his shorts and bare feet to write.

Danny gave up trying to eat in the kitchen, because all that bare skin and muscle was too distracting. If temptation got too much for her and she tried to brush against him as she walked behind his chair, Ross would suddenly become engrossed in the screen of his laptop and lean forward, propping his elbows on the table. She'd catch sight of him distractedly rubbing his jaw or the hair on his chest and have to leave the room to keep from diving onto his lap and offering to do it for him. Danny knew of only one form of defence — attack — so she seized on her grievances over the paparazzi invasion and nursed them into a temper tantrum that would have done a two-year-old proud.

The presence of the paparazzi camped on the doorstep didn't lend itself to romance. Ross knew exactly how many photographers were outside the house each morning, because most of them followed him down to the beach and took photos. He watched their comings and goings and did an occasional head count, but much to Danny's annoyance not much else happened.

'What's the point of counting them? What's the point of watching them? How will that get rid of them? Why don't you phone the police and get them to do something?'

'You mean you haven't already done that?'

She nodded grudgingly.

'And what did they do?'

'They said that so long as they weren't blocking the roadway or preventing access to my property, there was nothing they could do about it.'

'Exactly.' Ross went back to counting and watching. 'How do your neighbours feel about all the extra attention?'

'How do you think they feel? They hate it.'

'Good.'

Danny clenched her fists and stamped her foot.

'Don't make me have to send you to your room,' Ross warned.

Two days later, Ross said at breakfast, 'I've figured out a way to get rid of the photographers. I've spoken to Lloyd and the rest of the neighbours on the Walking School Bus route, but I need Jarvis Wainwright's number.'

'Why? What are you going to do?'

'I'll tell you when everything is arranged.'

Danny felt like the only kid in the class left out of planning the end-of-year party. 'It'd be better if I spoke to Jarvis. He doesn't like you, remember?'

'Just give me the number, will you?'

Ross refused to tell her what he was up to: all he would say was that Danny would need to send Matt and Mia to play at friends' houses on Saturday morning, and to make sure she was dressed in old clothes.

'Why?' she asked.

'Did I say old clothes?' Ross asked. 'I meant wear your everyday clothes.'

Danny grew worried. 'It's nothing illegal, is it?'

'Nope.'

It seemed everybody in the neighbourhood was in on the plan except Danny — even Joe knew what was happening. He climbed on the roof whenever he saw her coming his way, but Danny cornered him on Friday afternoon by blocking the way to his ladder.

She gave him her most evil look. 'Tell me what Ross has got planned for tomorrow, Joe.'

'Jeez, don't do that, Danny!' he said nervously. 'My missus made me watch *An American Werewolf in Paris* last night, and that's just how the werewolf looked before he bit somebody.'

'Tell me what's happening tomorrow and I promise I won't bite you.'

Ross was right: Danny was a dangerous woman. 'I can't. Ross will go apeshit if I tell you.'

She backed him against the ladder. 'I'm your cousin, Joe.'

'And Ross is my mate *and* my boss.' He rolled his shoulders uneasily as Danny narrowed her eyes at him. 'I'll tell you one thing.'

She smiled triumphantly. 'What?'

'There'll be cows. Lots of 'em.'

She tried unsuccessfully to pump Deryl, but all she got for her trouble was a pat on the hand and the cryptic comment: 'Ross has got it all organized, dear, just leave it to him. I'll be glad to see the back of those pastrami boys, I can tell you, and I'm going to give them a piece of my mind before they leave.'

Danny decided Deryl must be taking hallucinogenic drugs, because nothing else could explain the glow of approval on Deryl's face as she spoke about Ross, who still hadn't offered to move out or make Danny an honest woman.

By nine o'clock on Saturday morning, Mia and Matt had each been dropped at a friend's house for the day, and Danny was dressed in her lycra shorts, her *I Started With Nothing And Still Have Most Of It Left T-shirt*, her running shoes tied with string, and a battered Warriors cap. To mark the occasion, she'd painted her cropped hair orange and gold. It stood on end and made Danny look like a hyperactive fox as she rushed to the front door to do a head count of the photographers before reporting back to where Ross lounged on one of the chairs on the verandah, writing. She hoped all the hoopla didn't turn out to be a big fat disappointment — so far the only thing Ross had done to mark the occasion was put on a pair of cut-off jeans and a loud fuchsia-pink-and-blue Hawaiian print shirt that was *so* not him.

Danny instantly fell in love with it. 'That shirt is disgusting. Can I have it?'

'Don't I know it — and no, you can't. Your closet is bad enough.' Ross kept his eyes on the screen of his laptop. 'It was a birthday present from Deirdre.'

'A birthday present?' Danny was incredulous. 'What did you do to her?'

'I think it was in retaliation for *The Bride's Big Book for Her Bottom Drawer* I gave her for her last birthday.'

She squinted at him. 'There's a reason you're wearing it today, isn't there?'

'I'll get my photograph taken today, and with any luck Deirdre will see it and cringe when I make a point of telling everybody she bought it for me.'

'Your devious little brain never rests, does it?'

He smiled modestly. 'I do my best. How many of them are out there now?'

'Eight. What exactly are we waiting for?' Danny demanded.

Ross yawned, stretched and checked his watch. 'Guess that'll have to do, then.' He climbed to his feet. 'I just need to make a couple of phone calls.'

The phone calls were brief and left Danny none the wiser. 'Do we go outside now?' she asked.

'Not yet.'

Ross helped himself to an apple from the fruit bowl by the telephone and put another one in his pocket. He took a seat at the kitchen table, rubbed the apple on his shirt and bit into it.

Danny sat down opposite, propped her elbows on the table and her face in her hands and watched him eat the apple. A minute ticked by on the clock by the door. 'Now do we go outside?'

'Nope.'

Munch, munch.

She tapped her fingers against her cheekbones. 'Now?'

'No.'

Munch, munch. Munch, munch, munch.

'What about now?'

Ross finished the apple and looked at Danny, his eyes brimming with laughter.

She snapped to attention. 'You pig!'

He laughed and fired the apple core into the bin by the fridge. 'Come on, Rocky.'

The quiet country road outside the house was filled with Danny's neighbours, who all stood about glaring at the photographers. Danny was relieved to see that none of them were carrying pitchforks or guns. When she walked onto the front lawn with Ross, the photographers began taking pictures.

Danny gritted her teeth. 'This had better be good, Fabello.'

Ross pulled the apple from his pocket and bit into it. He seemed to be oblivious of the cameras aimed at them.

'What do we do now?' she asked.

'You'll see.'

Gradually the sound of distant mooing drifted towards them from the cliff end of the road. Everybody turned in the direction of the noise and the cloud of dust that accompanied it. The dust cloud increased, and the mooing grew louder. A slow smile spread across Danny's face as two hundred of Jarvis Wainwright's cows came over the rise in the road, a moving blanket of black and white, filling the narrow strip of tarmac and spilling over onto the rough country verges banded by batten-and-wire fences.

It was like something out of a spaghetti Western. All that was missing was the theme song from *The Good, The Bad and The Ugly* and Mexican bandits dressed in wide hats and ponchos shouting *Yee-hah!* and shooting guns into the air. In lieu of bandits, Jarvis Wainwright and his Silver Shadow brought up the rear of the herd, pushing them inexorably onwards, towards the photographers' sleek, expensive SUVs, Audis, Volvos and a particularly nice BMW convertible, all parked on the grass beside the road.

Jarvis gently tapped the accelerator and the cows broke into a trot. The photographers suddenly realized that their precious vehicles were on a collision course with a herd of hungry cows headed for the paddock full of lush, green grass beside Deryl and Lloyd's house. They rushed for their cars, fumbling at door handles and dropping cameras in their haste to escape the bovine apocalypse headed their way. The arrival of a police car at the other end of the road complicated matters by blocking their escape route.

Danny looked at the expressions of unholy glee on her neighbours' faces, and the smile curving Ross's mouth as he calmly finished his apple. She put her arms in the air and yahooed. It was better than winning the lottery.

The cows reached Danny's house and angled across the road

towards Deryl and Lloyd's gate, bumping clumsily up against the stranded cars as they went by. The BMW was dealt a hefty kick by an anxious youngster while the car's owner shrank behind the steering wheel. It wasn't until the paddock gate had closed behind the last cow that the photographers felt safe enough to emerge and inspect the damage to their vehicles.

'You're a prick, O'Rourke!' A redheaded individual with a bad case of sunburn pointed at a large dent in the side of the BMW. 'Look at my car!'

Ross threw away the apple core and wiped his fingers on his ugly shirt. 'Damn, that's a shame. You'll just have to take up running instead.'

'I'll sue you! See if I don't, you smug arsehole!' Red stepped in a fresh cow pat, skidded and promptly fell on his own. 'Shit!'

'That's about the most truthful thing I've ever heard you say, Hickford.'

Deryl descended on the hapless Hickford like an avenging angel in polyester. 'You've caused nothing but trouble hanging around outside our homes. My Felicity and Chantal have been so upset they've stopped eating.'

At Ross's questioning look, Danny mouthed *pigs*. He shook his head: only Deryl would name a couple of pigs Felicity and Chantal.

'Hey, Hickford!' Danny yelled exuberantly. 'We're getting the septic tank pumped out next week, if you get your car fixed in time you should come take a photo. You never know, the hose might accidentally get disconnected!'

Ross watched as Danny danced across the front lawn in her droopy shoots and shapeless T-shirt, with her cropped orange hair standing up on her head, looking like a punk-rocker cockatiel, and understood why Lloyd thought Deryl was beautiful in her awful dress and knee-highs.

'You were brilliant!' Danny tucked her thumbs in a pair of imaginary braces and high-kicked around the kitchen table. 'You were brilliant! *You were brilliant!*'

Ross stood at the open back door with a shoulder propped against the doorjamb and watched. She'd climbed out of her emotional bunker, but had he done enough to keep her from slipping back again?

Danny stopped dancing. 'Why are you looking at me like that?'

'Like what?'

'Like I've suddenly grown facial hair or need to wipe my nose?'

He shook his head slowly. 'You'd never believe me.'

She propped her hands on her hips. 'Try me.'

'No.'

The opportunity to delve inside his head was gone.

Danny opened the dishwasher and looked inside. 'Is this clean or dirty?'

'Clean,' Ross replied. 'I've arranged to do an interview at a hotel in Auckland today,' he continued. 'If you really want to lay this thing to rest, you should come with me.'

She filled two glasses with water, handed one to Ross and took a drink from her own. 'Come with you? Why?'

'To tell everybody who Danny is.'

Danny choked on a mouthful of water. 'Are you serious?'

'Are you that much of a chicken?' Ross emptied his glass and put it down. 'I'm meeting the journalist at one o'clock. If you want to come, you'll need to get changed.'

'I don't want to come.'

He shrugged. 'Fine, suit yourself.' He headed for the bathroom. 'But you're only giving a five-minute wonder an extra breath of life instead of facing the music and turning it into old news.'

'I wouldn't have had to face *any* music if you hadn't opened your big mouth in the first place!' Danny went to the kitchen door and shouted along the hallway. 'If — *if* I come, I'm going to wear my Coco the Clown pants! Do you still want me along?'

'Fine by me.' The door to the bathroom closed.

Danny was sitting cross-legged in the middle of his bed when Ross returned from his shower, naked but for a towel draped around his hips. He was surprised; she usually avoided coming into Nella's old bedroom.

'I thought I told you before: if you want to see a naked man, buy a magazine.'

'The staples are always in the wrong places.'

He fought with a smile; she had an answer for everything. He reached for the towel. 'I'm dropping this.'

'You can't, I'm a virgin, pure as the driven snow.'

Ross loosened the knot. 'It's coming off — close your eyes.'

The towel hit the floor.

'Pervert,' said Danny.

'Hussy,' said Ross.

The heat in her golden eyes aroused him; he stepped towards her, but Danny held up a hand.

'I won't have to say anything, will I? You'll do all the talking?'

Ross took a slow, deep breath. She'd be the death of him. He went to the closet. 'OK, now you're scaring me. Are you coming or not?'

Danny wiggled her bottom lip between her teeth and looked at Ross hungrily. She didn't want to go to an interview with him, she wanted to go to bed with him. But she mustn't, and if she didn't leave she was going to take a bite out of his gorgeous bum. She crawled off the bed.

'I'll have a quick shower and iron my clown pants.'

His head shot up. 'Like hell you will — can't you wear your blue skirt?'

'I do have some other nice clothes, and just this once I'll pay attention and make sure they match.'

Three quarters of an hour later, they were riding across the harbour bridge in the Explorer. Ross was wearing jeans, a denim shirt, sunglasses and — Danny inhaled deeply — Dolce & Gabbana aftershave.

Danny wore wide-legged white linen pants and a cream crushed-silk sleeveless top decorated with a line of roses made of the same fabric. The cream silk complemented the bronze and gold streaks in her hair and her honey-coloured eyes and skin. Ross kept looking at her. He was deeply puzzled. 'You look nice.'

'I always look nice; when it comes to fashion, I'm ahead of my time.'

'Yeah, you're a fashion icon to bag ladies the world over.' Ross sniffed. 'You're wearing Poison.'

'Don't let it go to your head.'

The journalist's name was Gaynor. She was waiting for Ross in a quiet corner of the hotel foyer. As soon as she saw Danny, her gaze sharpened with interest. Gaynor shook hands with Ross and introduced the photographer she'd brought along. Danny eyed him tepidly. She was off photographers.

Gaynor's eyes kept darting to Danny. When they were all settled on the sofas, Ross said, 'This is Daneka Lawton.'

'Ross's *sister-in-law*,' Danny added.

'Daneka?' Gaynor sat up straighter. 'Do you sometimes go by the name of Danny?'

Danny wished she'd kept her trap shut. 'Sometimes.'

Gaynor arranged drinks. Danny wanted to suggest arsenic for

Gaynor; instead, she accepted a glass of orange juice and tried to make herself invisible. Gaynor had other ideas. When Ross mentioned his Italian/Irish heritage, Gaynor remarked what a passionate combination it was and slanted a look at Danny. 'And is he?'

Danny was crunching on an ice cube. 'Izzywha?'

'Passionate?'

Her hackles rose. Like every other time in her life when somebody she cared about was under attack, Danny prepared to defend Ross, but instead he came to her rescue.

He looked at Gaynor and said flatly, 'Danny told you: she's my sister-in-law.'

Danny relaxed and let Ross take care of it. She popped another ice cube in her mouth and listened as he continued answering Gaynor's questions about his writing.

Gaynor wasn't the only one who was disappointed when their time was up. Ross was an eloquent, witty and thoughtful interview subject. When he spoke about his books and writing, his passion and love for his work became clear.

Gaynor tried one last time to include Danny in the interview. 'Could we get a photo of you and Danny?' she asked sweetly.

'No,' Ross told her bluntly.

Danny crunched an ice cube and smiled. She could get used to this.

'So when can my agent expect to see a draft of your article?'

The valet pulled Ross's car up to the entrance of the hotel. Danny plucked at one of the roses on her top and watched Ross hand over a $50 tip. Ross waited for her to lay into him for giving away so much money, but she didn't say anything, just climbed into the passenger seat when the valet held the door open.

'OK,' Ross said when Danny still didn't speak as they drove away. 'What's wrong now?'

'I think Gaynor got the wrong idea about us.'

Ross wanted to say, *No, Gaynor didn't get the wrong idea at all.* Instead he said, 'I barely spoke to you. We accomplished what we set out to do.'

'I don't think so. I'm sure Gaynor got the wrong idea.'

They stopped at traffic lights. 'What idea?'

'That we're a couple.'

Ross decided to take a chance. 'Why is that wrong?'

The lights changed.

'Think about it,' he said.

Chapter 21

For dinner, he cooked a wonderful Irish dish called colcannon. Mia and Matt wolfed it down before disappearing to the living room to watch *Freaky Friday* on DVD.

Danny studied the empty plates. 'You're drugging them, aren't you?'

Ross looked pointedly at hers. 'My cooking is the drug.'

'I was trying to be nice.'

'You don't know how to be.'

He poured two glasses of red wine and picked up his laptop. 'Come outside.'

She was still shaken by what he'd said in the car. Ross hadn't pressed her for an answer, just changed the subject and collected Matt and Mia.

Danny remained at the table. 'I'm not that kind of girl.'

His voice deepened. 'Oh yes, you are.'

He disappeared through the back door and out into the darkness carrying his laptop.

Her bare toes curled around the rung on the kitchen chair. 'If you're going to write, I'm not coming,' she called after him.

'I want to show you some photos,' he called back. 'You bring the wine.'

'*Yes, Mustah!*' Danny dropped her feet to the floor and muttered, 'Great, now he's going to show me his etchings.'

She told Matt and Mia where they'd be, collected the wine bottle and glasses and followed Ross outside.

He'd booted up the laptop and was sitting in his favourite spot on the verandah, the light from the screen shining on his face. Danny took the other chair and placed the wine and their glasses on the deck between them. She considered getting drunk. If she was comatose, she wouldn't have to concentrate so hard on keeping her hands off him. Ross made things worse by dragging Danny's chair closer.

'These are photos of my family,' he said. 'I've seen what yours look like.'

She tapped her fingers nervously on the arm of her chair. There was something very serious about a man showing a woman photographs of his family. 'Have you got one of Uncle Carmine's nose?'

Ross ignored her.

Breda Fabello had silvery blonde hair and hardly any wrinkles. She had Matt and Mia's sapphire blue eyes and Ross's determined jaw.

'I don't believe she's your mother,' Danny said. 'She doesn't look haggard enough.'

'Next time she calls, I'll get her to tell you about the night I was born — that should alleviate any doubts. She'll give you all the grisly details about how I got stuck and they needed forceps to get me out. It wasn't as if I planned it.'

Danny looked at his nose. 'I bet I know which part of you got stuck.'

'Cruel, Daneka, very cruel.'

Ross had inherited his black eyes from his father, but not the mellow, contented gaze. Vito was as dark as Breda was fair. He had a thick black moustache, black hair threaded with grey, and a wide, handsome smile.

'Oh, my goodness,' Danny leaned closer, 'he's so handsome.'

Ross picked up his wine and took a sip. 'I'm a chip off the old block.'

'And so modest,' she cooed.

'They used to fight like cat and dog when we were kids, and then disappear to their bedroom to make up. Of course, they've mellowed a little as they've gotten older, but the spark is still definitely there.'

Danny thought about Daniella and Patrick disappearing in the middle of the day and how she'd disapproved. It didn't seem to have done Ross any harm knowing his parents settled their differences by making love. He showed her a photo of a hugely pregnant woman with long, blonde hair and almond-shaped eyes a surprising shade of nutmeg brown. 'That's Carmel, right?'

'Right before she hatched Kevin and his amazing nose.'

'How is his nose, by the way?' Danny enquired.

'When I saw it last week — blooming.'

'They're redheads!' She exclaimed when Ross showed her a photo of Aoife and Annie. 'Where did that come from?'

'Granny Concepta O'Rourke, bless her heart.'

The twins had curls like Ross and Matt. Their hair hung about their shoulders in a shawl of red, gold and copper ringlets. Annie the artist had a sweet smile and limpid brown eyes, but Aoife's challenging gaze and wild red mane reminded Danny of a lioness.

'I must remember to tell her that, she'll love it.' Ross pointed at the screen. 'That's Deirdre, the youngest.'

'The Big Girl's Bottom Drawer?'

He tutted. *'The Bride's Big Book for Her Bottom Drawer.'*

Danny topped up her wine. 'She looks just like Patrick, except her skin's fairer.'

Ross was silent for a moment. 'Pat hated her from the moment Ma brought her home from the hospital.'

She waited to see if he'd say anything more, and when he didn't asked, 'Why?'

'Because he wasn't the youngest anymore. He was always doing things to her, hurtful, nasty things. We had to watch him all the time. Once Pat deliberately took Deirdre up into a tree and left her there crying because she couldn't get down again.' He stared at Deirdre's smiling face. 'My mother always made excuses for him, but eventually even my dad lost patience and whaled the living daylights out of Pat, but it only made him more sneaky.'

Taking her cue from Ross, Danny kept her eyes on the screen. 'I didn't like him much.'

'Neither did I,' he admitted.

'I was jealous of him.'

Ross turned to look at Danny. 'Jealous?'

She huddled in the chair. 'It'd always been just me and Daniella, just the two of us, and suddenly along came Patrick and . . . well, she had somebody else who meant as much to her as I did, *more* in fact.'

'It was bound to happen sometime. Daniella probably would've felt the same when you found somebody.'

Danny snorted. 'That was never going to happen. Nella was the home-and-hearth type, not me.'

Danny, you're a lot more 'home and hearth' than you know, Ross thought, *judging by the way you guard those kids.* He wondered if she realized how firmly entrenched she'd become in the role of family guardian. 'Aoife and Annie are total opposites — were you and Daniella the same?'

She took her time answering. 'She was the kind, sweet, *good* twin. My mother said I was just like my father, and he walked out on us when we were teenagers. I could be naughty, but I wasn't that bad. Half the time I got into trouble was because I was sticking up for Nella.' Old resentments simmered in her voice.

Ross wished he could tape what she'd said and play it back to her and then her grandparents and uncles. It might make Danny wake up to the lousy way she'd been treated by her family in the past, and ensure her newly discovered relatives took better care of her in the future.

'Danny, what was it like when you found out that Nella had breast cancer, just like your mother?'

She seemed surprised by the question — nobody had ever asked her before.

'They didn't have regular examinations, and by the time I realized . . .' Danny shrugged, 'it was too late.'

There it was again, the assumption that it had been her job to take responsibility for her mother's and sister's health.

'My grandmother's a twin, too. Her sister died of breast cancer, and one of my mother's cousins.'

Ross struggled to keep his voice even. 'Do you get checked regularly?'

'Of course I do. I've got an appointment soon.'

He cupped Danny's chin and turned her face towards him. 'Don't *ever* miss an appointment, do you hear me? Not ever. If you do, I'll—'

She seemed taken aback by his intensity. 'What?'

He forced a smile. 'I'll make you do the cooking for the rest of the year.'

'Now who's being cruel?'

'Danny . . .' Ross caught her face between his hands. 'Seriously . . .'

She shook her head. It had been a wonderful day. Why spoil it by talking about something so ugly? It was a beautiful night. *He* was beautiful. Danny leaned over and kissed him.

Ross resisted. 'Can we just— '

'No.' She kissed him again.

'You're just trying to distract me.'

'Is it working?'

He caught her by the arms and put some distance between them. 'Danny, I want to talk about this.'

'I don't.' She grabbed him by the hair and dragged him back.

'Ouch! Is this your idea of seduction?'

So much for moonlight *or* seduction. 'No. *This* is romance.' She got to her knees. 'Seduction comes later, when I knee you in the balls, you moron.' She clambered onto his lap, forgetting it was already occupied. His laptop crashed onto the deck. 'Oh my God!' Danny gasped, 'I've broken it! Your writing!'

Ross didn't care about the laptop. 'Forget about it, I've got back-ups.' He wrapped his arms around her hips. 'I want to talk about your breasts.'

Danny was annoyed. She'd wanted the day to end the same way their birthday had, but he'd ruined it. She grabbed the hem of the cream silk shirt and jerked it up. As usual, she was bra-less. 'Here!' she yelled. 'Ask them anything you want!'

Startled, Ross lowered his eyes and exhaled, a sigh of pure male appreciation. 'Hel-*lo*, little darlings.'

Dumb move, Danny's left brain semaphored to the right side, *really* dumb move. She tried to yank her top down, but Ross trapped her hands against her shoulders.

'Can you shut up? You're interrupting a private conversation.'

Danny tried to wriggle away, but he slid lower in the chair, taking her with him. She started to wobble and clamped her knees around his hips to keep from falling. When the bulge in his jeans brushed against her crotch, Danny gave up the fight. A girl could only resist so much temptation before she folded. She lowered herself onto him. 'So that's where you keep your light sabre, Darth.'

Ross pushed against her. Danny pushed back, trying to wrap her legs around his waist, but the chair got in the way. When he leaned forward to make a gap, Danny crossed her ankles in the small of his back and did a little bump and grind against him.

Ross yanked the silk top over her head and dropped it on the deck, taking one of her breasts into his mouth. Danny bucked against him as he sucked, digging her heels into his back. Reaching between them, she unhooked the button and lowered the zipper of his jeans and slipped her hand inside.

'Auntie Danny! Uncle Ross!'

They froze.

'Mia!' Danny squeaked, hastily scooting backwards and falling off Ross's lap in the process.

'Auntie Danny! Uncle Ross! Where are you?'

Danny snatched her top from the wooden deck. 'Stay where you are, Mia, I'll be there in a minute!'

Ross slumped in the chair with a hand across his eyes and shook his head. Who needed contraception with Mia in the house?

'Put that away!' she hissed.

He looked up. 'What?'

She pointed to his unzipped fly. '*That.*'

'My light sabre? Come back here and I will.'

'*We can't!*'

'But you want to, don't you?' He tucked himself into his jeans with difficulty.

She nodded.

'Auntie Danny!'

'I won't be a moment, Mia!' Danny shouted back. 'Go into the kitchen and wait for me!'

Ross inhaled and exhaled slowly. 'It's time the kids were in bed. I'd help, but I'm a little preoccupied right now. After Matt and Mia are in their rooms, *we* are going to bed; I don't care if it's yours or mine. I'll even settle for the chook house and risk getting my bare ass pecked by those damned chickens.' Ross checked his watch. 'You've got twenty minutes.'

She turned and ran.

Danny got the children into bed in record time. Ross had been different tonight, different all day. He'd let her see inside his head, revealing parts of himself she sensed he normally kept private. She recalled Gaynor's rapt expression as Ross cracked open the door to let a dreaded journalist get a glimpse inside — and knew Gaynor wasn't the one for whom he'd been opening the door.

As she'd settled the children, she heard the shower running in the bathroom — Ross was showering again, even though he'd already washed that morning. The gesture made Danny's fluttering belly flutter some more. She showered herself, brushed her teeth and ran Ross's razor over her legs. She slapped on some Poison, and pulled on a short purple silk nightgown that Nella had bought her some long-ago Christmas, which she'd never worn.

By the time Danny stepped out onto the verandah running along the side of the house between their rooms, a fine, soft rain had begun to fall. It released a warm, earthy smell from the sun-baked earth and blew gently inwards. She moved closer to the edge of the verandah, filling her lungs with the scents from the garden.

One of the French doors opened, the light from Ross's bedroom casting a pool on the wooden boards. He was bare-chested and barefoot, and wearing the same blue jeans he'd worn earlier, except the top snap was undone. Danny watched him search the deck and find her.

He joined her and looked at the thin silk moulding her body. 'Take it off,' he said.

She looked at his jeans. 'You, too.'

Ross reached for his zipper as she reached for the hem of the nightgown.

The jeans hit the verandah.

The nightgown landed on a flax bush.

The wind shifted and the summer rain blew. They made love in the warm, dark night, bathed in moonlight, with the raucous whirr of cicadas to serenade them. Later, when the rain had stopped falling, they lay in the wet grass, Ross's chest to Danny's back, his knee between her thighs and his hand cradling her breast.

'You sent a private investigator to Rotorua to find my family, didn't you?'

'Yup.'

'That was . . .' Did a word exist that would adequately describe what it meant to her? 'Very kind of you.'

'I should have known you didn't need my help,' he grumbled. 'It was a waste of time and money.'

Danny stroked his knee. His bark was so much worse than his bite. 'Was it expensive?'

'I'll have to write a book just to cover the cost,' Ross complained sleepily.

Her hand slid down his thigh. 'I'll help pay for it.'

He was suddenly wide awake. 'How? You are, as you so poetically put it, *on the bones of your* arse.'

'I'll work it off,' Danny promised.

She pushed him onto his back and climbed on top of him. 'How long do you think it will take?'

'About fifty years.' He reached for her hips, settled her in the right spot and groaned. 'That's if you don't kill me first.'

The interview with Gaynor was published the following weekend, accompanied by a photograph of Ross taken at the interview and another of him on the red carpet at one of the *John Doe* premieres, flanked by Kevin Spacey and Marisa Tomei. Gaynor had managed to add a few hints about the true nature of RF O'Rourke's relationship with the mysterious Danny who insisted she was only his sister-in-law.

'Cow,' Danny said when she finished reading the article. 'She's got no right to lead people up the garden path.'

Ross was sprawled in his chair on the verandah, enjoying the morning sunshine and reading the sports section. He wore a pair of raggedy jean shorts and no shirt. It amused Danny how much more Ross liked those old shorts and his Chargers T-shirt than the Armani suits hanging in his closet.

'Speaking of gardens, I've got grazes on my elbows and knees. Can we please just cut the crap and go to bed in my room tonight?' he asked.

'No. All that clandestine running between rooms twice a night turns me on.'

Danny didn't want the children to know they were sleeping together. She still didn't believe that what she had with Ross would last. He reined in his frustration. Physical intimacy, Danny understood; it was the intimacy between a couple that happened after they climbed out of bed that she struggled with. Watching her grapple with it was like watching a baby take its first steps. All Ross could do was be there to help her up when she fell.

He'd spoken with Danny's grandmother that week.

'So you're Uncle Ross?' Pania asked.

'Yes, ma'am,' Ross replied.

'Yes, *ma'am*, he says.' She sounded amused. 'You sound like a boy scout, but I saw you on the television and you're no boy scout, Uncle Ross. I hope you've got my granddaughter's best interests at heart.'

'Absolutely, Mrs Smith — and besides, I've seen a photo of her uncles.'

She chuckled. 'Uncle Ross, I think I might like you.'

Ross handed the phone over to Danny. She pressed it against her shoulder. 'What was that all about?'

'None of your business.'

He *was* glad she'd made contact with her mother's family. Family was important. A fact which Ross knew he'd lost sight of in the past couple of years. But at the same time, it helped strengthen Danny's stubborn resolve to remain independent and never rely on anybody but herself. At this rate it might take Ross years to wear her down, but he was every bit as stubborn as she was, and wouldn't give in until he got her up the aisle and a ring on her finger, which shocked the hell out of him. Ross knew that Danny loved him. Her body told him every night when they made love. It was just her brain that was having trouble catching up. Everything would work out.

He just needed to give her time and space to adjust.

At least that's what he thought until Danny came home a couple of days later and suggested he might like to take the children home to San Diego to spend Christmas with his family — without her.

Danny had gone for her breast screening with a smile on her face and a spring in her step. Nobody in their right mind actually enjoyed the trip to the breast clinic, but Danny had been through it many times and she had far nicer things to occupy her thoughts. She closed her eyes, listened to the music playing through the headphones, and thought about what Ross had done to her in the damp grass outside his bedroom the night before. *Twice.* She was still smiling when the doctor took her into the room to say they'd found a small change in her left breast.

Danny listened in silence, too dumbfounded to take in what

she was hearing. She made arrangements to return the following week. The doctor wasn't happy at the delay. 'Danny, we need to see you right away. It might be nothing, but we need to get onto this.'

'I know. I need to make some arrangements first for the kids. *Please* — just give me a week, OK?'

Reluctantly, the doctor agreed.

She touched her left breast. It didn't feel any different, and Ross had certainly never mentioned feeling anything wrong, and he was on more intimate terms with her boobs than she was. The other shoe had finally dropped.

Danny was too numb to cry. Her first thought was to make sure the children were going to be alright in the weeks and months to come while she got on with the job of trying to defeat this monster that kept devouring the people she loved.

She loved Ross; he was the other half of her, closer even than Nella had been. He understood her better than her sister ever had, because they were so alike. Ross cared about her, really cared. He didn't make empty promises the way her father and Patrick had. Ross showed what he felt and thought about the people he loved by doing things for them, even things he didn't want to, like coming to New Zealand when he'd much rather have stayed in his turret writing — and paying for somebody to find Danny's family, even though it was in his best interests for her to become more dependent on the Fabellos.

Danny now understood why Nella hadn't wanted Patrick to know she was sick. If the expression in Ross's eyes when he looked at her turned to pity and revulsion, it would kill her more surely than any cancer. Danny didn't know if she could stay strong for Ross and the children and fight the disease as well.

At first, when she told Ross she thought it would be a good idea if he took Matt and Mia to San Diego for Christmas, he looked pleased. 'You've got leave over Christmas?'

'No, I've got to work. What Emergency Department ever shuts down for Christmas?'

He frowned. 'Why would I want to take Matt and Mia to the States for Christmas if you can't come, too?'

'Why not?' Danny asked. 'You've been saying how much your family wants to meet them ever since you came here. I'll be at work the whole time, so it doesn't make sense for the three of you to hang around here.'

He searched her expression for clues, but Danny had on her best poker face. 'It won't bother you being here on your own for Christmas?'

'I won't be alone, I've got Van and Dee and Lloyd. Somebody from the hospital is always throwing a party most nights between Christmas and New Year, so I won't miss out.'

'I don't believe you,' Ross said abruptly. 'What's wrong?'

Danny's resolve wavered. 'Nothing's wrong. I need some space. You're not the only one who likes your solitude, you know. I thought if anybody would understand, you would.' She summoned a look of exasperation. 'Come on, Ross, you *know* neither one of us is cut out to be half of a couple! We're too much alike.'

Ross's expression hardened. 'Speak for yourself, Daneka. Call me an idiot, but I thought the reason we were so well matched was because we *were* alike.'

Danny shrugged.

'You know what you are?' he asked.

'No, but I guess you're about to tell me.' She braced herself.

'You're a coward. When are you going to stop making excuses for why something shouldn't happen and start finding reasons why it should?'

She wouldn't look at him. 'Be quiet: Matt and Mia will hear us fighting.'

'Stop treating them as if they're five years old! People fight! The important thing is that they learn to compromise and make up again! You've never learned how to compromise.'

'Oh?' Danny spat. 'Like you have?' The anger drowned out her fear and helplessness — if there was one thing she could rely on Ross for, it was a good fight and an even better fuck. Danny winced at how easy it was to make something so special sound so ugly and crude.

'You realize Matt knows we're sleeping together?'

That took the wind out of her sails. 'He does?'

'He's not blind. He's going to be twelve next month.'

'I know that.' Danny didn't need him to remind her when Matt's birthday was; she'd been around for every single one.

Ross was hurt and furious, and lashed out with the most lethal weapon he had — his tongue. 'You're incapable of having a positive, adult relationship because you're still a child. You're emotionally retarded, Danny.'

She flinched.

Thanks to a last-minute cancellation, Ross managed to get three seats to the States close to Christmas. Matt and Mia were excited at the thought of meeting their American family, but upset that Danny wasn't coming with them.

'I'll be right here waiting when you get home,' she reassured them. 'Uncle Ross will be with you. Just think of how great it will be to meet all your cousins.'

Danny and Ross were barely on speaking terms, so she gave Matt and Mia the Christmas presents.

'I'll call you as soon as we get to my parents' house,' Ross said stonily when the time came to leave.

'Thank you.' Her smile was strained.

Doubt niggled at him. 'Danny, are you sure everything's OK?' '

Yes. See you in two weeks.'

Chapter 22

Ross spent the first couple of days at his parents' house in San Diego helping Matt and Mia try to keep track of their new aunts, uncles and cousins. His mother had asked the rest of the family to wait until Pat's children were comfortable with the immediate family before second, third and fourth cousins descended, but Ross knew it was like trying to hold back the tide, and it was only a matter of time before they began to arrive on the doorstep bearing gifts, hugs and painful cheek pinches.

'Two things to remember,' he advised Matt and Mia. 'As soon as Aunt Lucia hugs you, duck and run, otherwise she'll pinch you on the cheek and she's got a grip like a Rottweiler. The other thing is to never ever let Cousin Bruno get you in a headlock and rub his knuckles on the top of your head; he's got hands like concrete. And don't play cards with your cousins Brad and Raul, because they cheat.'

His parents and sisters were charmed by Mia and Matt's accents. Ross was proud of them; they had beautiful manners, and were just shy enough to make them appealing instead of awkward. Breda burst into tears when she saw Matt, and Vito blew loudly into his handkerchief.

'Don't they like me?' Matt whispered anxiously to Ross.

'They're crying because you look so much like your father,' he explained.

'Oh. That's OK, then.'

Mia clung to Ross. She crept from her bedroom and spent each night with him in his old childhood bed, curled against his back. Matt slept in the same room, in Pat's old bed.

Ross kept replaying the horrible things he'd said to Danny. During the day he put on a brave face and hid the anguish he was feeling. But at night the feeling that something was wrong with Danny grew. He felt the same way he had in London when he'd instinctively known something important was happening to her. It was like having a gremlin sitting on his shoulder, taunting him.

'Damn,' he muttered into the darkness, taking care not to wake Matt and Mia. 'I've turned into Danny's twin.'

He explained to his family that Danny hadn't been able to come because she had to work, and everybody agreed that it was a shame because they wanted to meet her. Ross phoned and left a message to say they'd arrived safely, but after that he only dialled the number for Matt and Mia when they wanted to speak to her.

His sisters were amazed by the way he took care of Matt and Mia, as if he'd been doing it for years, and to be honest that was the way it felt.

Ross couldn't imagine life without them; it was as if they had always been there. Mia found her way onto his knee when the sight of too many new faces overwhelmed her, and Matt looked to him for reassurance and approval.

'I can't believe what I'm seeing,' Carmel told Aoife. 'It's like they're his.'

'Yeah,' Aoife smiled maliciously. 'Pat would be *so* pissed.'

The following day when Ross discovered Mia playing in the garage with several of her older cousins, he whisked her away and steered her firmly in the direction of the back yard. 'It's not a good idea to play in the garage with your bigger cousins, Mia.'

Ross knew all about what took place out in the garage. When he was ten, he'd had his first look at a pair of naked breasts in there, courtesy of his thirteen-year-old cousin Lucrezia. He took Mia inside and handed her over to Carmel with a brief explanation of where he'd found her. Carmel plonked Kevin in Mia's lap and said, 'Here, honey, cuddle him — he's safe enough for another few years.'

'Ross, go tell your father to hurry up with that wine, lunch is nearly ready,' Breda ordered, as he tried to slip through the kitchen to the quiet of the den. He reluctantly retraced his steps through a wall of humanity which included several aunts and female cousins and Deirdre. How did his mother manage to cook anything with no room and so much noise? He'd almost made it to the door leading to Vito's wine cellar when Aunt Lucia popped up and grabbed him.

'So handsome!' She pinched his cheek between her thumb and fingers and waggled his head from side to side. 'So clever! So rich! Why is this one not married yet, Breda?'

Breda whacked the long-handled spoon she was using to stir cake batter hard against the side of the mixing bowl. 'Don't get me started, Lucia. It's a painful subject.'

Deirdre sniggered.

'Yeah, Aunt Lucia,' Ross tried to ease away. 'Don't get her started about why Deirdre and I aren't married yet.'

Deirdre scowled.

Whack! Whack! went their mother's spoon.

Lucia hauled Ross back down. 'What's the matter? Are you gay?'

Ross struggled free.

'He's not gay!' Breda exclaimed indignantly.

'He's got a phobia about commitment, you know — like those guys you see on *Jerry Springer*,' Deirdre said through a mouthful of roasted nuts.

'Ahhh!' Lucia and several of his cousins nodded understandingly.

He wrenched open the door to the cellar, muttering '*For*

chrissakes.'

'Ross Fabello! Do not blaspheme!' Breda shouted as the door closed behind him.

Vito stood in the cellar with a bottle of wine in each hand and his glasses perched on the end of his nose, studying the labels. The cool, shadowy room was an oasis of calm after the chaos in the kitchen. Vito looked at Ross over his glasses. 'Lucia got you.'

Ross sank onto a seat that he'd made in woodwork class when he was eleven. The legs were uneven and it wobbled. He rubbed his abused cheek. 'Twice, first she grabbed my cheek, and then she asked if I was still single because I'm gay. Deirdre joined in and said I had a phobia about commitment. They're worse than a coven of witches.'

'You don't look too bothered about it,' his father observed.

Ross shrugged. 'Of course not.'

Vito nodded thoughtfully. 'You've changed since you went to New Zealand.' He set about opening a bottle of red wine. 'You used to be a big bundle of anger and impatience, something was always wrong with you. Your mother and I worried, but when you came to visit when you were doing the movie stuff we noticed a big difference. You looked a lot happier.'

Ross didn't answer. He watched his father open the bottle of wine. Vito treated it like a religious experience. He could tell by the aroma or the look of a wine whether it had grown on the sunny or the shady side of a hill. He not only sniffed the cork, but checked the size and how porous it was. He liked to taste it with a variety of foods, first bread, then bread with salt, and finally bread with cheese.

'When you come home *this* time, you no longer look so happy Instead, you look sad — very sad and very troubled.' Vito sniffed the wine, sipped it, rolled it around in his mouth and swallowed. 'I think about it, and I know the reason why you're unhappy.' He pulled another wineglass from a rack mounted on the wall and filled it halfway. 'You love Danny and you had a fight with her.'

Ross took the glass and nodded. 'Promise me you won't tell Ma.'

Vito tipped back his head and tried to identify the flavours in the after-taste left by the wine. Blackcurrant, plum and spice. 'OK.'

Ross bought time by sniffing, sipping and rolling the liquid. 'We had a fight, a bad one. I said some terrible things, and then she pretty much kicked me out of the house. She said she couldn't come with us because she had to work.'

'You believe her?'

'No.'

Vito removed his glasses and put them in the pocket of the plum-coloured sweater that Breda had knitted him the Christmas before. 'You don't know what's wrong between you and Danny?'

'I don't have a clue. I've never met a woman who's so damned difficult and unreasonable and . . .' he trailed away shaking his head.

'Sounds like your mother.'

If that wasn't a good enough reason to stay away from Danny, then what was? Ross propped his elbows on his knees and rubbed his neck. 'I just keep feeling there's something wrong, that I shouldn't have left her alone or that I missed something.'

'Then you've got to go back to New Zealand.'

Ross stopped rubbing. 'You think so?'

Vito nodded. 'If you got a voice inside you saying something is wrong, you mustn't ignore it. If I'd done that the day your mother had the twins, they all would have died.'

Ross had heard the story about how Vito had suddenly got a feeling that something was wrong at home. At the risk of being fired, he'd walked out of work and come home to find Breda in early labour and haemorrhaging.

'Imagine what would have happened if I'd ignored that feeling?'

There was a sound of feet thumping down the wooden stairs, and Matt appeared with Ross's cellphone in his hand. 'It rang, but I didn't get to it in time. The caller ID said it was Auntie Danny. She left a message.' He held the phone out to Ross.

Ross and Vito exchanged looks.

Ross punched the keypad to access his voicemail, and heard Danny say, 'Ross, it's . . . it's Danny.' She sounded nervous and upset. 'I . . . I wondered if you . . .' Her voice broke: *'Ross, please come home . . . I need you.'*

Ross enlisted Deirdre and his brother-in-law Tom's help in finding the earliest flight to Auckland, while Carmel and his mother packed his bag. He took Matt and Mia aside and told them he needed to talk to Auntie Danny about something really important, and he couldn't do it over the telephone. Matt looked worried.

'Are you going to ask her to marry you?' Mia asked.

Ross was momentarily speechless. Fortunately, his fertile imagination came to his rescue. 'Auntie Danny beat me to it. She asked me the first day I met her.' Or at least, that was how he chose to interpret Danny's suggestion he get knotted.

Mia's eyes widened. 'She did?'

'Yes.'

'What did you say?'

'I told her I'd think about it.'

Ross could tell that Matt wasn't buying it.

'That's good,' Mia said. 'If you're going to keep doing that sex thing with each other, Deryl said you should get married.'

'Mia!' Breda reproved. She, Lucia and the cousins were unashamedly eavesdropping from the kitchen.

'Sorry, Granny Breda.'

'That's alright, darlin'.' Breda swept her away from Ross, adding,

'It's not *your* fault.' She nudged Lucia. 'See? I told you he wasn't gay.'

'What about his phobia?' Lucia asked.

'He got over it,' Breda retorted and hustled Mia away.

Aoife and Annie arrived with their husbands, Pete and Joe, and their kids, and wanted to know what all the fuss was about. Vito told them about Ross's feeling that something was wrong with Danny and her message.

'Oh!' Annie breathed. 'Who'd have thought Ross would turn into a sensitive New Age guy?'

Joe looked at Pete, who looked at Tom.

'None of us, that's for sure,' Tom said.

'Sensitive New Age guy, my ass,' Aoife snorted. 'He's turned into Danny's twin.'

'I'll never make that fucking flight at this rate!' The sensitive New Age guy yelled from upstairs.

'Ross Igor Padraig Oreste Fabello, mind your language!' Breda shouted back. 'You're setting a bad example for your children!'

'I bet you each a twenty that Danny fluffs his names during the wedding service,' Joe told Tom and Pete, but neither of them took his bet: it was a given that anybody marrying a Fabello would make a mess of that part of the ceremony, because the kids all had four names apiece, and they were a mixture of Italian and Irish.

Ross hurried downstairs carrying a small holdall and shrugging into his black leather jacket. 'I'll never make it.'

Pete dangled a set of car keys. 'Sure you will. We'll take the squad car.'

Ross arrived in Auckland at 5.30 a.m. local time, two days before Christmas. The face staring back at him from the mirror in the airplane toilet was haggard, red-eyed and sported thick, black stubble — he'd gone way past five o'clock shadow somewhere over

Hawaii. He looked like a serial killer.

First and Business Class were full, so he'd had to suffer the indignity and discomfort of travelling Economy. He hadn't slept, and pushed away the airline meals. The flight seemed to take forever: if Ross could've got out and pushed the plane, he would have.

It took ages to clear Customs, so he caught the early morning traffic heading into Auckland and didn't arrive at the house until after nine o'clock. Danny wasn't home and her car was missing from the garage. Next to the phone in the kitchen was a sheet of paper with a blue logo and Danny's name, date of birth, address and hospital number printed in the top left-hand corner. Beneath that was an appointment for a biopsy for a lump in her left breast.

Ross sagged against the counter.

Danny had a lump in her breast. And she was having a biopsy . . . *Right about now.*

A receptionist sat behind a sleek white counter tapping away on her computer. She looked up at Ross, and her professional smile of welcome faltered as six foot one of tired, anxious combustible Irish/Italian male loomed over her. She took in his rumpled clothes, bloodshot eyes and stubbled chin, and the way his black curls stuck up in two points like the Devil's horns, and shuddered.

'I'm here to see Daneka Lawton,' Ross told her hoarsely. 'Can you show me where she is?' He gave her his name.

'If you'd just like to take a seat, sir, I'll find out if we have anybody by that name.' The receptionist scurried away.

Ross looked around the waiting room. Several women who were waiting to be called for their appointment watched him warily from behind their magazines. Fear and impatience oozed from his pores like sweat.

Minutes passed and the phone rang and still the receptionist didn't return. Ross gave up waiting and leaned across the desk to check the computer screen. Daneka Lawton was in Consulting Room 6 — he saw a sign saying *Consulting Rooms* and followed it.

The receptionist met him in the corridor outside the rooms. 'You're not allowed down here!' she cried. Ross counted the numbers on the closed doors and apologized to two women sitting in an alcove wearing pale-pink hospital gowns and not much else. 'I'm Danny Lawton's fiancé.' He reached Consulting Room 6, grasped the door handle, and hoped he hadn't gotten it wrong.

She was sitting sideways on an examination table wearing one of the pink gowns, looking small and lost and unbearably sad. Her eyes widened when she saw him. *'Ross!'*

Ross crossed the room and gathered her into his arms, hugging her so tightly it was a wonder he didn't break a rib.

'I . . . can't . . . breathe . . .' Danny gasped.

'Sorry.' He let go and cupped her face between his hands. 'Why didn't you tell me?'

She gulped and swiped at the tears running down her cheeks. 'I did.'

'I mean, why didn't you tell me sooner? You knew before I went away, didn't you?'

'I didn't want to be a bother.'

'For an intelligent woman, you can be really stupid.'

Danny put her arms around his waist beneath the leather jacket and rested her cheek against his chest. She sighed and closed her eyes. 'I know.'

The door burst open and the receptionist and a security guard rushed in.

'That's him!' the receptionist cried. 'He looked at my computer!' She turned to Danny. 'Are you alright?'

The guard looked at Ross, and Danny snuggled in his arms. She didn't look like a woman in need of protection.

The receptionist was feeling braver now that she had the guard in tow. 'He *said* he's your fiancé,' she told Danny.

Danny didn't care what Ross had said.

'You'll have to make him leave,' the receptionist told the guard.

Danny clung to Ross. 'But I need him!'

'Is this man your fiancé?' the guard asked.

'Yes,' she said.

The receptionist wasn't convinced. 'Where's the ring?' she demanded suspiciously.

Danny could tell Ross was getting angry, so spoke up quickly before he said something that would get him thrown out. 'Do you think I'm going to let him choose it? I want something nice and big. Despite the way he looks, he'll go for small and tasteful.'

If anybody thought it was strange that a woman waiting to have part of her breast removed was quibbling over the size of her engagement ring, nobody thought to mention it. The receptionist had seen stranger things, and as for Danny — just having Ross with her made everything better. With him beside her, she could weather any storm.

'Oh.' The receptionist looked disappointed. It would have been nice to have something exciting happen for a change. 'Well, the radiographer will be along in a moment to collect Ms Lawton, and then you'll have to sit in the waiting room.'

Not in a million years, Ross thought, but forced a smile for Danny's sake.

The moment the door closed behind them, he stopped smiling. 'I'm sorry I said those terrible things to you when we fought. You're not emotionally . . .' He couldn't finish.

'It doesn't matter. I've said worse to you.' She stroked his stubble. 'You look like a serial killer.'

'Thank you.'

Danny clutched the edges of her gown. 'I've got a lump.'

'I know. I saw the letter on the kitchen counter back at the house, and figured you'd left it there for me to see.' Ross covered her hands with his and gently prised the edges of the gown apart. He looked at Danny's small, beautiful breasts and up into her vulnerable, tear-filled eyes. 'Where?' he asked quietly.

She pressed her fingers against the side of her left breast.

He laid his big hand over her hand and breast so tenderly that Danny started crying again. 'I'll probably have to have a mastectomy. I wish I could have them both removed rather than sit around waiting for the cancer to get me.'

He couldn't speak, only nod.

'It wouldn't bother you?' She cupped his hand. 'Not having these?'

Ross covered both her breasts with his palms. 'These I can do without.' He pressed a hand against her heart. '*This* I can't.'

Tears slid down Danny's cheeks, and her nose ran. 'You glib-tongued serial killer, you,' she sobbed. 'I love you.'

'Thank you, sweetheart. I love you, too. Do you know your nose is running?'

She laughed and buried her face against his chest and let him hold her while she waited for the radiographer. He wouldn't wallow in pity and pussyfoot around. He'd kick her in the butt and help her fight.

'What made you change your mind and call me?' Ross asked.

Danny thought about it. 'I grew up,' she said simply.

A young woman in navy blue trousers and a white tunic stepped into the consulting room. Her jaw dropped at the sight of her patient sitting on the examination table with a big, dark, dishevelled-looking man holding her naked breasts.

'It's alright,' Danny explained, 'he's my fiancé.'

Ross wouldn't leave. He stayed and held Danny's hand while

they did the biopsy. Danny didn't even flinch, but Ross felt as if he was going to pass out.

The doctor saw them afterwards in her office. She explained the results would be delayed due to the Christmas break.

'Whatever the results show, Danny, we've caught this early. In the meantime, try and get some rest. Stay home from work.' She looked at Ross. 'Can you make sure she does that?'

'Yes, even if I have to tie her to the bed.'

On their way out, the receptionist stopped them. Some of the patients sitting in the waiting room had alerted her to just who Ross was and who Danny must be.

'Tell me, are you who I think you are?' she asked.

'Not now,' Ross said curtly. But she was looking at Danny, not him.

'You're Danny! That writer bloke's sister-in-law.' Danny nodded. The writer bloke scowled.

'This is him,' she said. 'The writer bloke: RF O'Rourke.'

The receptionist still hadn't forgiven Ross for looking at her computer. 'Never heard of him.' She smiled at Danny. 'Get plenty of rest won't you, dear? We'll contact you the moment we get the results.'

They spent the week waiting for the biopsy results driving slowly northwards to the Bay of Islands. Ross was amazed at how strong and cheerful Danny was, and wished he had her strength and optimism. He was humbled when Danny told him that her positive attitude was largely due to him.

'You made me see that this isn't the worst thing that could happen. If the results are positive and it's cancer, I'll have treatment; and if they're negative, I'll count my blessings.'

The Bay of Islands was a magical place with its pale jade waters, pretty islands and golden beaches fringed by pohutukawa trees with their scarlet blooms. Danny warned they might have trouble finding somewhere to stay at this time of year, because the whole of New Zealand went on holiday to the beach, and the country shut down for almost a month.

They got lucky and found a little bach with an outdoor toilet and shower. Possums ran across the roof at night, and moreporks called in the trees. It was idyllic and provided just the kind of rest the doctor had ordered. They called Matt and Mia on the speaker phone in Ross's car on Christmas Day to wish them a Merry Christmas.

'I opened your present from Auntie Danny, Uncle Ross,' Mia told him.

Danny protested. 'Mia! You shouldn't open other people's presents.'

'What did Auntie Danny give me, Mia?' Ross asked.

'A whole lot of socks — and none of them match.'

'Uncle Ross said you asked him to marry you,' Matt said.

'No, I didn't,' Danny replied.

'Yes, you did,' Ross insisted. 'How could you forget something that important?'

'Because I never asked you, that's how!'

'Yes, you did: you told me to get knotted.'

'That doesn't mean—'

Ross kissed her to shut her up. He looked into Danny's startled golden eyes and murmured against her mouth, 'I'll think about it.'

Three days later, Danny received the news. She didn't have cancer.

Epilogue

In February, Danny sat in the audience at the Kodak Theatre in Los Angeles and watched Ross accept the Academy Award for Best Adapted Screenplay for John Doe. He looked like a woman's dream-date in his Armani tuxedo — tall, dark, handsome and just a little bit cranky. Danny's taste in clothes hadn't improved. Ross had chosen her amber Marchesa gown, and had topaz and diamond earrings shaped like Darth Vader made especially for her. Danny added her own personal touch by painting a topaz-and-gold-coloured streak through her fringe.

Ross had completed what Danny, Aoife and Annie referred to as his "twin" book and sent it in to Wanda, who said it was his best work yet. Afterwards, he took Danny and the children to Ireland to meet Granny O'Rourke and the family. Predictably, Concepta took exception to Danny's name.

'What kind of a name is that, for goodness sake?' she cried. 'Everybody will think Rory is marrying a man.' From then on, all his Irish relatives called her Dymphna.

After years of being alone, Danny had family in Ireland, Italy, America and Rotorua. Like all families, being a member came with baggage, like Granny O'Rourke's renaming, and Breda's constant questions about exactly when Ross and Danny were going to get engaged and tie the knot.

'You're not getting any younger,' she said in her usual tactful manner. 'If you want to give Matt and Mia a brother or sister, you need to get a move on. I saw something on television about how a woman's eggs start going rotten once she turns thirty-five.'

Danny placed the blame firmly at her son's door. 'He hasn't said yes yet.'

'He's thirty-seven years old, which is on the shelf in anybody's book. I accept on his behalf.'

Things were looking more promising on the marriage front for Deirdre. Breda didn't know that the glow in her youngest daughter's cheeks was due to quiet, unassuming Darren giving Deidre her first orgasm and continuing to deliver the goods.

'He's nice enough, I suppose,' Breda said. 'I just wish he wasn't so awful quiet. The poor man can hardly string two sentences together.'

'He's exhausted,' Aoife replied, and Deirdre kicked her.

Ross had visited Danny's grandparents and uncles in Rotorua and passed muster. He'd helped on the farm, played touch rugby with a crowd of Danny's cousins, which included Joe, and been coached in the correct pronunciation of the traditional Maori greeting *Kia ora*.

'You know I talked to you about those special reasons?' Pania asked Danny as they watched a Maori hangi being opened. She pointed at Ross, who was fascinated with the way the food was cooked in the ground, and was deep in conversation with several of the older women. 'Well, that man's a good reason. Don't let him get away.'

'What about me?' Danny protested. 'Don't you think he's lucky to have me?'

'Too bloody right he is,' Ted agreed.

Danny and Ross had agreed to spend most of their time in New Zealand and visit his family and house in San Diego during the school holidays. They were extending the house in Auckland,

and Ross was going to build a turret like the one at his home in San Diego. Mia had already suggested they could use it for bungy jumping.

Danny watched Ross accept his Oscar and step up to the podium to speak. She overflowed with happiness, the good, quiet sort that lasted, not the flashy, roller-coaster variety — although with Ross in her bed she had some of that, too. She had a man who loved her even when she was impossible, and two beautiful, happy children.

And her health.

There wasn't anything more Danny wanted.

Ross thanked the Academy for the award, and the people involved in making the film.

'I apologize in advance for not having a psychiatrist or analyst to thank; if I'd known that I really stood a chance of winning this award, I assure you I would have gone straight out and signed up with somebody.

'I want to say a big hi and an even bigger thank you to my mother, father, sisters, brothers-in-law, and nieces and nephews sitting at home in San Diego, probably screaming the neighbourhood deaf. Also hello and much love to my relatives in Lombardy, Italy and County Clare, Eire.' He held up his Oscar. 'Look, Granny O'Rourke, at what Rory has done. Kia ora to my family in Rotorua, New Zealand. Forgive my pronunciation — it can only get better.

'Hi to my two children, Matt and Mia: I love you, and now it's time you were in bed.'

Ross paused and looked across at where Danny sat, watching him in the audience with a huge smile on her face.

'And to my beautiful Danny — yes, *the* Danny.' His voice deepened as it always did when he was feeling emotional. 'I love you, I treasure you, and I'm so glad I have you. As wonderful as this little golden statue is, it'll never ever be as precious to me as you and our kids.'

'Oh, and one last thing, darling,' Ross added, 'I accept.'

Acknowledgements
Thank you to Dixie Carlton and Ammie Christiansen from Indie Experts for getting me started again, and Katie Fisher for the wonderful cover art.

www.ingramcontent.com/pod-product-compliance
Lightning Source LLC
Chambersburg PA
CBHW020416010526
44118CB00010B/272